Service Chain Management

Christos Voudouris · Gilbert Owusu
Raphael Dorne · David Lesaint

Service Chain Management

Technology Innovation
for the Service Business

 Springer

Christos Voudouris
Gilbert Owusu
Raphael Dorne
David Lesaint

British Telecommunications plc
Orion Building pp 1/12
Adastral Park, Martlesham Heath
Ipswich, IP5 3RE
United Kingdom

chris.voudouris@bt.com
gilbert.owusu@bt.com
raphael.dorne@bt.com
david.lesaint@bt.com

ISBN-13 978-3-540-75503-6   e-ISBN-13 978-3-540-75504-3

DOI 10.1007/978-3-540-75504-3

ACM Computing Classification (1998): K.6, H.4, J.1, J.7

Library of Congress Control Number: 2007936681

© 2008 Springer-Verlag Berlin Heidelberg

Cover design: KünkelLopka, Heidelberg
Typesetting and Production: LE-TEX Jelonek, Schmidt & Vöckler GbR, Leipzig

Printed on acid-free paper

9 8 7 6 5 4 3 2 1

springer.com

Foreword

Since the emergence of the digital networked economy, companies are undergoing significant changes in the way they manage their businesses. The technology revolution is bringing changes that will affect companies for decades to come. Service enterprises, being the engine of today's Western economies, stand to be transformed the most. Digital service delivery over broadband networks on a global scale opens new horizons for service businesses and consumers creating not only new opportunities but also threats. BT's response is: "Don't just survive: *thrive!*" This book supports this message by presenting a range of technologies and methods that can be the source of innovation to help the services sector address its challenges and take advantage of its opportunities.

BT is experiencing these challenges and opportunities first hand together with its service partners, customers and suppliers. Trends such as liberalisation of services and outsourcing have profoundly affected our industry and others by unbundling vertical service companies, giving rise to new and competitive service chains. By using modern digital communications these chains now span the globe from India and China into Europe and the US.

With everincreasing customer expectations and a proliferation of service offerings, the management of these chains has become a priority for business leaders; this book can provide the inspiration. From the strategic planning perspective to the day-to-day operational scheduling, and from people management to network planning and design, the book covers a range of topics that cut across the enterprise bringing both a bird's-eye view and a holistic perspective.

Beyond the technological considerations, it is often the journey to the successful implementation and continuous usage of solutions that really transforms an organisation. This book offers unique management insights from a hands-on perspective, presenting best practices, risks, and difficulties, and suggesting ways to mitigate them. Methodologies to accelerate solution development and ensure successful implementation are also discussed, something often found wanting in texts solely focusing on the engineering details.

Moreover, this book touches upon emerging customer and technology trends from the perspectives of the Web 2.0 generation, through to digital service chains for software and content, real-time personalisation, service chain collaboration, employee empowerment, and others. These subjects debated today are likely to shape the services and companies of the future. They will have a profound impact on the evolution of services and their economics, and more importantly on how customers will be experiencing the digitally networked world in years to come.

Andy Green
Chief Executive of Group Strategy and Operations, BT Group plc

Acknowledgements

We would like to thank all the contributing authors to this book. They were invited as either members or collaborators in our R&D programme at BT's Chief Technology Office to survey specific areas that fall under (or relate to) Service Chain Management. Their input was integrated into the book by cross-referencing it with the other content and by removing overlaps between related subjects. The material was enhanced in places with additional text, figures and citations added by the main authors. Finally, a "flow" was created by restructuring sections and creating links between chapters so this becomes a comprehensive and easy to read textbook for the subject.

We would like to especially thank Paul Cleaver (General Manager, Field Force Automation) and his team in BT Global Services for their kind support, encouragement and assistance in our efforts to create this book. They were enthusiastic about the idea from the start with Paul also contributing a chapter with invaluable insights and experiences from his longstanding career in management and IT automation solutions.

Beibei He helped with several aspects of the book and her efforts are deeply appreciated. Eric Chin, Zhan Cui, Robert Ghanea-Hercock, Nadim Haque, Sachin Karale, Duong Nguyen, Sid Shakya reviewed parts of the content and assisted in the editing. Last but not least, Nader Azarmi and Paul O'Brien with the help of Rika Nauck wholeheartedly supported the effort and facilitated the publication.

Contents

Part I Resource Planning

Part III Process, Communications and Information

Epilogue

Contributors

[1] British Telecommunications plc
[2] Infosys Technologies Limited
[3] Lancaster University, Management School

[4] University College London, Department of Computer Science
[5] Warwick Business School
[6] University of Essex, Department of Computer Science

Chapter 1
Defining and Understanding Service Chain Management

1.1 Introduction

The growth of the services sector in recent times has been phenomenal with services displacing manufacturing as the main driver of western industrialised economies. However, a disproportionate part of the yearly productivity growth in OECD countries is still due to improvements in manufacturing (Wölfl 2005). In this context, *Service Operations Management* (Johnston and Clark 2001; Schmenner 1995) is becoming increasingly important for companies and government alike to achieve productivity growth and a cost advantage over their domestic and international competitors. This includes technologies and systems for automating and optimising service operations within and across companies which we will refer to them collectively as *Service Chain Management*.

Service Chain Management can be seen as analogous to *Supply Chain Management* (Simchi-Levi et al. 2000; Vollmann et al. 2004) but for services. Supply Chain Management is concerned with the planning and management of activities from raw materials to the delivery of finished goods. Similarly, Service Chain Management is concerned with the planning and management of activities from support functions to the delivery of end-user services. The flow of materials is negligible in Service Chain Management thus techniques developed under Supply Chain Management are of limited direct value. The names *Services-Oriented Supply Chain Management* (Anderson and Morrice 2000) and *Service Management* (Fitzsimmons and Fitzsimmons 2001) are also in use to refer to related areas but either in a more specific context to service chaining or in a more general context to service operations respectively.

To a certain degree, Service Chain Management was until recently confined to studying the operations and systems of large and vertically integrated service organisations such as airlines, utilities, healthcare providers, banks, or the after-sales functions of manufacturers as in Lee et al. (2005). Nonetheless, there is an increasing trend of services outsourcing and offshoring; initially focusing on customer support such as call centres but recently moving onto a broader range of activities including

C. Voudouris, G. Owusu, R. Dorne, D. Lesaint, *Service Chain Management*
DOI: 10.1007/978-3-540-75504-3, ©Springer 2008

engineering, software development and other tasks requiring high-skilled human capital (Bjerring-Olsen 2006). This trend, combined with the proliferation of service providers and resellers in telephony, the Internet, gas, electricity, insurance and other services, has resulted in cross-organisational service chains of three or more tiers making chain efficiency increasingly important.

From an IT perspective, Service Chain Management enables service organisations to improve customer satisfaction and reduce operational costs through intelligent and optimised forecasting, planning and scheduling of the service chain (internal or external) and its associated resources such as people, networks, information and other tangible (or intangible) assets. Despite the transition to a service-driven economy, logistical solutions for services lag significantly behind to what is available for product-driven industries. Enterprise Resource Planning (ERP) and Material Requirements Planning (MRP) systems have been in use in factories for years and they have substantially matured both in terms of breadth and depth of functionality, nowadays supporting fully the *Sales and Operations Planning* processes (Vollmann et al. 2005). Hopefully, Service Chain Management and related technologies could one day play a similar role in service firms.

1.2 Book Objectives

In this book, we present the latest innovation and technologies that can manage the operations of a service company. Our viewpoint is based on our experiences at BT plc as well as associated research and development in universities and partner companies such as Infosys Technologies. Several subject experts have contributed to the book each providing his/her unique perspective on their respective topics. The area is quite broad, covering field force and workforce management, network and asset optimisation, customer relationship management and also the linkages between them.

Our intention in this book is to not only look at Service Chain Management from the enterprise viewpoint but also from the service customer and service professional viewpoints. Service companies are human-centric which creates the need for enabling technologies for service personnel and customers alike. These human-centric technologies span areas such as customer analytics, process management, information management and unified communications.

The book investigates beyond traditional areas such as Operational Support Systems (OSS) which, despite standardisation efforts (TM Forum 2006), still lack a detailed framework for facilitating enterprise-wide resource planning. In addition, we are presenting the technical ground for bridging the large functionality gaps not filled by platforms such as CRM (Customer Relationship Management), HR (Human Resources) and ERP/MRP[1] when they are implemented in a service context.

---

[1] In services, ERP/MRP are mainly relevant in financial management and also, where applicable, inventory management for parts and spares

We put a strong emphasis on customer requirements and trends, methodologies for successfully developing and deploying enterprise solutions while provide advice on how benefits can best be realised out of technology investments.

In the next section, we detail the challenges faced by service firms which Service Chain Management and associated technologies are coming to address.

1.3 Challenges in Service Operations

Service companies are required to effectively plan and schedule their resources to offer an efficient service to customers. This is no different in principle to Manufacturing Planning and Control (MPC) (Vollmann et al. 2005) that gave rise to MRP, ERP and the more sophisticated Supply Chain Management systems. However, the main focus in services is on people and assets rather than materials management which is at the heart of MPC.

People are the core and essence of a service business. In the context of many services, they are not even confined to a particular facility (e. g., like the factory in a manufacturing context) but are mobile, offering service across a geography. Furthermore, in cases where the demand needs to be satisfied near-instantaneously (e. g., calls to emergency services); there is no inventory of finished products to protect operations whilst long waiting times are unacceptable. The enterprise needs to plan staffing so that demand is met with adequate supply for every minute of every hour of operation across several geographical areas; this represents a huge logistical exercise to plan and execute. On the financial side, the costs associated with staffing come under Operational Expenditure (or OPEX for short) and represent a large percentage of the costs associated with running a service business.

Assets are often networked and represent critical and expensive infrastructure. Examples of networked assets include telecommunication, electricity, gas, water, rail and road networks. Facilities are also important and they are either integral part of the network (e. g., telephone exchanges, railway stations, electricity stations, etc.) or stand-alone (e. g., hospitals, airports, retail outlets, warehouses, etc.). Equipment is either fixed and housed within the facilities or mobile and carried by service personnel. It can range from very expensive specialist hardware (e. g., medical scanners in hospitals, network switching equipment in telephone exchanges, etc.) to everyday tools such as mobile phones, laptops and various handheld devices. On the financial side, facilities and equipment come under Capital Expenditure (or CAPEX) and dominate the investment of service companies, nations or even multinational groups (e. g., multinational energy or transportation networks). Materials are also required and managed but they often represent only a small percentage of the overall turnover (e. g., 5% or less in businesses such as telecommunications).

It is a characteristic of the service industry that, in the majority of cases, the enterprise and its people and assets such as networks, facilities and equipment have to follow customers in terms of geography. This is generally not the case with manufacturing where production facilities can be centralised. In this respect, services are less suitable to offshoring to lower cost geographies although service digitisation and modern communications have facilitated that in recent times (e. g., call centre migration to India). There are indications that this offshoring is actually having a productivity enhancing effect for service firms (Bjerring-Olsen 2006).

Constrained to operate in high cost geographies with an expensive asset base, it is sometimes puzzling why services have not excelled in Service Chain Management approaches across their operations. Why have systems not emerged for systematically planning resources at the enterprise level thus optimising the OPEX and CAPEX profile of companies? If materials management was the main issue then Supply Chain Management and manufacturing could lend a hand to bring inventories under control but, as mentioned above, materials account for only a small percentage of overall operations.

Clearly, competition is not as intense as in product industries with several service industries moving to privatisation only in recent years (e. g., telecommunications, energy and water utilities) or being under the state umbrella as with health, policing and education. Even in industries that have undergone privatisation, it is sometimes in the service "wrap" that competition is heavily emerging. The main assets such as electricity, water, rail and telecommunication networks are often owned and maintained by near-monopoly and heavily regulated players. Furthermore, several sectors are still enjoying high profit margins leaving room for the operational inefficiencies to "fly under the radar" so to speak.

Growth of services is also a factor working contrary to productivity as identified by Fixler and Siegel (1999). It could be the case that improvements are eventually motivated by intensified competition when demand (e. g., from manufacturing to outsource its services side to specialists) subsides relatively to production capacity in the services sector.

Overall, the situation is not static and, increasingly, services are following the manufacturing route searching for productivity gains. Increased competition will eventually lead to lower profit margins and a drive for efficiency to reduce operational and capital expenditure which, if it does not translate into better service, is ultimately passed on and burdening customers and tax payers. Call centres, transportation and retail are examples where this drive for efficiency is already taking place and it will not be long before other areas follow the same trajectory especially as a result of service liberalisation initiatives, e. g., within the EU (Bolkestein 2004).

1.4 Key Success Factors in Services

Given the increasing strive for productivity and other improvements, one may reasonably ask what should a service business aim for when it comes to Key Success Factors (KSFs)? One key success factor in manufacturing is to reduce inventories and associated costs, and it can be met by introducing techniques such as Just-in-time (Tersine 1998) and Vendor Managed Inventories (Disney and Towill 2003). What is the equivalent objective(s) in Service Chain Management? A number of unique features, attributed to services, have been identified in the literature (Zeithaml and Bitner 2003; Fitzsimmons and Fitzsimmons 2001) and may provide direction in answering the question. We summarise these features below:

- *Services are intangible.* They cannot be seen, felt, tasted or touched in the same manner as tangible goods. The customer usually bases its judgment on peripheral cues and experiences.
- *Services are heterogeneous.* No two customers or employees are precisely alike. Human interaction makes defining quality a challenge and it may vary from one customer to the next.
- *Services are simultaneously produced and consumed.* Mass production is difficult. Customer satisfaction is in "real time" with the customer "observing" and "participating" in the process.
- *Services are perishable.* They cannot be saved, stored, resold or returned. More importantly, they cannot be inventoried. A service company may use inventory management (e. g., for spares) but this accounts for a very small part of the overall service operations.

Let us focus first on the last point from the list which is service perishability. Capacity management is definitely a key factor when addressing the perishable nature of services and different strategies have been proposed (Sasser 1976; Armistead and Clark 1994). Customers are sometimes highly critical on this subject (especially on public services) arguing that organisations with overcapacity and idle resources are offering long waiting times due to gross operational inefficiencies within them and across their service chains. Whichever way this is perceived externally by customers and the specific strategies internally followed by companies, efficiently *matching supply with demand* is a key success factor for services and should particularly focus on the two following goals:

- Minimisation of *waiting time* for customers
- Minimisation of *idle time* for resources

But it is not all about minimising "hard" and measurable targets that makes the difference here. Services are human-centric and issues arising from intangibility, heterogeneity and simultaneous production and consumption also need to be taken into account too. Addressing these areas is that leads to superior efficiency and quality, and this is expressed by the further goals:

- Maximisation of *performance* for employees and other resources
- Maximisation of *experience* for customers

The performance of employees is not confined to productivity but extends to areas such as behaviour, quality of the work and also company culture. Similarly, customer experience is not confined to the service itself and satisfaction with it but extends to the peripheral tangible cues associated with its delivery such as facilities, websites, vehicles, equipment, personnel and everything else that affects the customer's perception of a service provider (Shostack 1977; Bitner 1990).

The four objectives outlined above, *Waiting, Idling, Performing* and *Experiencing* (we use the term *WIPE* for short) represent a set of meaningful and widely applicable key success factors for services which can be detailed by organisations and management into appropriate measures and scorecards when applied to specific contexts. More interestingly, the four objectives are not standalone but interconnected. For example, waiting times have an impact on how customers are experiencing a service, but they are also dependant on the level of resource capacity and how it is put in place to avoid extremes such as overworking or idling[2]. If such extremes are not controlled then they impact on work quality and staff morale[3] leading to a drop in productivity and rework required to remedy faults, thus increasing further the waiting times and so forth. It is not difficult to see how companies can end up in vicious circles with "positive" feedback loops making a bad situation worse due to demand amplification effects across a service chain, see Akkermans and Vos (2003) for a case study.

Given the negative publicity over the years, and criticism on both public and private services, with regards to failing on one or more of the four objectives, one may argue that the *WIPE* challenge for the service industry as a whole is of equal scale to the inventory challenge faced by manufacturing. To achieve the above goals, services need to embrace technology rather than trying to remedy isolated problems from a solely marketing or management perspective. Technology and management methods need to work hand-in-hand towards a common goal to be able to help an industry as a whole. Furthermore, a Service Chain Management blueprint, similar to Supply Chain Management, would be required that represents best practice in *Service Planning and Control*. This blueprint, implemented through software suites from different vendors, could then be applied division after division, company after company, vertical after vertical, leading to efficiency improvements similar to those

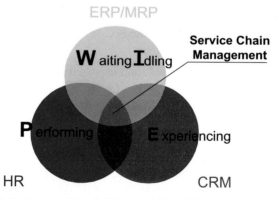

Fig. 1.1 The WIPE challenge and how it links to existing CRM, HR and ERP infrastructure with Service Chain Management covering functionality gaps and providing the orchestration across the system space

---

[2] Idling of resources is not always associated with a "lull" in demand but could be due to personnel being deployed at the wrong place, at the wrong time with the wrong skill

[3] Idling can sometimes be as demoralising as overworking if not more

experienced from the introduction of the MRP/ERP template and associated systems in the manufacturing sector.

The effort is not trivial, but it can draw on the existing CRM, ERP (mainly financials, possibly MRP where applicable) and HR systems with Service Chain Management technologies bridging the gaps and providing the orchestration across the system space in the context of a service business. A pictorial representation of these roles is provided in Fig 1.1.

In the next section, and as an example, we look at BT plc and more generally telecommunications/utility companies from a systems evolution perspective. We examine how they often arrive at a Service Chain Management blueprint and what elements such blueprint is likely to include.

1.5 Developing a Blueprint for Service Chain Management

In telecommunications but also in a general utility context, the main resources to be managed include call centre agents and field service engineers and also the networked assets of the company (e. g., telecommunication, electricity, rail, transport or other types of networks). Service companies employ field and office-based engineers, call centre agents and other personnel to install, deliver or terminate their services as well as upgrade, repair or maintain their assets. In addition to that, modern telecommunication and energy companies may incorporate an ever larger element of professional services personnel (i. e., ICT professionals in the case of telecommunications, risk management specialists in Energy, etc.). We examine here the trajectory of BT which can be considered as representative of leaders in this domain; they being a telecom, an IT-savvy company and one of the first large organisations to be recognised by the OR community through an INFORMS Franz Edelman Finalist Award for automating scheduling across its operations (Lesaint et al. 2000).

1.5.1 Automating Scheduling and Dispatching

The late 1980s and early 1990s saw the first efforts being made within BT to fully automate and optimise the planning and scheduling of resources in call centres and in the field. This constituted the beginning of efforts to systematise Service Chain Management. Work started on the operationally hard problems of scheduling shifts in the call centres and dispatching jobs in field operations. As the latter proved the hardest, we focus below on field service automation.

The dawn of this era in BT saw the creation of the Work Manager system (Laithwaite 1995), between 1989 and 1997, which automated work scheduling for field personnel. Field service is an essential element of many industries (Vigoroso 2004), and as field operations can sometimes account for up to 50% of Operational Expenditure (OPEX) in service companies they are therefore a major consideration. In the case of BT, the current field force exceeds 30,000 engineers in size; not long ago this number was over the 50,000 mark.

General examples of field service include the installation, repair and maintenance operations in utilities, emergency services such as ambulances and police, health visitors and community workers, automobile repair, construction and maintenance of buildings, equipment repair and maintenance. The area is also closely related to transportation and logistics and some times the two are treated under the same umbrella.

Field service is generally regarded as a challenging domain given that the mobility of resources increases the complexity in decision making by adding the spatial dimension on top of what is already required in terms of decision making in an office-based environment (e. g., planning and scheduling of shifts in a call centre).

Underlying optimisation problems such as the Vehicle Routing Problem in services can be seen as similar to the Job-Shop Scheduling Problem in manufacturing (Beck et al. 2003). Not surprisingly, the algorithms used in field personnel scheduling, which in the case of BT's system included simulated annealing and local search techniques (Lesaint et al. 2000), came from the same areas of Operations Research and Constraint Programming that were used in Finite Capacity Scheduling for manufacturing (Nuijten and Le Pape 1998). However, field personnel scheduling tends to be more of a reactive problem with many exceptions happening during execution due to external factors (e. g., traffic conditions, task delays and interruptions). This calls for dynamic scheduling systems which re-optimise the allocation of jobs to field resources at regular intervals to respond rapidly to emergencies (Laithwaite 1995; Lesaint et al. 2000).

1.5.2 Moving to Advanced and Systematic Planning

In the context of BT, and after the automation of scheduling processes, one question that was raised in the late 1990s amongst management was how automated capacity/manpower planning could be added on top of scheduling so that the company moves away from locally maintained solutions (e. g., specially-designed spreadsheets) and a system stack gradually develops similar to that we find in Manufacturing Planning and Control (Vollmann et al. 2004) linking Sales and Operations Planning down to capacity/manpower planning and to personnel scheduling. This desire was motivated by the fact that BT, as with other telecom operators, had begun to venture into new growth areas and products. This meant that an increasingly complex set of resources (engineers, call centres, professional services including the network assets) with hundreds of skill types had to be mapped to an increasingly complex set of services and properly planned to align with the overall company strategy.

It was at this point that the analogy between Supply Chain Management approaches in manufacturing and specifically Advanced Planning and Scheduling or APS (Stadtler and Kilger 2000) and how they can be adapted to services in their entirety became a priority. In the case of BT, this motivated the creation of an integrated Service Chain Management blueprint in the form of the BT Field Optimisation Suite (FOS) (Voudouris et al. 2006; Owusu et al. 2006).

1.5.3 FOS: An Example Suite for Integrated Service Chain Management

FOS incorporates dedicated applications for forecasting demand, planning resources, scheduling work, reserving capacity and managing employee, customer, supplier links across a service chain in a way similar to Supply Chain Management (SCM) (Stadtler and Kilger 2000; Vollmann et al. 2005) for product-driven industries. The suite is intended for service operations with high volumes of low-to-medium complexity work (i. e., not large scale project or programme management) that have a strong element of repetition and standardisation. It is also intended mainly for field service operations as the name implies, although modules are also suitable, and currently used, in office environments.

The overall architecture of FOS is depicted in Fig. 1.2 alongside its links to CRM, ERP and HR systems.

The main modules of FOS are the following:

- *FieldForecast* models and forecasts service demand over different geographies, skills and time frames. It links to ERP financial applications for exchanging budgeting information.

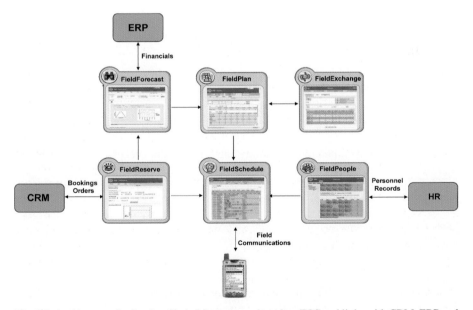

Fig. 1.2 Architecture for Service Chain Management based on FOS and links with CRM, ERP and HR enterprise systems

- *FieldPlan* plans resource capacity to meet expected demand. It supports "what-if" scenario modelling to balance cost against quality of service criteria.
- *FieldSchedule* schedules work to resources. Constraint technology allows for efficiently handling the variety of requirements which real-life schedules must comply with such as skill-matching, due dates, working shifts, staff breaks, regulatory constraints, temporal dependencies between tasks, and so on.
- *FieldPeople* manages all people specific information relating to rosters, attendance, skill and geography. A single system providing human resource visibility across the organisation. It receives personnel records from the company's general HR application.
- *FieldExchange* allows the balancing of resource capacity between divisions and subcontractors (i. e., supporting cross-organisational service chain management). Users can negotiate the acquisition, release, loan, or hire of resources with *collaborating internal or external partners.*
- *FieldReserve* is an automated reservation system enabling a customer to create or change bookings and appointments to suit his/her own circumstances. This module together with the scheduling application is normally interfaced with a CRM system to handle interactions with end-users over multiple channels although direct access through a web portal is also possible.

Contrasting the FOS architecture above with Supply Chain Management suites for manufacturing may provide clues to the essential elements of a blueprint for Service Chain Management and also how current enterprise platforms for services are likely to evolve.

1.5.4 Contrasting with Supply Chain Management

For that purpose, we use SAP's Advanced Planner and Optimizer (APO) product here as a contrasting example. SAP APO (Dickersbach 2003) provides a toolset for planning and optimising supply chain processes in manufacturing industries. The FOS and SAP modules, which address analogous problems, are identified and listed in the table below.

Having been developed independently and for different end-problems, it is worth highlighting that the same pattern of high-level functional blocks emerges for advanced planning and scheduling irrespective of whether it is a service or product.

Table 1.1 Feature comparison: BT FOS with SAP APO

FOS service modules	SAP APO modules
FieldForecast	Demand planning
FieldPlan/FieldExchange	Supply network planning
FieldSchedule	Production planning and detailed scheduling
FieldReserve	Global available to promise
FieldPeople	SAP ERP human capital management

Nonetheless, this similarity does not necessarily extend within the applications. In services, the focus is on manpower planning and operational issues centre on personnel scheduling while in product industries materials planning is key and operational issues centre on machine scheduling.

Service chain collaboration in FOS is supported by the FieldExchange application though functionality is not as extensive as that found in specialist products dealing with *supply chain collaboration*. Furthermore, compared to its manufacturing cousins the FOS architecture, is to some extent, incomplete as it deals with just one aspect of the resources, i. e., people, and does not integrate the planning of networks and other types of assets under the same umbrella. Network and asset planning, which represent a major resource management area for utilities and telecommunications, are usually addressed separately and under a Geographical Information Systems (GIS) (Longley et al. 2005) banner. To start bridging this gap, we include and specifically cover the subject of network planning in the book. Potential synergies are gradually emerging, such as assessing network/asset planning from a service requirements perspective and aligning it with human resources planning. These synergies may one day provide a holistic strategic planning capability, which links CAPEX to OPEX, by modelling how investment in asset infrastructure may impact operations and vice versa.

Drawing on the case of FOS and likely future enhancements as discussed above, one can identify some major milestones during its evolution path which are indicative of the general steps required in developing a Service Chain Management blueprint. These steps based on the FOS experience are presented in Fig. 1.3.

To expand on these findings further, we discuss below the situation across several service industry verticals.

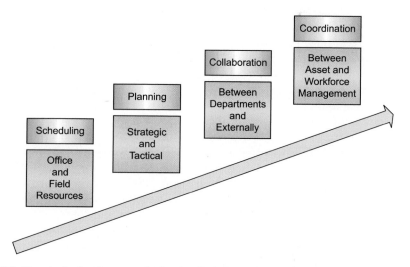

Fig. 1.3 Steps in the development of a Service Chain Management blueprint

1.6 The Broader Picture Across Verticals

Service Chain Management having to deal with the unpredictable human-centric nature of services is a notoriously complex and uncertain domain to be attacked at its entirety with readily available technology tools. Market needs in certain areas have begun to be addressed such as call centres or field service, in the case of utilities, but as yet, no solutions exist for managing a service business in the way that ERP manages production in a manufacturer.

Even in utilities, as discussed above, managing the networks, assets and personnel using a single platform which translates business planning to capacity planning and then to discrete schedules for network or people resources, all in an optimised way, is not presently available. We are simply describing, here, the equivalent of an ERP logistics module for manufacturing yet the reader may appreciate the challenges involved when attempting to apply a similar template to all the different and complex service contexts and situations.

There is one exception to this, namely with the airlines. They currently have what can be described as an integrated service chain management approach. This is due to the pioneering work of the internal departments of companies such as AMR, the parent of American Airlines. This, in turn, gave rise to companies, such as Sabre (Cook 1998; Horner 2000), which subsequently transformed the IT side of their industry. With regards to the other verticals, solutions are largely embryonic addressing only specific operational problems and areas (e. g., nurse scheduling, police dispatch etc.).

Overall, we would rather be optimistic about the future. The "point" solutions or early software suites of today are likely to be enhanced in the next 2–5 years into integrated application suites. Increased automation will start to penetrate additional domains such as rail companies, retail, health care and emergency services which are generally lagging behind in managing their service chain element. In 5–10 years from now, we can expect collaborative solutions also to emerge that automate cross-company transactions through service markets (e. g., between companies and/or with their subcontractors) to squeeze costs out of cross-organisational service chains. We may also see process and information holistically managed using the same solutions.

Obviously, there are a number of scenarios as to how this is going to play out. Certain aspects may be delayed or brought forward depending on macro-economic factors and technology advancements. Complementary technologies such as RFID and location-based services are showing promise too with respect to their application to service verticals (Woods 2005; Lopez et al. 2007) thus accelerating adoption of service chain management (e. g., solutions combining scheduling with tracking for field resources are increasingly popular, see Chaps. 10 and 20).

A rather insightful picture is presented in Fig. 1.4 where we project a potential future for Service Chain Management solutions over the next decade in terms of the following dimensions:

1. *sector coverage* of solutions in terms of substantial penetration and impact;
2. *operations coverage* in terms of processes and functionality to be gradually integrated under a single enterprise platform;

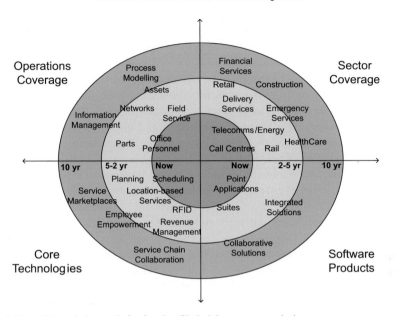

Fig. 1.4 Potential evolution path for Service Chain Management solutions

3. *core technologies* to be developed and incorporated into commercial off-the-self solutions;
4. maturity of *software products* available from vendors.

The figure was compiled on the basis of several analyst reports and the state of current IT solutions, as observed through interactions with companies, in addition to the trajectory of vendor offerings in the now mature area of Supply Chain Management which, as a pattern, is likely to repeat itself here.

1.7 Technologies for Services and Book Structure

The book provides information on foundation technologies for Service Chain Management. These technologies can provide the basis for innovation within companies and across service chains, leveraging the fact that we are increasingly operating in an increasingly digitally-networked and information-rich world.

As with supply chains, advanced planning and scheduling lies at the core of our chosen subject. Planning for services is covered in Part 1 of the book. We look at strategic resource planning in Chap. 3, demand forecasting in Chap. 4 and tactical planning and resource deployment in Chap. 5. These areas are highly interlinked, underpinning Service Sales and Operations Planning processes; demand forecasts drive decisions on strategic resource planning which in turn constrains tactical planning. This, ultimately, enables the management of short term demand fluctuations by optimising the configuration and deployment of resources. Network planning is examined in Chap. 6 providing a more complete picture (as discussed in Sect. 1.5.4) of the technological capabilities and options in optimising assets as well as people resources.

Part 2 deals with the operational timeframe and the execution of services. The area is heavily reliant on reservation and scheduling techniques. We examine, in Chap. 7, how reservation systems operate and their links to CRM. The pricing of services to complement a reservation function and underpin customer segmentation strategies is discussed in Chap. 8. The scheduling of shifts and work allocation, which are the most complex and challenging areas, are examined in Chaps. 9 and 10 respectively. Chapter 11 examines the all-important IT side of human resources which can act as a data hub, providing information to scheduling and other systems.

Several complementary and supporting technologies work in synergy with the above. These technologies are covered in Part 3 of the book. In Chap. 12, we examine workflows and service-oriented architectures which are vital in the design and modelling of digital service processes, more so when they are geared for flexibility and human-centricity. Personalised communications, which can empower customer and employees, is examined in Chap. 13. Chapter 14 examines customer analytics and business intelligence; the main bridge between marketing and operations management and an important tool in a service chain for sensing and acting upon internal and external signals.

Part 4 examines technologies for the future service chain. Chapter 16 looks at emerging cross-organisational issues and ways to develop a truly collaborative forecasting process across tiers. The impact of the Internet and opportunities in online revenue management are examined in Chap. 17. The use of electronic marketplaces for trading services is explored in Chap. 18, while Chap. 19 explores the application of similar concepts to implement employee empowerment by moving services away from the "command and control" mentality.

Finally, the above technology-oriented chapters are complemented with three important chapters placed at strategic points in the flow of the book which examine emerging customer trends (Chap. 2), agile methods for successfully implementing technology solutions (Chap. 15) and ways of ensuring realisation of benefits from technology investments (Chap. 20).

Before jumping into the main content of the book, we explore one final and emerging dimension that the reader should bear in mind when considering the technology and management insights to be presented in this work.

1.8 The Emergence of Digital Services and Chains

Current perspectives of the Service Chain Management and related subjects are focused on improving the management of physical resources and services as delivered by the mainstream established industries of today. This chapter would have been incomplete if we did not examine another concept and dimension, which is that of the *Digital Service Chain*. The digitisation of services is an ever increasing trend introducing efficiencies in the design and delivery of services. It is also promising to boost cross-country commerce in services which, although it is in the increase, is still far behind goods which constitute the main form of international trade (Wölfl 2005). The "fuel" for this digitisation is the Internet, which enabled by Web 2.0 (O'Reilly 2005) and the ever increasing computing power and network connectivity, creates opportunities for existing products/services to be delivered electronically in complementary, or totally new, ways with new underlying business models (Jopling 2006).

Given this background, we are starting to experience digital service chains which, to a large degree, depend on the digital transportation and processing of information from "raw" inputs to "finished" outputs delivered over bandwidth-rich computer networks to a variety of computationally powerful consumer devices. Prominent emerging such chains can be found in:

- Software Services and
- Entertainment and Media Services,

although other areas such as e-Health and e-Government are also experiencing growth (European Commission 2007).

None of these areas are entirely new. They rather represent the natural switch to digital delivery and, in the form of services (e. g., Software as a Service), of existing "products" in the broader sense. More specifically, *Software Services* can be seen as the evolution of the hosting and networking business into on that provides turnkey and fully configurable ICT solutions on demand which previously would have required a complex physical delivery and installation of hardware/software into the customer's environment. Similarly, *Entertainment and Media Services* focus on the digital delivery of movies, music and other content over the Internet with ever increasing quality (e. g., High Definition TV) without the involvement of physical resources such as CDs, DVDs or the requirement for dedicated service facilities (e. g., Cinemas).

The above mentioned examples have clearly created opportunities for new business models and ways of using software functionality or experiencing content (e. g., as demonstrated by the iPod and iTunes from Apple or Salesforce.com in the CRM on-demand space).

The structure of these digital service chains is not dissimilar to traditional service or product chains and it consists of the following steps:

1. Content Creation: This is often an intense human process to create complex content such as enterprise software, computer games, movies, music, artwork, etc.;
2. Aggregation: This is often a step that gathers together digital information into a useful collection such as a software application suite, television channel, image gallery, etc.;
3. Distribution: In this step, the software or information is placed on a networked computer platform which is using the appropriate distribution system to manage

delivery to multiple users as a digital service (i. e., IPTV platform, Music Server, Software Application Server);

4. Data Transport: A fixed/mobile network and/or a terrestrial/satellite broadcasting platform transfers data on the forward and (increasingly) the reverse path to/from customers;

5. Digital Experience: The digital service is experienced through a variety of devices with convergent products which combine several functions spurring interest and creating new experiences (e. g., media centre which marries PC with TV functionality, smartphone which combines PDA with mobile phone, camera and MP3 player functionality).

The above steps for the two examples mentioned of software and media are illustrated in Fig. 1.5.

Although the domain is fairly new, we can already see some potential opportunities for applying Service Chain Management. For example, one main advantage of current supply chains is the extensive availability and use of Point Of Sales (POS) data in planning. A similar electronic feedback loop is currently largely missing in the digital world with little information captured in real-time on what digital services or content is accessed and by whom. Such a feedback loop possibly based on customer analytics (as examined in Chap. 14), if it is anonymised and non-intrusive, can assist in advanced planning and scheduling of resources across all the service chain steps.

Personalisation of digital services (discussed in the context of communications in Chap. 13) is a largely unexplored area. With ever increasing bandwidth and emerging software/content configurability, capturing user preferences and then using them to customise the experience has obvious potential. Service design and operations would need to adapt and be ready to support mass customisation; learning from similar experiments in manufacturing (Seifert 2003).

Revenue management and online dynamic pricing (examined in Chaps. 8 and 17) have a lot to offer given that the variable cost of digital offerings is often minimal

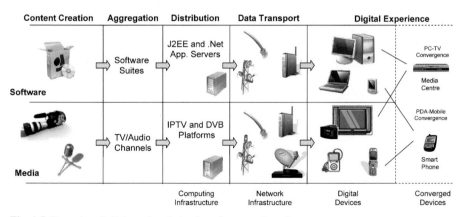

Fig. 1.5 Emerging digital service chains in software and media

(i. e., production of additional units once the first one is produced). Fierce competition can sometimes lead to heavy discounting converting once premium products into cheap commodities, as past cases like CD phone directories have shown (Shapiro and Varian 2000).

Electronic marketplaces (as discussed in Chap. 18) also present us with opportunities. From advertising slots to software components to games, music and movies, communities involving businesses or individuals as in (Kirovski and Jain 2006) could develop and leverage Service Chain Management technologies to digitally trade between them.

1.9 Summary

In this chapter, we defined and then elaborated on the general area of Service Chain Management. The inspiration in defining and analysing this area has been its parallel with manufacturing, known as Supply Chain Management which has received extensive attention by business and academia in recent times.

We believe that services with an ever growing economic influence deserve similar, if not a more, concerted effort to improve productivity through technology and make it easier to trade globally. Using planning and scheduling at its core, Service Chain Management can take advantage of recent advancements in communications, workflow, analytics, mobility and the ability to "digitise" services. This will allow the gradual emergence of an architectural blueprint and associated systems that can help an enterprise institute best practice in the planning and control of its service operations.

In that context, we examined the case of BT and utilities with FOS presented as example of a Service Chain Management platform. Similar, if not better, progress has also seen in airlines, with all service sectors increasingly looking at automation for addressing their service challenges. The emerging concept of the Digital Service Chain was also presented with two example service chains discussed.

The technologies, as they will be presented in the book, were outlined with links made on their utility and relevance in the management of the present and future services and chains. Emerging customer requirements and trends can provide additional insight in this direction by highlighting developments in customer service and their likely impact on operations. We provide this customer angle and perspective in the next chapter.

Chapter 2
Customer Service: Emerging Requirements and Trends

2.1 Introduction

In the previous chapter, we provided an overview of the general area of Service Chain Management and the subjects to be covered in the book. One important source of requirements and inspiration for Service Chain Management applications are the enterprise's customers and their emerging requirements and expectations on customer service. This area also known as *Services Marketing* has been covered by books focusing on the subject of integrating customer requirements across the service enterprise, see Zeithaml and Bitner (2003). However, we focus here on emerging customer service trends emanating from service digitisation and electronic communications which are increasingly impacting service management systems.

Customer service can be seen as the key differentiator in the 21st century global economy and more so for service industries since they centre their operations around it. The modern business faces global competition, low barriers to entry, high levels of innovation and growing user expectations. Businesses need to engender loyalty in their customer base if they are to survive the inevitable disruptions this dynamic and competitive environment brings.

Research consistently points to the importance of customer loyalty and the role customer service plays engendering loyalty in customers. Galbreath and Rogers (1999) in their seminal survey across a number of industries concluded that it costs 5–7 times more to find new customers than to retain current customers and that an increase in customer retention by 2% was equivalent to cutting operating expenses by 10%. Reichheld (2003) recognised that "Loyalty leaders (i. e., companies that have a greater than average loyal customer base) on average grow (over 10 years) at twice the growth of other companies." Similarly, Shaw and Ivens (2002) found 85% of business leaders believed that differentiation by price or product is no longer a sustainable business strategy, with 71% viewing customer experience as the new battleground as also highlighted in the context of the WIPE challenge in Chap. 1. More recent research by Cusumano (2006) concluded that IT businesses that combined a strong service wrap around their core products generated higher and more

C. Voudouris, G. Owusu, R. Dorne, D. Lesaint, *Service Chain Management*
DOI: 10.1007/978-3-540-75504-3, ©Springer 2008

stable profits and higher market valuations. Customer service is the front line in the battle for both customer loyalty and business success.

2.2 Emerging Trends

This chapter identifies six emerging customer service trends changing the way businesses interact with customers. These six trends are transforming markets; changing traditional operational models and helping companies win in the digitally-enabled world. They also increasingly impact requirements and expectations from Service Chain Management and associated processes and systems. Figure 2.1 outlines the six trends and how they ultimately link to customer loyalty.

In more detail, they are as follows:

- The growth of customer intimacy and personalisation of service treating customers as individuals not segments.
- The emergence of the extended and open enterprise, blurring the boundaries between customer, supplier and business.
- The growth in customer and employee advocacy, customers as well as employees can be a business's best asset in delivering service and loyalty.
- Exploitation of customer analytics to enable pro-active service, changing the engagement flow from reacting to customer demands to anticipating them.
- The increased tempo of service delivery and the move towards real-time service and operations, service organisations need to achieve the types of flexibility and

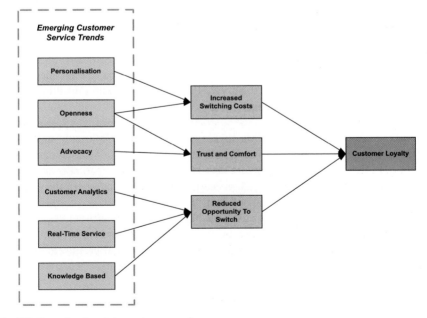

Fig. 2.1 Emerging trends in customer service

control over their operations and suppliers that manufacturers achieved in the 1980s with ERP.

- The deep knowledge-based enterprise leveraging all its information assets to service increasingly complex needs.

The trends impact customer loyalty by enhancing customer perception of brand, increasing their perceived switching costs and minimising the opportunity to churn as also illustrated in Fig. 2.1. The strength of these dependencies varies, but there is a growing body of evidence on their importance in determining customer loyalty and subsequent business success.

2.3 Becoming a Real-Time Enterprise

The basics of good customer service, availability, accessibility and responsiveness, remain at the core of service delivery. However, there is pressure to improve the responsiveness of business to customer needs following the advent of the Internet. The Internet has extended the number of channels available for customers to engage with an organisation and introduced the possibility of real-time control. Online visibility of product or service availability, delivery schedules, catalogues, fault alerts, flight times, all provide information and functionality to customers previously accessible only through retail outlets or call centres. Furthermore, more complex services are increasingly available via the Internet. Health advice such as NHS Direct[1] provide online healthcare decision making, numerous banks specialise in on-line services as do insurance companies. Never has so much information and choice been directly accessible by end customers with many delivering a real-time response to their needs.

This immediacy and expectation of much reduced waiting times, impacts the backend operations and service chains supporting the customer experience. Inevitably this leads to increased automation and a focus on the usability of services when extended into the customer's domain.

Wittgreffe et al. (2006) provide a good example of this trend in the corporate telecommunications solutions and the wider impact a move to real-time service has on systems and operations. In their example, corporate customers are provided with real-time SLA (Service Level Agreement) management which automatically flexes resource capacity on-demand to suit the applications being used by the customer. This requires not only a portal for customers to monitor and adjust their SLAs on-line, but a billing system which can rate and charge in real-time; the ability to monitor and automatically optimise a variety of resources in real-time (storage, processing and network capacity) when SLA breaches are experienced and a policy manager to automatically interpret the SLA thresholds given by the customer. An extension of control to the customer has a broad impact on the functioning and performance of the underlying operational systems.

---

[1] www.nhsdirect.nhs.uk

To the business customer, they experience a user-friendly dashboard for monitoring and controlling SLAs and response times of seconds rather than days. To the service provider, they realise cost savings but need to re-engineer systems and processes to enable real-time delivery. In a recent survey by Gartner Research (Scott 2007), 63% of businesses viewed real-time infrastructure was an imperative for their organisation and that the main driver for this was service quality and cost.

In the consumer markets, there are many examples of the advent of real-time service. The airline industry is one that has seen significant disruption, with on-line ticketless booking, self selection of seats, check-in on-line. These have reduced costs, impacted fares and reduced overall cycle-times by removing traffic from travel agents and call centres, as well as slimming down the airport operations. Forrester Research (Harteveldte and Rotman Epps 2007) reported that 86% of US leisure travellers used on-line check-in facilities in 2006. The average cost of an agent check-in is $3.02 versus between $0.14 to $0.32 for a self-service option. Customers experienced savings in time waiting and queuing; airlines reduced costs.

In a competitive marketplace, providing real-time control and immediate resolution of issues is a key market differentiator through the dramatic reductions in response times experienced by customers and the cost reductions experienced by business. This, as evidenced by the airline industry, can reshape markets and customer expectations.

Several chapters in the book describe specific technologies that can underpin real-time service. Chapter 7 and 10 provide insights on automating service reservations and work allocation which are both instrumental in real-time order reception and processing. Chapter 8, 16 and 17 examine approaches to online pricing and other types of information exchange in B2C and B2B contexts allowing companies to communicate faster demand and supply parameters (e. g., price, volume) across their service chains.

2.4 Making Service Personal

At the heart of CRM (Customer Relationship Management) is the "relationship" between a customer and a business. However, many organisations take an operational view of their CRM systems focusing solely on operational measures and ignoring the softer side of customer relationships which often have a greater impact on customer loyalty. There is a growing range of technologies aimed at supporting increased personalisation of service to customers.

The Internet is a growing channel for customer service. The first generation of personalisation technologies on the Internet employ user profiling based on a user log-in, allowing systems to recognise the user and subsequently provide a context sensitive service. The customer experiences this through recognition of personal preferences, a history of engagement such as previous interactions, access to tailored information such as order updates. A new generation of personalised service uses subtle analysis of user interactions to tailor the experience. Urban (2007) web morphing engine analyses mouse clicks to classify users against different cognitive models. These are then used to tailor the subsequent rendering of content to suit the user's preferences.

In a similar way, Tateson and Bonsma (2003) presented *eShopping Garden* which monitors user preferences when browsing an on-line catalogue, characterising the types of images selected, resulting in it offering images that is believes will be of interest to that user based on its experience of other similar users. This has been subsequently applied to supporting the on-line catalogue for the Tate Modern gallery[2].

Call Centres are also exploiting a new generation of technologies supporting increased personalisation of service. CLI (Calling Line Identification) allows call centres to detect the identity of the caller and subsequently call up profile and history data prior to answering. This is increasingly used to predict the likely cause of the call by combining this with customer analytics capabilities allowing the call to be directed to the agent best placed to handle the call. An emerging technology that is being employed in call centres is non-linguistics analysis of a call, which analyses non-linguistic signals such as tone of voice, pace of conversation to predict the behavioural outcome of a call. These can both detect cues which can be flagged to the agent in order to improve the likely outcome of the call. Picard (1997) and more recently Pentland (2004) describe how such signals can both detect customer emotional states such as stress, and be used to predict the likely outcome of the call.

A more fundamental shift in an enterprise's ability to personalise is through the adaptation of its processes to suit customer needs. Thompson et al. (2006) outline Kreno, a prototype system which can compose an end to end business process on the fly in response to a customer's needs. This extends the traditional manufacturing model of mass-customisation epitomised by companies such as Dell, to the service sector, and is a strong indication of the type of agility envisaged for the service industries in the future.

There will be an ever growing trend towards customisation of service where organisations tailor and adapt their offering to meet customer needs. This will eventually go beyond the service wrap and customer support aspects focusing on the actual service itself and how it can automatically evolve to suit the customer's particular situations, roles even moods and general lifestyles. Chapter 13 focuses on this subject by examining the personalisation of communications when provided as a service. Technologies described in that chapter are generic and they can be utilised to assist in the configuration and adaptation of services at the provision and execution stages so that services become more precise and dynamic.

2.5 Exploiting Customer Analytics

Central to excellent customer service is customer intimacy; the understanding a business has of its customers and their experience of their products and services. It is with customer analytics where we start to see a convergence of the marketing and operations functions of a business.

---

[2] http://www.tate.org.uk/collection/carousel/index.htm

Customer analytics is a strong differentiator in the marketplace. The UK supermarket chain, Tesco (Humby and Hunt 2003) introduced a loyalty card in 1995 which captured customer spending habits and allowed the issuing of discount coupons. Its analytics gave it insight into its customer base and their spending habits helping to drive the design of its stores and Internet shopping business. Tesco issues 7 million variations in its product coupons based on customer analytics, increasing redemption rates to 20–50%, the industry average being 2%. This has played a key role in driving customer loyalty and revenue growth.

Capital One, a US financial services company, is another proponent of customer analytics, running multiple experiments per day to find the best levers to improve customer retention and profitability. Davenport and Harris (2007) report how their approach resulted in an increase in customer retention of 87% with one product set and lowered the cost to acquire customers by 83%.

Recent research points the way to increasingly sophisticated approaches often refer to as customer lifecycle modelling. An example of this is provided by Nauck et al. (2006) who describe the application of advanced data analytics techniques for predicting individual customer lifecycles and the events a customer is most likely to experience. They analyse operational data on past customer events and predict a sequence of most likely future events. This allows businesses to anticipate customer events, such as complaints or churn events, and where appropriate act proactively. Nauck et al. (2006) report that exploiting customer analytics to anticipate potential customer complaints and subsequently contacting the customer, both reduced complaints "significantly," saved costly complaint escalation, and improved the overall customer experience.

An additional benefit of customer lifecycle modelling provides a stronger basis for predicting customer lifetime values which allows churn reduction activities to focus on prioritising the most profitable customer accounts.

Operationalising the outcomes of customer lifecycle modelling provides a powerful business tool for improving operations. By monitoring customer behaviour, anticipating needs, taking action in response and then measuring the impact, a business develops a data driven feedback loop for operational improvements. It has a com-

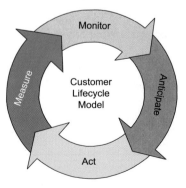

Fig. 2.2 The use of a customer lifecycle model in an operational context

pass by which to assess change and improve its relationship with its customers. The proposed approach is depicted in Fig. 2.2.

Chapter 14 is devoted to the subject of customer analytics and more generally business intelligence. In there, we present state-of-the-art approaches for companies to utilise to improve in this area.

2.6 Engendering Customer and Employee Advocacy

Often service companies rely heavily on customer satisfaction as the key measure of customer service. Many fail to appreciate that satisfaction is not necessarily a strong indicator of customer loyalty. Reichheld (2003) concluded that the overwhelming majority of customers that leave a company say they are satisfied and that of 84% of customers who are satisfied only 41% are loyal. Jones and Sasser (1995) noted that in highly competitive markets there is a large difference in levels of customer loyalty between satisfied customers as opposed to completely satisfied customers. Satisfaction is too simplistic a measure for capturing customer loyalty.

Urban (2006) recognises the importance of going beyond traditional customer relationship management and traditional satisfaction measures, towards what he terms as customer advocacy as the key to delivering a loyal customer base.

Customer advocacy aims to make customers strong advocates of products and services, thereby placing customers at the front of a company's engagement with its customers. Customer advocacy by its nature is a longer term strategy and difficult to measure as it is essentially an emotional response to a brand, product or service. However, it is evident in many leading brands, FirstDirect; Apple; Harley-Davidson; Amazon.com how powerful customer advocacy can be. At the root of this relationship is the trust.

Advocacy is a powerful capability for generating customer loyalty relying on the core concept of "word of mouth" marketing, whereby customers become advocates of a company's products.

Creating customer advocates starts with the employees. Heskett et al. (1997) found a strong correlation between employee satisfaction, customer satisfaction and profit. All employees in a company need to be service advocates focused on customers not just the front line staff. Big River Telephone (Band and Schuler 2007) is an example of transforming customer loyalty and acquisition rates by focusing on the personal engagement between the company employee and the customer. The achieved 98.6% customer satisfaction and grew their customer base by involving senior executives in customer engagement.

Employee empowerment and commitment to servicing customers, combined with a customer base willing to advocate a business's products is a powerful combination when weathering market disruptions and pressures. Although the above is more of a marketing subject, we examine technologies for employee empowerment in Chap. 19. Empowerment is often the neglected factor to achieve staff engagement (beyond better compensation and training) and through that customer satisfaction and advocacy. The subject of empowerment is strongly linked to Service Chain Management and a promising way to improve service operations by establishing a high performance and entrepreneurial style culture.

2.7 Becoming a Knowledge-Driven Service Enterprise

A new generation of Internet tools commonly known as Web 2.0 are increasingly being adopted both by businesses in their day to day operations. Blogging, Wikis, podcasts, social networking, webchats, forums, instant messaging, and collaborative working – all support a new generation of users which epitomise a knowledge-based enterprise. These solutions provide a broader range of channels for collaboration between employees, between businesses and with partners across a service chain. The outcome of this is a business which leverages both formal structured data in its systems as well as the tacit knowledge held in its employees, customers and partners in supporting its service operations.

Aral et al. (2006) identified a strong positive correlation between the structure and size of a workers communications network (such as email, messaging and social networks etc.) and their productivity. Such results are also seen in large scale deployments in industry.

In June 2005, IBM (2006) launched "ThinkPlace" to allow all employees to create, exchange and develop ideas, supporting new products and services. ThinkPlace is an open collaborative environment where ideas are jointly developed, overcoming barriers of access to expertise and resources. This open, collaborative forum for innovation combines the best practices of jams, online communities and marketplaces. ThinkPlace exceeds 90,000 IBM users, of which approximately 40% were repeat users. In 2006, ThinkPlace had generated over $10 million in revenue for new services or productivity savings, with ideas focused upon new revenue generation (14%), cultural (36%) and productivity/savings (50%).

By leveraging the collective knowledge of an extended enterprise, employees, customers, suppliers and partners can:

- share information so that they may learn more about customers and how they use products, about suppliers and how to improve end-to-end processes, about employees and how to improve performance,
- share ideas and improve upon them providing channels for innovation and improvement and finally
- share work practices so that all parts of the business may benefit from doing things the best possible way.

Such change will impact operational performance, however the key benefit is the agility it introduces into the organisation so it adapts and it evolves when faced with changing customer needs. By embracing an open culture of learning and collaboration, organisations can both improve their responsiveness and ability to satisfy their customer base.

The majority of chapters in the book strongly link to and support the vision of a knowledge-driven service enterprise. Service Chain Management and related approaches provide the necessary (and often largely missing) technology infrastructure required to collect, organise, process and maintain structured operational data which are essential to manage a service company in lack of a full blown ERP. These service management approaches and systems have the potential to make an organisation better by driving operational excellence.

Complemented with light and user-friendly knowledge management approaches from Web 2.0, we probably look at new powerful and holistic systems to emerge that are capable of "sensing" and "acting" upon a variety of internal or external signals and structured or unstructured data that is collected across the enterprise and also from customers and suppliers both upstream and downstream the service chain.

2.8 Opening-up the Enterprise

Alongside the emergence of the Internet, a new generation is emerging, known as Generation C (for Content), this generation is adept at using digital technologies and invariably creating their own content.

Resulting from this shift in consumer behaviour is the emergence of more collaborative channels for customer engagement. Customer forums supporting, advising and sometimes confusing customers are commonplace. Originating in the computing industry where forums often supported programming networks, evolving into IT support forums and are now emerging across the full spectrum of products and services. It is now commonplace for people to look to the Internet to interact with others on topics ranging from medical complaints to tracing family trees. Forums provide a unique insight into customer behaviour and viewpoints previously hidden.

However, forums appeal to customer altruism. Securing active customer engagement requires a light touch from business so it is not perceived as exploiting customer goodwill. Too much corporate control stifles user engagement and can reduce the level of trust placed in that channel.

An example of a more recent shift in opening up an enterprise has been around the production lifecycle. BBC Backstage[3] and NikeID[4] are examples, from different industries, of customer co-production where customers take a very active part in the product creation process. Rather than companies designing for users, users design for themselves. The seed of this new form of engagement can be seem in the plethora of collaborative content tools MySpace, Wikipedia, LinkedIn[5], Yahoo Pipes[6], Flickr. These services have blurred the traditional business-customer boundary. More enlightened companies view this as an opportunity to tap into a broader

---

[3] http://Backstage.bbc.co.uk

[4] http://Nikeid.nike.com

[5] http://www.linkedin.com

[6] http://pipes.yahoo.com/

knowledge base, extending an organisation to include not only its employees but its customers and suppliers. Again, as with many on-line offerings, the biggest impact is on the backend systems and operations. NikeID allows customers to design their own trainers, have them manufactured and delivered. This requires a sophisticated manufacturing supply chain supporting mass customisation.

Research (Prahalad and Ramaswamy 2004) has shown that the co-creation experience is both a positive experience for customers and a source of value creation for an organisation. Additionally, it can create enhanced customer loyalty by increased the perceived switching costs to a customer. As Auh et al. (2007) conclude in their study of co-production in financial services:

> "... drawing the customer closer to the service production and delivery process has positive outcomes for the firm. Far from feeling overwhelmed and burdened by the co-production process, customers who participate ... feel more closely tied to the organisation and demonstrate a stronger intention to use the firm for future purchases."

An open enterprise offers both a broader opportunity for customer engagement and an opportunity to source a wider spectrum of views when introducing new products and services. It recognises that new ideas are not the reserve of the enterprise and innovation is a collaborative process that needs to involve customers. The Internet provides a powerful channel for facilitating this engagement.

Opening up the service enterprise and engaging the customer deeper in co-production is not an easy challenge and requires flexible resources and processes to provide customised services while maintaining a competitive price. Although the marketing side is a major consideration once the decision is taken to move the enterprise down that route most issues to be discussed and resolved are heavily operational. Resource flexibility can be achieved by advanced planning and scheduling approaches as detailed in Parts 1 and 2 of the book. Emerging approaches such as flexible workflow examined in Chap. 12 can provide the necessary foundation for managing process variation while staff empowerment (see Chap. 19) can help counteract organisational rigidities preventing successful service delivery in an open environment.

2.9 Summary

In the growing service economy, a customer's experience of service is increasingly the key differentiator for a business. The way in which businesses operate when selling, provisioning, supporting, billing, and repairing services, often determines customer loyalty, their value and profitability, and indeed will contribute to a company's market value. Customer expectations of service never stand still. Growing competition, an increasing tempo of innovation and globalisation means there is a continuous escalation of expectations which business needs to respond to.

In order to stay competitive and drive business growth, organisations can exploit several current trends both in terms of marketing strategy but also with regards to operations and service management systems. This advice can be summarised to the following.

- Grow customer intimacy and personalisation of service.
- Extend your organisation to involve and collaborate with customers.
- Engender advocacy in both customers and employees.
- Exploit customer analytics to enable pro-active service.
- Strive for real-time service and operations.
- Leverage your enterprises knowledge base.

We have seen a shift from a viewpoint where customer service is the add-on or wrap to the core product, to one where it is the core product itself and more so in the services sector where maximising customer experience is a key success factor. Service companies are increasingly designing this experience their customers have, ensuring it is a driver of business processes and systems rather than a by-product. These changes are reflecting the increased strategic and operational value placed on customers as the main stakeholders in a service business.

Part I
Resource Planning

A key element of optimising a service chain is the effective utilisation of resources – a process we term *resource planning*. As noted in Chap. 1, a service organisation is characterised by two types of resources: people and assets. Decisions on how best to utilise an organisation's resources can be made for the long (i. e., strategic), medium (i. e., tactical) or short (i. e., operational) term. Strategic decisions primarily affect capital expenditure (i. e., CAPEX). On the other hand tactical and operational decisions affect operational expenditure (i. e., OPEX). In order to minimise OPEX and maximise investments related to CAPEX, decisions regarding resource utilisation will have to be optimal. There are two basic components of resource planning – demand forecasting and supply planning. Visibility of both demand and supply profiles is a prerequisite for optimal resource planning.

This part is about developing systems to automate resource planning. Implementation of a resource planning system requires a framework that articulates and supports the modelling of the process – i. e., from capturing of demand and supply data; through matching supply to demand; and to acting on recommendations. One of the challenges in implementing a resource planning system is to ensure the accuracy of the demand forecasts. Inaccurate forecasts will lead to non-optimal plans. Optimality is key to recommendations being acted on.

In this part, we also outline other challenges of automating resource planning systems notably, stakeholder involvement, data integrity, security and budget; and then describe the approaches required to address them. The approach taken in this part is to start from a high level and then go into specific techniques. The first chapter looks at strategic resource planning. It argues the case for an automated resource planning system and outlines a framework for implementing one. This provides a high-level view of resource planning. We then address the challenges in generating accurate demand forecasts in the second chapter. The last two chapters focus on optimising resource planning. The first of these two focuses on human resources with emphasis on generating capacity and deployment plans for the medium to short term. The last chapter is on network planning (i. e., assets). Here we describe the techniques needed to optimise the planning and design of networks.

Chapter 3
Strategic Resource Planning

3.1 Introduction

One of the cornerstones of successful organisations has been the optimal use of their workforce[1]. Two types of resources characterise service organisations: *front* and *back* office resources. These resources are defined by their capability (i. e., skills), location and availability. Front office resources handle incoming demand whilst the back office resources execute the services related to the demand. Planning of such resources can be carried out at one of three levels: strategic, tactical and operational; referring to long-, medium-, and short-, term planning respectively. The three levels for planning may overlap or may be distinct. Either way there is a flow of information from strategic to tactical and from tactical to operational. The loop is then closed by flow of information from operational back to strategic (see Fig. 3.1). In this context, strategic planning provides information on the overall balance of customer demand with available resource capacity. Tactical planning suggests a coarse-grain allocation of resources to tasks with no consideration given to when those tasks must be executed. And operational planning[2] represents the allocation of specific resources to specific tasks; detailing the specific times of execution. The level of detail required for planning increases as one moves in time from strategic to operational. For strategic planning it is sufficient to analyse resource requirements based on the number of resources and their levels of productivity. On the other hand, for operational planning it is imperative that details such as starting location, preferred working location, scheduled hours, and availability for overtime are identified for accurate deployment to be realised.

The focus of this chapter is twofold. The first is to examine the extent to which strategic resource planning[3] has been automated in service-oriented organisations. The examination highlights the fundamental organisational, research and software engineering issues that have to be addressed before a fully automated system can

---

[1] Hereafter referred to as resources.

[2] Also referred to as scheduling in this book.

[3] We use *strategic resource planning* and *strategic planning* interchangeably.

C. Voudouris, G. Owusu, R. Dorne, D. Lesaint, *Service Chain Management*
DOI: 10.1007/978-3-540-75504-3, ©Springer 2008

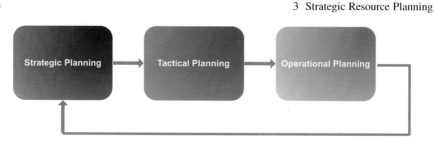

Fig. 3.1 Information flow from strategic to operational planning

be realised. To underpin our discussions of the challenges for automating strategic resource planning, we define the strategic resource planning process. The second objective is to provide a set of guidelines on implementing an automated strategic resource planning system. The remainder of this chapter is structured as follows. We examine the motivations for strategic resource planning in Sect. 3.2 and argue the case for automation. In Sect. 3.3 we define the strategic resource planning process. We outline and address the challenges that must be addressed before a fully automated resource planning system can be realised in Sect. 3.4. In Sect. 3.5 we provide some guidelines on implementing an automated strategic resource planning system. We provide a summary of the chapter in Sect. 3.6.

3.2 The Case for Strategic Resource Planning

Fundamentally strategic resource planning involves forecasting long term demand for services and identifying the resource requirements needed to deliver those services. It can be viewed as the process of analyzing key success factors, economic drivers and the forces that drive change in an industry (Shaw et al. 1998). The process is analytical and convergent with a view to developing strategies for managing risk (Heracleous 1998). Through strategic resource planning, the contingencies, uncertainties, trends, and opportunities that are often unanticipated can be identified, evaluated and acted upon (Miller and Waller 2003).

We adopt Vancil and Lorange's (1975) definition of strategic planning – the process of *progressively narrowing of strategic choices* which have to be implemented on yearly, quarterly, monthly and weekly basis. Oftentimes, this process involves two main elements: *multiple stakeholders* and *disparate sources of information*. It also requires information exchanges among the stakeholders. The successful coordination and synchronisation of information exchanges among stakeholders coupled with an integrated single-truth information source are hallmarks of successful service organisations. If organisations spend most of their time reacting to events, this is symptomatic of either a poorly articulated and/or implemented strategic plan.

High level choices in strategic planning revolve around four key areas: *investment* in new services, *provision* of existing services to customers, *repairing* (i. e., assurance) of "broken" services; and *ceasing* of services. Investment, provision, repairing and ceasing of services are inter-related. For example, investing in a new service may lead to a reduction in the number of faults that may arise from existing services. Identifying such relations and the impact they have on an organisation's resources involve the process of analyzing lots of data from different parts of the organisation. Clearly, the level of complexity and the sheer volume of data involved in this process necessitate an automated approach for efficiency and effectiveness. Indeed there have been attempts to automate strategic resource planning in service organisations. However, automation has been limited to the front office with either specialised statistical packages or spreadsheets used for the back office resource planning. Specialised statistical packages require expertise with statistical knowledge which limits the usage of such tools. On the other hand, spreadsheets are easy to use but do not lend themselves to collaborative decision making; become complicated with time as new features are added and are brittle.

There is an emerging desire in service organisations to move away from developing disparate spreadsheets and bespoke statistical packages to an integrated single truth, strategic planning system for business users. Clear evidence of this is to be found in the attempts being made to develop such systems for service organisations – see analysts' reports from Forrester (Herrell 2007) and Aberdeen Group (Vigoroso 2004). As noted earlier, the success of strategic planning systems is dependent on the richness of the data it uses. Data gathering is a laborious process. Thus, an automated strategic planning system will allow business users to focus on what they are supposed to do – that is, making decisions rather than data gathering or model building. Strategic decision making also includes analyzing investment opportunities; environmental change and market competition; and business performance.

3.3 Characterising the Strategic Resource Planning Process

Service organisations operate in financial cycles. A cycle is defined as a year, encompassing a 12 month period, which is further broken down into quarters. They budget and report to their investors within a typical financial cycle. The strategic resource planning process provides a mechanism for soliciting inputs from multiple stakeholders (see Fig. 3.2) on customer demand predictions and resource requirements. The process is repeated several times in a financial cycle. Each cycle is a joint review by all stakeholders with focus on analyzing variances between what has been budgeted and what has happened with the aim to address issues that arise. Accurate demand forecasting is *sine qua non* for optimal resource planning. In his paper, *Four Steps to Forecast Total Market Demand*, Barnett (1988) note that history is replete with stories of organisations making strategic errors because of inaccurate demand forecasts. He cites the case of over forecasting of demand by the US electric utilities between 1975 and 1985 which led to an adverse effect on the financial situation in the electric utilities industry. Barnett also refers to the effects of inaccurate forecasts in the petroleum industry in the 1980s in his paper. In 2006 a leading Communi-

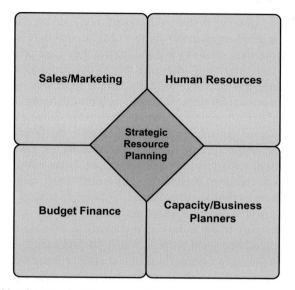

Fig. 3.2 Stakeholders in strategic resource planning

cations Service Provider in the UK underestimated the demand for their premium broadband package, which resulted in an increase in customer complaints (Durman 2007).

Barnett argues that without demand forecasts, decisions on investment, marketing and resource allocations will be based on hidden, unconscious assumptions about industry wide requirements. As noted earlier, drivers for forecast in service organisations can be classified as one of the following: *investment, provision, repair* and *cease*. These four top-level drivers give the total market forecast. Analyzing the demand curves for these drivers will highlight the impact of one driver on another. For example, it will bring to the fore the effect of product substitution when an investment is made for a new infrastructure.

Once the forecasts for these high-level drivers have been agreed upon, they must be decomposed into their constituent products. The process of decomposition over a time frame is termed demand planning (Owusu et al. 2002; Vitasek 2006). The purpose of demand planning is to be able to translate the demand forecasts into skill requirements. The procedure for demand planning may include split ratios using statistical techniques (Makridakis et al. 1983) or some form of heuristics using intelligence from sources such as the environment (e. g., weather), competition, industry regulation and so on.

Once demand has been identified at the skill level, only then is it possible to know how many resources are required. Thus, the output of the demand forecasting phase can be directly translated into a requirement for resources. Naturally questions such as the following arise. Are *there enough resources? Do they have the right skills? Are they well positioned to serve customers?* The process of answering these questions is referred to as resource, capacity or manpower planning (Vitasek 2006). In essence resource planning provides the mechanism to match available manpower resource capability and capacity to the demand forecast. Resources tend to be multiskilled; mobile (i. e., have multiple areas of work), and have different attendance patterns. The procedure for matching supply to demand involves either (i) flexing capacity to meet the demand or (ii) constrain the demand. The latter approach is termed constrained as opposed to the former which is, unconstrained resource planning. Capacity can be flexed along three dimensions: *skill*, *geography* and *availability*. Flexing capacity in the constrained mode, in most cases, tend to focus on the geography dimension. Flexing capacity is making decisions. Decisions related to skill involve retraining. Those along the geography dimension include permanent deployment, recruitment, layoff, and retention. When it comes to availability, decisions such as productivity improvements, shift patterns and overtime allowance can be made. Decisions have cost implications. In the case of strategic planning, the costs affect budgets that have been set. Most times budgets are set and the resource planning process is about identifying the variance between the budget and the resources required to match the forecasted demand. Invariably, this involves some negotiations between those who set the budgets and the strategic planners. These negotiations iterate until a state of "reconciliation" has been achieved. Only then will

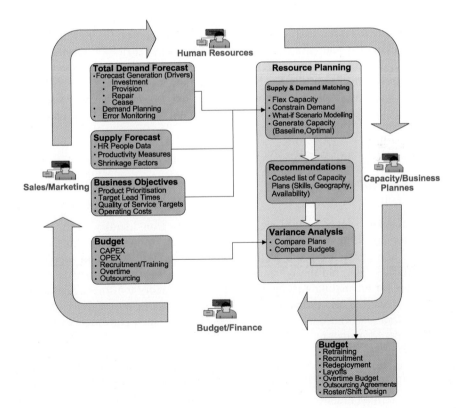

Fig. 3.3 The strategic planning process

the resource/capacity plans be communicated to the tactical/operational planners for execution. A "reconciliation" state defines how many resources with the relevant skills are required in each geographical area; their shift patterns; and the amount of overtime allowed. We summarise the strategic planning process in Fig. 3.3.

3.4 Barriers to Implementing an Automated Strategic Resource Planning System

Decision making is at the heart of strategic planning. Effective decision making is underpinned by a wealth of relevant data. Bill Gates in his book "Business @ the speed of thought" (Gates 1999) emphasises the importance of flow of information to the survival of organisations. He argues that good actionable data is needed to get the most out of an organisation's resources. The questions that arise are: *who are the decision makers? What data is required for strategic planning? Is the data up to date? How will decision makers use the data?* As noted earlier, decision making in strategic planning is centred on resource utilisation. Resource utilisation is influenced by demand priorities, budgets and other organisation-wide objectives. Thus, from a user-centric perspective, a strategic planning system must provide the user with the ability to (i) forecast, view and adjust demand curves; (ii) view and model resource behaviour; and (iii) create and modify product attributes and their associated mapping to skills. The strategic planning process described in the previous section begins to highlight the key barriers to automation – challenges around demand management; resource planning; enablers such as data standardisation, security, strategy and governance and budget management. We examine these challenges as follows.

3.4.1 Demand Management

Demand management is a set of activities that range from identifying the demand from customers, through translating specific customers' orders into promised delivery dates, in order to achieve a desired balance between demand and supply. Two main activities underpin the demand management process; first there is *demand forecasting* for estimating customer demand and secondly the forecasted demand has to be converted into estimated promised delivery dates – an activity known as *demand planning*. The output of demand planning is then converted to resource requirements for matching with the supply. With the time to market being a differentiator amongst service organisations; the questions that arise are how quickly can one forecast demand? How resilient is the demand management system? In view of the fact that the accuracy of any forecast depends on the interpretation of historical data and external influences, how does one ensure that historical data is interpreted in a consistent manner? We examine these challenges below.

3.4.1.1 Flexible Multi-Forecasting Approach

It is worth noting that historical data is not the only data required for strategic fore-casting, e. g., how does one forecast at strategic level when historical data does not reflect current and future situations? In such scenarios, details about current and fu-ture projects can be used. Demand tends to be hierarchical in nature (see Fig. 3.4) to reflect the different types of users in an organisation. From a strategic viewpoint, resource planners may be interested in investment and provision programmes and so on. Whilst on an execution level, business users will be interested in specific prod-ucts. Typically customers order products – an example of this could be the forecast for broadband connections in the South East of England.

The need for forecast applications to be customised for specific requirements can not be overemphasised – for example, providing the ability to forecast based on var-ious customer types, geographic locations, required skills and time windows. Cus-tomis ing a system so that it is able to provide a forecast for specific requirements is a complicated task as it involves considerable reconfiguration of the forecasting al-gorithms. A structured approach which allows users to represent their requirements in an intuitive manner is needed.

Generating a forecast requires the use of statistical models. The use of statistical models in forecasting demand is well recognised. For example Erlang-C (Angus 2001) is used extensively in forecasting demand that is visible to the front-office. However, when it comes to visibility of demand that require action by back office resources, various models and thus specialised packages exist. Besides, there may also be external events that may influence baseline forecasts. This leaves open the problem of seamless integration of different models with the view of combining them in a user friendly manner to strategic planners.

Demand planning specifies delivery dates, lead times, priorities, specific skill requirements and their sequence. There are two approaches to demand planning. The first approach uses a bootstrapping method (Hansen 2000) to sample histori-

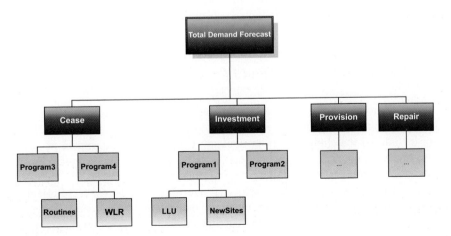

Fig. 3.4 Example demand hierarchy

cal jobs to convert the forecast volumes into forecast jobs. Thus, the jobs will have specific attributes needed to match them against some resources. The second approach is based on templates – equations that define the relationships between jobs. The first step in using the second approach is to identify the activities or skill set required to deliver the order. The second is to define the sequence of the activities with their durations. Demand planning may involve using either a simple heuristic or a sophisticated template to convert forecast volumes to jobs. The challenge with demand planning is to provide a mechanism to capture user specific equations and heuristics.

3.4.1.2 Resilience in Managing Demand

Forecasting is an operation that demands constant accuracy monitoring. Once a baseline forecast has been generated; users will adjust the forecasts. There are four approaches to adjusting a forecast. The first approach is to exclude exceptional events from future forecast. Clearly such events don't follow any specific pattern. Once an event is excluded, a heuristic is used to compute a value from previous data points which will then be used in generating future forecasts. The second approach to adjusting a forecast is to override it for a specific time period. The third approach involves applying a template to the forecast generated. These templates tend to be mathematical equations; such as positive/negative gradient; normal distribution; and exponential growth. Once a template has been identified; users apply it to a baseline forecast to increase or decrease the forecast. The last approach to adjusting a forecast is used when multiple baseline forecasts have been generated from different sources.

How accurate are the adjustments? How resilient are the forecasting models to changes? In most organisations, more than one forecasting model will be in use. This poses a real challenge when it comes to tuning the various models. The challenge arises from the relationships among the models. How can these relationships be represented so as to facilitate automated self-tuning?

3.4.2 Supply Management and Planning

If demand is to be matched to supply well, the data of the resources (see Fig. 3.5) – i. e., supply must be accurate, timely and appropriate. The activities in resource planning include (i) matching supply to demand; (ii) assessing the impact of service levels and backlogs; (iii) suggest optimal resource plan; and (iv) compute the cost associated with the plans. Resource planning tends to be constrained by business objectives. Business objectives may include (i) overtime budgets; (ii) recruitment and training budget; (iii) outsourcing target; (iv) investment and maintenance targets, denoting priority of demand; and target lead times reflecting service level agreements.

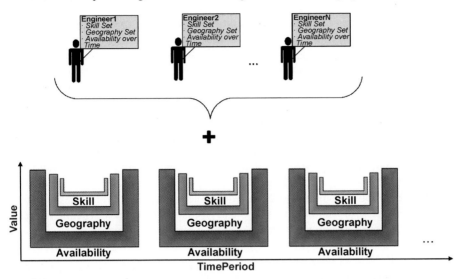

Fig. 3.5 Supply attributes aggregation

Business objectives allow users to engage in scenario modelling. Four types of input are required for generating resource plans:

- Budget constraints on resource acquisition schemes, overtime and so on.
- Demand forecast and job profiles.
- The *initial supply forecast*. This is a baseline estimation of the available manpower based on the current workforce. While it is often fixed with regard to geography and time, it is variable with regard to the skill breakdown due to multiskilled labour.
- Business objectives include the following:

  - The supply *shrinkage*. This considers absences such as leave, sickness or training which lead to a reduction of the average working time of the resources.
  - *Overtime*, on the other hand, allows the stretching of the resource working time.
  - *Intake* describes the employment of additional workforce and can be permanent or temporary in nature, and thus leads to an increase of the available head count.
  - *Wastage* specifies the loss of labour and hence a head count reduction due to reasons such as layoff or retirement.
  - Hiring of *contractors* enables an organisation to bring in additional workforce on a temporary basis.
  - Quality of service targets.

The main objective of the matching phase is to ascertain whether the demand in each geographical location and during each considered time period can be satisfied with the available resources. Besides, multiple products can require the same skills and hence can compete for the same resources. How does one determine the optimal utilisation of resources with such conflicting objectives? One approach is to order products according to their priorities. There may be other approaches depending on business objectives. The issue here is that of flexibility in incorporating new approaches in a system. Classical Operational Research (OR) techniques (Simpson et al. 1995), although relatively successful in matching supply to demand; tend to be slow for large data sets and tend to be limited in their representation capabilities. Recently, heuristic based methods (Silver 2004) are becoming increasingly popular in workforce optimisation applications because they provide solutions in reasonable time and their representational capabilities. The challenges here are that of generating optimal solutions within reasonable time; and providing explanations of solutions in a user friendly manner. Clearly, what is needed is a dynamic capacity flexing and multi-objective system for matching resources to demand.

3.4.3 Variance Analysis, Recommendations and Reports

Two possible scenarios could arise from matching supply to demand: under- and over-resource utilisation. The former is characterised by a lack of sufficient manpower to deliver the requested services, and thus will lead to a reduced quality of service and loss of potential revenue. The later sees a proportion of the resources unused and thus will result in inflated business costs. Both situations are undesirable for a service business. The question is how does one close existing gaps? In order to close the gap, it is imperative that a list of recommendations and their associated costs be made available. There are four classes of recommendations that could arise from the matching phase. Three of the four classes are resource centric with one focusing on demand. The first class relates to decisions that affect the geographical locations of the resources. The second requires decisions to be taken on the skill requirements of the resources; and the third has to do with the availability of the resources. It should be noted that these decisions have long term implications. We refer to the process of generating these recommendations as *variance analysis*.

During the variance analysis stage, there is a requirement to alter the parameters of the supply and the demand models in order to reduce existing mismatches. What are the available parameters? As noted earlier, resources (i. e., supply) are defined by their capability, location and availability (i. e., attendance patterns). For instance, Jensen et al. (2006) suggest the use of the secondary skills of surplus resources. This way, resources will be shifted from one skill to another skill. On location, Burnham et al. (2007) suggest that resources can also be moved permanently to areas where they will be needed – i. e., move the resources to where the work is. Similarly, they provide some guidance on altering the availability of resources. They argue that one can influence the available resource volumes by managing shrinkage and overtime factors. They explicate their argument by offering examples such as shifting leave absences to less busy periods of the year, reducing time lost due to training and bringing more resources in on overtime during work-intensive periods. Burnham et al. also note that one can control the head count of the workforce by altering intake and wastage, and thus influence the overall resource volume. Sasser (1976) proposes the "Chase" strategy which describes how additional resources, such as agency workers or contractors, can be brought in from outside suppliers during peak periods. On the demand side, the possibilities for influencing and altering the forecasted work volumes are limited as demand is customer driven and is thus beyond the control of the business. The "Level" strategy described by Sasser can be used to control demand (Sasser 1976). Options for levelling demand as suggested by Sasser include the use of (i) appointment and reservation system, (ii) differential pricing to increase demand for non-peak periods and (iii) advertising and promotion. Another approach suggested by Lesaint (2006) is to shift demand in time by postponing or bringing forward initiatives such as product launches or promotions.

Identifying the parameters needed to eliminate discrepancies between supply and demand marks the start of the variance analysis process. Generating the scenarios/recommendations for the possible combinations of all the parameters is a challenging task. The challenge is to generate accurate scenarios in business time. It is obvious that one can automate the process. The question that arises is how does one generate scenarios that demonstrate gradual improvements until demand and supply are aligned; and can not be improved further? What is a gradual improvement? How does one generate an improvement within user-specified ranges that adhere to budget restrictions? This is an open question! Since decisions taken during the variance analysis phase have to be judged not only by their benefit in terms of product delivery but also by their financial implications.

Another challenge in variance analysis is the ability to visualise the recommendations/scenarios in a manner that will allow users to look at the same problem scenario from different angles, thus focusing on different factors. It is imperative that the data visualisation is simple and intuitive in the core, without losing sight of the potential significance of each individual piece of information in the decision-making process. The way data is represented is of paramount importance as a means of augmenting human ability to make decisions efficiently and effectively. Effective data representation requires the presentation of information in a manner that is consistent with the perceptual, cognitive, and response-based mental representations of the user (Bermudez et al. 2000).The ability to visualise data and drill down to its constituent parts will accelerate the process of highlighting any major gaps between supply and demand.

3.4.4 Enablers and Planning Environment

3.4.4.1 Strategy and Governance

History is littered with cases of failed IT projects. Analysis of these failed projects highlights the lack of proper governance structure and organisational strategy. The impact of introducing an automated strategic system on those involved in the process should not be underestimated. How does one minimise the risk of failure? Soft Systems Methodology (SSM) (Checkland 1990) has been applied successfully in system development projects to identify all the relevant stakeholders and eliciting their specific requirements. Users should be involved in every stage of the development process. The challenge will be to identify the relevant change management programmes that should be put in place in order to ensure the system is introduced in a smooth and a well thought out manner.

3.4.4.2 Data Definitions and Standardisations

Communication is at the heart of strategic resource planning. And when it comes to effective communication, the key issue is *what* is being communicated. Automating the strategic resource planning process requires that a vocabulary of common concepts be defined among the multiple stakeholders. We refer to these core concepts as entities and these are used to describe demand and resources. Examples of these entities include product; geography, and time periods. There must be an agreement of the definitions and the acceptable values for these entities. Without such agreements machine to machine interaction becomes impossible. *Product* sets define demand types. Delivering a product in most cases requires the co-ordination of multiple activities. The principle here is similar to Bill of Materials (BOM) (Vitasek 2006) in the manufacturing industries. These activities in turn may represent skills. *Geography* defines the organisational structure and tends to be hierarchical in nature. For example, the top level of the hierarchy could be a particular country, underneath that could be larger geographical areas; which are then broken done to smaller geographical areas and so forth. The lowest level tends to be where demand is captured. As an example, for a telecommunications company, the lowest geographical level could be the telephone exchange since all demand types are associated in one form or another to an exchange. Another example would be in the case of the police department, the lowest level will be the police station since every police incident can be tied to a police station. *Time periods* define the acceptable periods for planning purposes e. g., weekly, monthly and so forth. How does one administer these entities (i. e., concepts) with the view to ensuring that changes are propagated to all interested parties and systems? For example, how should one treat forecasts based on an organisation that has been changed? What about skills that have become obsolete because of new technology – how should one treat related historical demand? We believe standardizing entities could benefit significantly from input from other industrial initiatives such as the Collaborative Planning Forecasting and Replenishment (CPFR 2007) and ebXML (ebXML 2007).

3.4.4.3 Security

One of the key requirements outlined in Sect. 3.3 is to be able to allow multiple stakeholders to use the system. Multiple users of system require an audit trail of user interaction. This raises security challenges. There are two aspects to security: *authentication* and *authorisation.* Authentication defines who can access the system whereas authorisation defines what can or can not be done. Despite advances in authentication and authorisation technologies, their impact on system change leaves much to be desired. For example how does one add new business functionality without having to rewrite routines that enforce security concerns? Besides, at what level should authorsiation rights be defined?

3.4.4.4 Budget Management

Budgeting is part of the strategic resource planning process. The allocation and modifications of the available resources is subject to cost restrictions. This means that decisions on how to best utilise an organisation's resources have to be judged not only by their benefit in terms of delivering services to customers but also by their financial implications. As an example, employing additional workers is often only justifiable in situations of significant under-resourcing as they involve large financial commitments. On the other hand to fill smaller resource gaps temporary solutions, e. g., increasing overtime allowances, might be the better choice. There are two approaches to budgeting with regards to strategic resource planning. One approach is to set the budget and enforce it. The other approach is to have an initial budget and then use the resource planning process to refine it. One of the challenges facing most service organisations is the globalisation of their workforces. Outsourcing is becoming a strategic opportunity and many companies are moving to outsourcing most of their cooperate functions. The question that arises is which projects should be outsourced? The other challenge is how does one determine which specific investment projects the organisation should undertake? How much of the budget should be allocated to capital expenditure and the operational running of the organisation?

3.5 A Framework for Implementing an Automated Strategic Planning System

Having outlined the challenges that must be addressed before an automated strategic resource planning system can be realized; this section outlines the high level requirements of such a system. The goal is to provide a set of guidelines for implementing an automated strategic resource planning systems.

(i)   The system should provide the facilities for creating and maintaining core entities – product hierarchies, organisational structure, availability sets. More importantly, it should provide a mechanism to define the relationships among these core entities.

(ii)   The system should support collaborative demand modelling and resource planning.

(iii)   The system should have the facility to generate demand forecasts taking into consideration environmental impacts such as

     a.   global and localised marketing campaign;
     b.   changes to business strategy;
     c.   incorporating local knowledge such as competitor activity;
     d.   weather forecasts which may affect demand.

(iv)   The system should enable the modelling of strategic planning targets, e. g., recruitment targets, productivity targets, quality of service targets; with the ability to present an ordered and costed list of management options to meet given criteria. Such options should include overtime, use of contingency resource, training plans, etc.

(v)   The system should support the graphical visualisation of work demand data and resource profiles.

(vi)   The system should provide the ability to integrate with existing systems.

(vii)   The system should provide the means to capture budget details and its corresponding breakdown by location, product sets and so on.

(viii)   The system should provide user authentication and authorisation functionality.

Strategic planning systems can be viewed as having three parts – namely inputs, processing and outputs (Lederer and Salmela 1996; King 1999). Input will include *core entities, user profiles*; demand and resource profiles. *Processing* will include the processes for *demand forecasting* and *planning*; and *resource planning*. For *output* it will be *reporting*. In deciding whether to build or buy, it is imperative to go for a modular approach – identify the modules for *inputs, processing* and, *outputs*.

It is worth addressing the issue of *build* or *buy*. This question comes up whenever a new system is required. There are various arguments for choosing either approach, most of them documented by technology analysts like Forrester, IDC, Gartner, Aberdeen Group, just to mention a few. When it comes to *strategic* resource planning systems however, little or no such analysis exists. With regards to the question of *build* or *buy*; our view is to go for both approaches. Buy from best of breed and build where a system doesn't exist. With the advent of service oriented architectures, the focus has now shifted to integrating components. This equates to best of breed components for demand forecasting, resource planning and so forth.

We end this section with a sample of strategic resource planning systems. The vendor landscape is divided into two camps. The first camp is a list of vendors who develop solutions for the front office resources – workforce management solutions for call centres. Included in this camp are Genesys and Pipkins. The second group refers to those who develop solutions for the back office. Two vendor types categorise this group: *field force* and *professional services*. For field force, players include Clicksoftware, @Road and Field Optimisation Suite (aka FOS). On the professional services side, we have vendors such as Computer Associates, Compuware, and Primavera Systems.

3.6 Summary

There is an adage which says when *you fail to plan; you are planning to fail*. An organisation is as good as the resources it has. Jim Collins (2001) in his book *From Good to Great* refers to this as getting the right people on the bus and getting them aligned to the objectives of the organisation to ensure optimal delivery. This chapter was about strategic resource planning. We highlighted the importance of automating the strategic planning process. We live in an Internet age, where timely access to data and the ability to reason with data quickly in order to make quality decisions is crucial to the profitability of service organisations. We defined the process of strategic resource planning. The process we outlined is generic, though variations may exist for specific organisations. We also proposed the requirements for an automated strategic planning system. We conclude with the key message of this chapter: Clear visibility of total demand and resource availability to an organisation is *sine qua non* to effective strategic resource planning. The next chapter examines the sources of demand and the mechanism of making them visible to the resource planning process. It also offers some practical tools for forecasting and planning demand – necessary prerequisites for success resource planning.

Chapter 4
Forecasting and Demand Planning

4.1 Introduction

Compared to traditional manufacturing and supply chain, forecasting in the service industry is in a nascent stage. Forecasting in the service chain is not limited to forecasting of sales, raw material or components but it could be as varied as forecasting internet bandwidth requirement, call volumes at a call centre or the customers walking into restaurant between 8 pm to 9 pm on Saturday evening. The variety and complexity of forecasting requirements changes from business to business.

Forecasting is carried out to predict the volume of service requirement where some kind of resource (e. g., staff or infrastructure) is deployed. The Forecasting and Demand Planning functions in the service industry are aimed primarily at optimising resource utilisation. Tactical or operational forecasting seeks to help in day-to-day demand planning, while strategic forecasting is aimed at providing valuable inputs for the planning of resources in the long term.

The first section of this chapter provides a general introduction to the complex tasks of *forecasting* and *demand planning* within the service industry and how they are interlinked. We will elaborate on the challenges faced by service organisations in achieving higher forecast accuracy in Sect. 4.3. Section 4.4 provides an overview of the forecasting process and the various steps involved. The section also looks at different forecasting methods and forecasting measures. The impact that forecasting can have on demand planning is illustrated in Sect. 4.5 and Sect. 4.6 discusses how to deal with unprecedented events in the service chain.

4.2 Demand Forecasting and Planning

Demand in the service industry may pertain to skill, human power, effort, space or time. For example, a logistics service sells warehouse space as a product; while the

C. Voudouris, G. Owusu, R. Dorne, D. Lesaint, *Service Chain Management*
DOI: 10.1007/978-3-540-75504-3, ©Springer 2008

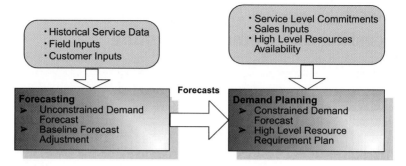

Fig. 4.1 Relationship between forecasting and demand planning

space, in this context, is tangible, other services that comprise the solution (invoicing, tracking, inventory management, etc.) are non-tangible. Herein, we are specifically focusing on services which are primarily delivered by people.

Forecasting and demand planning are used interchangeably at times; however they are both distinct functions. The objective of forecasting is to predict demand whilst the aim of demand planning is to shape the demand and produce a resource requirements plan. The primary goal of forecasting is, therefore, to enable the resource planning function, which in turn, optimises resource allocation and utilisation.

Traditionally, demand planning is a process of identifying, aggregating, and prioritising all sources of demand for the integrated supply chain of a product or service at the appropriate level, horizon and interval (Vitasek 2006). In the context of the service industry, this relationship can be defined as shown in Fig. 4.1.

The inputs to forecasting are typically historical service data, information from field personnel and planners and feedback from the customer. This derives a baseline forecast, which is a vital input to demand planning. Frequently, the baseline forecast is exposed to the users for adjustments. Traditionally this is done within demand planning, but it could also be done within the forecasting function.

Demand planning takes various inputs such as contractual service level commitments, sales plans and estimated availability of skills or resources. Demand planning converts numeric forecasts of customer demand into skill requirements, usually incorporating business activities, and provides a high level resource requirement plan.

It is interesting to note here, that it is not always possible to constrain demand in the service industry, particularly, when the service levels are contractually bound. In such cases, flexing resources to meet upcoming demand is often the only option. Demand planning provides a fairly accurate picture of the gap between resource requirement and availability. The ability of any service organisation to plan the demand primarily relies upon the forecasting accuracy. Large deviations in forecasting accuracy can have a significant impact on demand planning and hence, service fulfilment. Forecasting accuracy depends upon appropriate usage of forecasting methods or algorithms. However, best forecasting models are vulnerable to unprecedented events. We will discuss these points in detail in Sects. 4.5 and 4.6.

4.3 Challenges in Demand Forecasting

For services delivered by people, their time is a revenue generating or service fulfilling opportunity for the organisation which, once lost, cannot be utilised. Thus the major challenge of forecasting service demand is directly linked to revenue/resource management as the loss of forecasting accuracy directly links to loss of revenue or increased cost. The service industry faces number of challenges which hinder accurate forecasting. We will discuss some of them in this section.

Gathering historical data and using it appropriately to generate forecasts poses several challenges. In a dynamic business environment, service propositions change regularly. Sales promotions and new products and services are frequently introduced. In such cases, historical data may not be appropriate and consistent. Furthermore, there is likely to be more inherent 'noise' in data recorded by service agents. It may be a result of human error or other inaccuracies due to business practices, for example, service agents (or managers!) striving to meet targets (Seddon 1992). This questions the reliability of data. While a forecaster might not have a luxury to investigate such factors every time, the data should be thoroughly investigated before it is used for modeling. Any discrepancy, aberration or irregular pattern should be explained to the greatest possible extent.

Normally, service businesses are data rich which creates a problem of plenty. It is extremely important to choose data with contextual relevance; however, this is not always straightforward. For example, a service centre can have multiple data for each service: the arrival time of demand at the call centre; the arrival time of demand at the local scheduling centre; the time when the service starts; the time of service completion, etc. It is possible to model any of these data to generate service demand forecasts. At this juncture, it is important to understand the demand planning process and the customer requirements to select the most appropriate data. For example, planning may be based on when the service demand arrives at the call centre. From the customer's perspective, a more appropriate approach may have been to forecast the actual time of the demand occurrence. However, as this data may be unavailable, the next best possible option (in this instance) is to use the call centre data.

A variety of modelling techniques are available for producing forecasts. Based on data patterns, forecasting horizon, data availability and business requirements the choice of technique differs. In situations where there are multiple products or services provided to differing customer segments across various geographies, it may not be possible to develop and run individual forecasting models for each different data set. In such circumstances, the data sets may be grouped into like categories and a generic model may be run for each category. Thus, efficiency is achieved, in such cases, at the risk of a loss of accuracy. We will discuss some of the forecasting methods in Sect. 4.5.

Differences in organisational culture and geography introduce additional challenges to forecasting. For instance, the same service function carried out in two different arenas (geographical regions or physical locations such as call centres) using similar approaches will yield different results. At times, it is not possible to include all these parameters in forecasting, but a simple adjustment factor based on past observations may need to be considered.

Other service businesses face different forecasting challenges. Retailers, for example, produce daily forecasts for large numbers of products in multiple geographies; such operations require large automated forecasting and inventory planning system with heavy computational power. Utility industries, such as electricity companies, require forecasts for very short horizons, e. g., the demand occurring in 10 minutes time. The financial industry requires short term forecasts, e. g., share market, and long term forecasts, e. g., futures and options. IT and consulting services require forecasts for specific skill sets. Internet service providers need to forecast bandwidth usage where telecom service providers have to forecast call volumes. They also have to forecast the type and quantity of service provisions, as well as service failures, occurring across geographically spread networks to provide timely service.

4.4 The Forecasting Process

The forecasting process begins with gathering of data. Meaningful and sufficient data is a prerequisite to any successful forecasting process. Once the data is made available, it needs to be freed from influencing events that are non-repetitive in nature (such as promotions or unprecedented events), outliers and missing values. This part of the process is called data cleansing. Once the data is cleaned, it needs to be analysed for historical patterns, seasonality, etc. Findings and interpretations of this phase helps in selecting appropriate forecasting methods. After a variety of models are created and tested for accuracy, the 'best' model is selected. No one forecasting measure can provide a true picture of model performance; hence, forecasting accuracy needs to be measured with different metrics. Ideally, the chosen model is then tested on data not included in the development stage, before the model is integrated with the Demand Planning function. This process is summarised in Fig. 4.2.

With so many methods and measures available, it is important to find one that yields and measures accurate forecasts. The practitioner needs to follow a number of steps in order to ensure that the forecasting methods and measures are as relevant as possible. The following section discusses each step in turn.

4.4.1 Data Analysis and Interpretation

The first step in producing forecasts is to understand any historical data that is available. The standard summary statistics, e. g., mean, standard deviation, are useful in providing a basic understanding of the data. In addition to identifying sufficient, appropriate data it is important, as with all statistical analyses, to identify any general patterns.

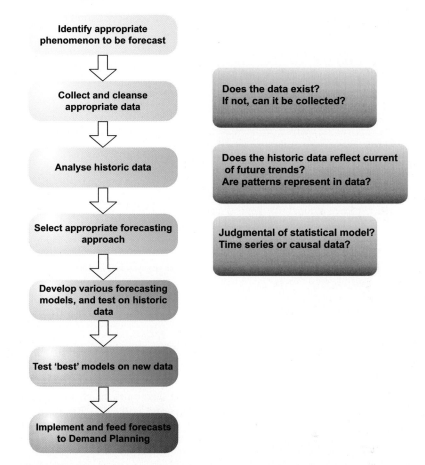

Fig. 4.2 High-level process for producing forecasts for use in demand planning

The use of scatter plots (to identify possible correlation or non-linearity) or time series graphs can indicate any patterns or unusual observations. When plotting time series data there are four common patterns to watch out for:

- horizontal (or stationary): data fluctuate about a constant mean;
- trend: a long-term increase or decrease in the data;
- seasonal: a repeating pattern that depends on 'seasonal' factors, e. g., days of the week, months of the year;
- cyclical: a recurring pattern that may be of different length or recurs at irregular intervals.

Figure 4.3 shows examples of these patterns. Additionally, unusual observations are more easily identified through plotting the data.

Furthermore, if forecasts are to be prepared for different products or for different geographies, summary statistics and plots may highlight any similarities and differences that can then be borne in mind.

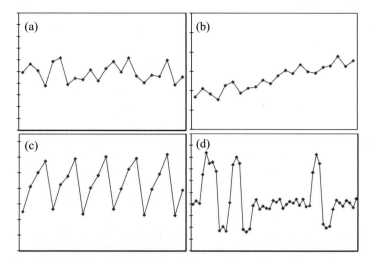

Fig. 4.3 Patterns in time series data (**a**) horizontal, (**b**) trend, (**c**) seasonal and (**d**) cyclical

4.4.2 Forecasting Methods

The branch of mathematics and statistics that represents forecasting has grown rapidly in the last few decades. Since the early work in the 1950s and 1960s on various extrapolation techniques (Brown 1959; Brown 1963; Holt 1957; Winters 1960), the advent of computers brought about the development of techniques that required much larger amounts of calculations (Box and Jenkins 1970). Further still, newer computational methods, such as Neural Networks, have been successfully adapted to Forecasting (Zhang et al. 1998).

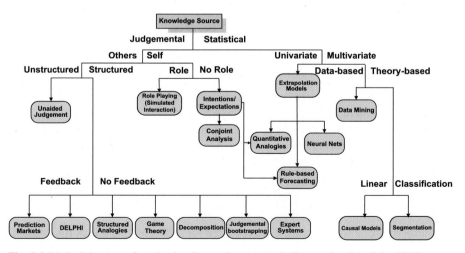

Fig. 4.4 Methodology tree for selecting forecasting approach (Forecasting Principles 2007)

So great is the variety of approaches that only a few can be addressed in this chapter. The Methodology Tree (Forecasting Principles 2007) shown in Fig. 4.4 illustrates the choice of approach available to the forecasting practitioner.

In general, there are two main types of forecasting methodologies: the scientific approach of statistical models based on historical data and the less mechanical approach using the judgement of experts. There are numerous statistical methods, varying in complexity from relatively simple (e. g., mean levels) to sophisticated or computationally intensive techniques such as Autoregressive Integrated Moving Average (ARIMA) (Makridakis et al. 1998). Judgemental forecasts are made by individuals based on their knowledge of the environment; this might include information about past events and expectations of likely future events or trends. In this section, we will explore some of these methods.

4.4.2.1 Statistical Forecasting Methods

Statistical forecasting methods fall into two major families: those that utilise explanatory variables and those that use time series data. Time Series methods produce forecasts using some combination of previous data values, thus the forecast of the next data point can be summarised as (4.1).

$$Y_{t+1} = f(Y_t, Y_{t-1}, Y_{t-2}, \ldots, e) \tag{4.1}$$

where e is an error term. These methods are most appropriate where an understanding of the patterns exists without, necessarily, understanding causality or, perhaps, the drivers of the forecast variable may be too complex to model. For example, a service outage (e. g., power supply or telephone network) may be due to one of many failings which, in turn, could be caused by one or a combination of many factors.

A variety of methods can be employed to forecast time series data, but in order to find the most appropriate method it is important to understand the nature of the data. Decomposition methods (Makridakis et al. 1998) separate the data into component parts, identifying cyclicality, seasonality and trend. Frequently, the first step in modelling a time series is to de-seasonalise or transform the data prior to the application of a smoothing method such as a Moving Average or Exponential Smoothing. The number of periods included in a Moving Average, or the amount of smoothing used in a Single or Double Exponential Smoothing, depends on the amount of variation in the time series. The greater the variability in the data, the more periods required to smooth the data. More sophisticated methods can cope with trend (e. g., Holt's Linear method) and seasonality (e. g., Holt-Winters' method) (Makridakis et al. 1998). It can also be useful to determine the correlation in the data using the Autocorrelation Function (ACF). The ACF can help identify seasonality and is often performed as the first step in developing ARIMA models (Makridakis et al. 1998).

Methods using explanatory variables seek out the relationship between the variable to be forecast and one or more independent variables. The forecast variable can then be summarised as (4.2).

$$Y_t = f(X_{1t}, X_{2t}, \ldots, e_t) \tag{4.2}$$

One of the most common methods is Simple Linear Regression which seeks to identify a relationship between two variables that represents the correlation between the two variables. The concept, based on minimising the errors of "fitted" values, i.e., the predictions of values based on the data used to create the model, can be extended to include any number of explanatory variables. Multiple Linear Regression identifies the best combination of these explanatory variables that minimises the errors of fitted values. The models can then be used to determine forecasts based on given values of the explanatory variables. For example, the sales of a particular service in a geographical area may be explained by the proportion of high-income earners living there. It may also be explained by the number of customers who have recently purchased another service. Of course, there could be a relationship between these two factors!

Whilst the linear regression methods usually cope very well with data that exhibits horizontal or trend patterns, care needs to be exercised in defining the models for seasonal data.

There are tools available to assist in deciding the most appropriate method to use (Forecasting Principles 2007), but there are some basic rules to follow; the first being ascertaining the availability of sufficient data. A statistical model is only possible if there is data available; which type of model depends on two further questions. Are there any patterns in the data that can be modelled? Is the historic data likely to reflect the future? This last question is certainly worth considering if the market is fast-moving or new products are soon to be introduced.

There are several advantages to using statistical methods: they make efficient use of the available data; they are reliable, i.e., two forecasts made with precisely the same input data will be identical; they are less prone to personal bias. However, these methods can only interpret trends that are present in the data.

4.4.2.2 Judgemental Forecasting Methods

Judgemental forecasts, using techniques such as structured analogies (Green and Armstrong 2004), can incorporate knowledge that does not exist in historic data, such as past events that are not expected to recur or expected future trends. Of the many disadvantages in using judgemental forecasting, perhaps the main problem is that bias may be introduced (Hogarth and Makridakis 1981). Single-expert judgements can be subject to bias resulting from personal opinion whereas judgements by groups of individuals can result in there being too many opinions and a lack of agreement, or by the group following a dominant individual. One approach, called DELPHI (Ludwig 1997), surveys several individuals in isolation and then shares the results before the same individuals re-forecast in the light of the shared information. Whilst this approach reduces bias, it can be time-consuming and, therefore, may not be appropriate for short-term forecasting.

4.4.2.3 Integrated Approaches

The distinct advantages of both statistical and judgemental forecasting methods have led to the integration of the approaches in an attempt to optimise the forecasts. Integrated forecasts can be successful provided sufficient quantitative data is available, the separate forecasts contribute different information and the judgement is not obviously biased. There are five common integration schemes, shown in Fig. 4.5 (Armstrong and Collopy 1998):

1. Revised Judgement: Experts make judgemental forecasts which are then revised based on statistical extrapolations;
2. Combined Forecasts: Experts make forecasts independently of forecasts produced by a statistical model. The two sets of forecasts are then combined (e. g., the average is taken);
3. Revised Extrapolations: Experts make adjustments to statistical forecasts;
4. Rule-based Forecasts: Judgemental forecasts are used as inputs to a statistical procedure which is tailored to the situation;
5. Econometric Forecasts: Judgemental inputs are used to identify the model, the coefficients of which are obtained using regression.

The approach needs to be selected according to a number of rules. For example, Revised Judgement or Revised Extrapolation should be chosen if the time series is unstable or there is a high degree of uncertainty and if experts have up-to-date information that is not present in the data set. Econometric methods should be used if there is a high level of domain knowledge (either past data or future knowledge),

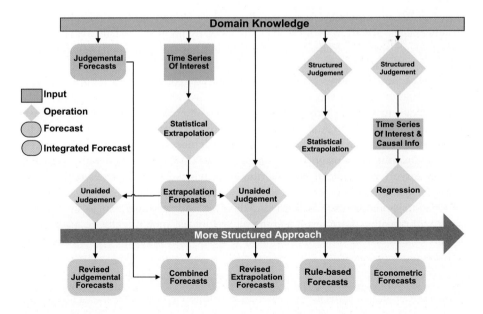

Fig. 4.5 Schematic showing different approaches to delivering combined forecasts

if there are contrary trends in the data and if there is information about causal variables.

The advantages of an integrated scheme are many but, in general, revised forecasts will be more accurate than judgemental or statistical forecasts alone if the time series data adds information to the expert knowledge. The drawbacks, too, are numerous. For instance, the expert may be overwhelmed by information, reluctant to adjust initial forecasts or may inadvertently introduce "double-counting".

4.4.3 Forecasting Measures

In order to assess the accuracy of the forecasts there are a plethora of measures available. To the non-statistician in an operational environment, however, it can be confusing when deciding which measure is appropriate, or to decide just how good the forecasts are.

If the error (e) associated with the forecast (F) of the observation (Y), then the error at time t is defined as (4.3).

$$e_t = Y_t - F_t \tag{4.3}$$

and the percentage error (PE) is defined as (4.4).

$$PE_t = \frac{(Y_t - F_t)}{Y_t} \times 100 \tag{4.4}$$

Some of the most popular measures of accuracy, along with their advantages and disadvantages, are given in Table 4.1. The list is by no means exhaustive; however, it provides a useful introduction to the precautions that the forecaster must take when assessing model accuracy.

None of these measures, however, allow for a comparative assessment to be made unless another set of forecasts are generated using another model. Consequently, it is difficult to know whether, in the context of the data, how good the forecasts are. The Forecast Value Add (FVA) (Galliland 2005) provides a comparison with a Random Walk[1] forecast. The FVA is the difference between the model MAPE (Mean Absolute Percentage Error) and the MAPE of the random walk forecasts. Any positive FVAs indicate that the model provides better forecasts than simply using the previous value.

Caution should be exercised if using the FVA with seasonal data as the random walk will provide a false result and the naïve forecast should really be made using the previous seasonal value (i. e., Monday forecasts should use the previous Monday values).

---

[1] The Random Walk forecasts the next observation by using the value of the current observation. This technique provides the user with a naïve "baseline" as no intelligence is used in preparing the forecast.

Table 4.1 Summary of some common measures of accuracy

Measure	Definition	Advantages	Disadvantages
Mean error	$ME = \frac{1}{n}\sum_{t=1}^{n} e_t$	Will indicate systematic under- or over-forecasting (bias)	Likely to be small as positive and negative errors tend to offset each other. Does not indicate size of errors
Mean absolute error	$MAE = \frac{1}{n}\sum_{t=1}^{n} |e_t|$	Overcomes disadvantage of ME by making each error positive before averaging. Is more interpretable and easier to understand	Difficult to interpret the result as value can be meaningless unless context is presented
Mean squared error	$MSE = \frac{1}{n}\sum_{t=1}^{n} e_t^2$	Each error is squared before taking the average. Inflates larger errors, so indicating poor forecasts	Difficult for non-statisticians to interpret the result
Mean percentage error	$MPE = \frac{1}{n}\sum_{t=1}^{n} PE_t$	Will indicate systematic under- or over-forecasting (bias)	Suffers from likelihood of being small as positive and negative errors tend to offset each other
Mean absolute percentage error	$MAPE = \frac{1}{n}\sum_{t=1}^{n} |PE_t|$	Overcomes disadvantage of MPE by making each percentage error positive before averaging. Is more interpretable and easier to understand	Difficulties arise when the time series contains zeros as PE cannot then be calculated
Standard deviation of absolute percentage errors	$SDAPE = \sqrt{\dfrac{\sum_{t=1}^{n}\left(APE_t - A\bar{PE}\right)^2}{n-1}}$	Indicates consistency of forecasts. Large values highlight some errors are small and others are large	Difficult for non-statisticians to interpret the result
Forecast value add	$MAPE(RW) - MAPE(model)$	Provides a simple comparison with a naïve forecast	Requires the Random walk forecasts and MAPE to be calculated

Ultimately, the measures to be used by the forecaster should be those that the user feels most comfortable with. The conversion of the error into a value that has a business meaning can be very helpful.

4.5 Understanding Forecasting Impact on Demand Planning

Even with meticulously developed forecasting models, it is possible that the expected benefits to the business may not be realised. Unfortunately, forecasting will never be 100% accurate; hence, the business process needs to have a provision to safeguard against this inaccuracy. Clearly, the better the forecast the lesser allowance needed. Failing to account for the inaccuracy in the forecast will lead to a failure in fulfilling demand.

In order to illustrate how the forecasts can impact on demand planning and be interpreted in terms of business drivers, this section uses an example of matching resource to a demand. Table 4.2 shows the daily demand (number of jobs) for a service company which requires the deployment of a certain number of service agents. The number of agents required is based on the expectation that each individual will complete 5 jobs per day.

The forecasts (shown in red in Fig. 4.5) are very good for the first three weeks where the daily percentage error for weekdays is, on average, about 5%; however, the forecasts for Week 4 are less accurate; the comparative percentage errors range between 9% and 17%. The inaccuracy of forecasts from Wednesday of Week 4 means that the business will be seriously affected.

The impact of the inaccuracy of the forecasts can be seen by examining the last three columns of Table 4.3. If the number of service people deployed is greater than that required the business will incur costs associated with employing surplus staff. Conversely, if too few people are deployed there will be insufficient service people to meet the demand, thus impacting on the customer. In this instance, the forecaster has continued to adjust the statistical baseline using their domain knowledge, but new sales initiatives have seen an increase in demand. Unless the forecaster and the demand planner are party to this information, the forecasts will continue to be inaccurate and affect business performance.

As shown in the illustration, forecasting accuracy can have a significant impact on demand planning. In the service industry, this could result in failure to provide contractual service levels and severe penalties. To mitigate this risk, service organisations tend to keep buffer resources. In practice it is uneconomical to keep these

Table 4.2 Daily demand of service

Week	Mon	Tue	Wed	Thu	Fri	Sat	Sun
1	237	214	232	249	243	31	27
2	213	197	218	194	241	50	30
3	202	232	212	204	199	28	19
4	234	236	272	251	231	30	21

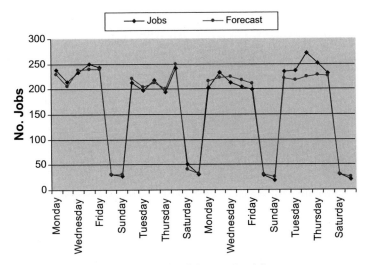

Fig. 4.6 Time series plot of the daily demand and the associated forecast

Table 4.3 Summary of the forecasts for weeks 3 and 4

Day	Jobs	Forecast	Error	Absolute percentage error	Service people deployed	Service people required	Business impact
Monday	202	210	−8	4.0%	41	42	1
Tuesday	232	227	5	2.2%	47	46	−1
Wednesday	212	220	−8	3.8%	43	44	1
Thursday	204	220	−16	7.8%	41	44	3
Friday	199	205	−6	3.0%	40	41	1
Saturday	28	31	−3	10.7%	6	7	1
Sunday	19	25	−6	31.6%	4	5	1
Monday	234	200	34	14.5%	47	40	−7
Tuesday	236	210	26	11.0%	48	42	−6
Wednesday	272	225	47	17.3%	55	45	−10
Thursday	251	220	31	12.4%	51	44	−7
Friday	231	210	21	9.1%	47	42	−5
Saturday	30	31	−1	3.3%	6	7	1
Sunday	21	26	−5	23.8%	5	6	1
			MAPE	11.0%			

spare resources solely for meeting unexpected demand and so the buffer is often created by flexing resources from areas of low utilization. Clearly, the higher the forecasting accuracy the lesser buffering is required.

4.6 Unprecedented Events and Risk Mitigation

To the dismay of some managers it is virtually impossible to forecast unprecedented events. However, it is possible to design an appropriate response to such events.

Scenario-modeling allows for different intensities of events to be simulated. If a similar event has occurred in past, relevant data points can be analysed to understand the impact on the service chain and mitigation strategies can be developed to meet similar situations in the future. However, there is no one answer to unprecedented events. For example, the terrorist attacks of 9/11 resulted in the instigation of multiple system back-ups in multiple geographies to mitigate the risk of loss of valuable business data. Airlines have analysed the 9/11 scenario to understand how demand will fluctuate in immediate and distant time post disaster.

From a forecasting perspective such events create a two-fold complexity. First, they adversely impact the demand data which then cannot be used to carry out regular forecasting without adjustment. Second, such events need to be modelled but, due to unique nature and impact of each event, a forecaster needs to maintain a library of such unprecedented event models.

A further risk of forecasting in the service industry is due to the nature of the industry. Most of the services are perishable with time and hence, to maximise it, the models are operated with an inherent positive bias. However, when both forecast error and bias are in the same direction, their cumulative impact can produce highly skewed forecasting scenarios. For example, to mitigate the risk of "no-shows," the airline industry over-forecasts demand in an effort to avoid flying with empty seats. This is, sometimes, at the expense of compensating some customers unable to travel on valid tickets.

There is no prescriptive approach to choosing a forecasting model. Factors concerning data, likely occurrences of unprecedented events and the impact on business will mean no two situations are ever the same. Ultimately, the decision lies with the forecaster who has to understand a variety of factors. Understanding these factors often requires a non-scientific approach, which is why forecasting is as much of an art as much a science.

4.7 Summary

In this chapter we looked at the definition and scope of forecasting and demand planning functions in the service industry. We discussed various challenges in achieving forecasting accuracy due to profusion of data and specific forecasting requirements. We discussed various statistical and judgemental methods for forecasting and measuring forecasting accuracy. We then described how unprecedented events add complexity to forecasting. The importance of understanding the impact of forecasting on demand planning was illustrated. Demand planning affects resource utilisation. Inaccurate demand planning will either result in over or under resource utilisation. Both scenarios have financial implications for service organisations. The subject of the next two chapters is about tools needed to ensure that resources are properly utilised in an organisation.

Chapter 5
Tactical Resource Planning and Deployment

5.1 Introduction

One of the key goals for service businesses is to find the right balance between the quality of service delivered to its customers and the incurred cost. The quality of service should be as high as possible in order to achieve high customer satisfaction and retention, and this often increases costs. Authorising overtime, for example, to guarantee timely service delivery has financial consequences. However, costs generally should be as small as possible to achieve high profitability. Clearly both objectives are contradictory and often cannot be fully satisfied at the same time due to the constraints on resource utilisation.

Resource planning is the mechanism to manage resources within the service chain. It ensures that resources are utilised effectively to provide services to customers. Tactical resource planning focuses on planning in the medium-term, i.e., it looks at planning periods from a few days to a few weeks. Similarly to strategic planning, it provides resource managers with an overall, condensed view of the balance between demand and supply as well as capabilities to influence this balance. On the other hand and interlinked with operational planning[1], tactical resource planning often involves the anticipatory deployment of individual resources and thus has to provide a detailed plan about the expected utilisation of the workforce. The requirement to generate both *coarse*- and *fine*-grain plans poses certain challenges to the development of tactical resource planning systems. Firstly, it has to address the balance between quality of service and cost reduction objectives of the business. Secondly, it must provide an automated approach for generating both *coarse*- and *fine*-grain plans. The usefulness of these plans is dependent on their quality. The more accurate and optimal these plans, the quicker they will be implemented. Firstly, generating an optimal plan is costly. Secondly, the enormous complexity of many real-life planning scenarios makes any optimisation particularly demanding. Thirdly, a tactical resource planning module has to seamlessly integrate with other

---

[1] Also referred to as scheduling or work allocation in this book.

C. Voudouris, G. Owusu, R. Dorne, D. Lesaint, *Service Chain Management*
DOI: 10.1007/978-3-540-75504-3, ©Springer 2008

information sources within the service chain; such as, absence and attendance; demand profiles and work allocation systems. And finally, end users, notably, resource managers have to be provided with full visibility and control of demand and resources.

This chapter is about tactical resource planning systems. It examines the aforementioned challenges in some detail and then presents approaches to overcome them. The chapter is structured as follows: the tactical resource planning scenario is introduced in Sect. 5.2 and the major challenges are examined in Sect. 5.3. This is followed by a study of available solution strategies and techniques in Sect. 5.4, and a case study in Sect. 5.5.

5.2 Defining Tactical Resource Planning

Resource planning, in short, is the process of shaping, arranging and flexing the available supply in order to meet the expected customer demand. It is a proactive process that ensures that resources with the right capabilities are available at the right location at the right time. As noted in Chap. 3 on strategic resource planning, this process includes strategically balancing demand and supply in the long-term, tactically deploying individual resources to expected work volumes in the medium-term and the scheduling of the actual service delivery to customers in the short-term. There is a flow of information from strategic planning to tactical planning; and then from tactical planning to operational planning with the decisions taken becoming more specific and detailed in the latter phase. For tactical resource planning, this means that it uses coarse-grain plans referred to as capacity plans generated during the strategic planning phase and produces detailed plans, i. e., deployment plans, which are fed into operational planning, as illustrated in Fig. 5.1.

Within this medium-term planning horizon, the service demand is often only known to a certain extent and, consequently, tactical resource planning involves a combination of actual and forecasted work. Analogically, resource availability within the medium-term planning horizon cannot be fully determined in advance and thus one has to complement actual data on resource working times and absences with the corresponding forecasted inputs from the strategic capacity plan. The combination of known and predicted data, depicted in Fig. 5.2, is unique to the tactical scenario as it bridges the gap from strategic planning, where data are predominantly forecasted, to operational planning, where mainly actual data are used.

Fig. 5.1 Tactical resource planning in the service planning chain

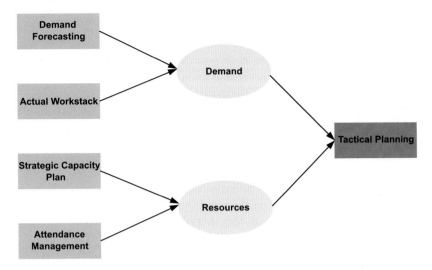

Fig. 5.2 Tactical resource planning environment

As noted in Chap. 3, customer demand and resource supply are generally captured along three main dimensions:

- *Capabilities* describe the required skills or qualifications of a resource to deliver a service and thus satisfy a customer demand. Typical examples here include (i) a repair skill of an engineer and (ii) the vaccination qualifications of a nurse.
- The *geography* determines the locality of the service provision. This could be, for instance, the customer premise where a meter reading takes place.
- *Availability* refers to a time slot or time window, such as a shift or a day, a service has to be provided in.

Additional demand properties such as customer and appointment types, supplementary resource attributes such as driving qualifications, and legal requirements such as health and safety regulations place further constraints and limitations on the planning process, but all scenarios share the basic principle of matching resource supply to service demand along the capability, geography and availability dimensions. In other words, resource planning revolves around constraining the resources' choices so that they cover and match the demand for services. Reducing resource flexibility this way leads to increased certainty about their usage and hence leads to increased certainty about the expected service delivery. In the tactical context, this means that individual resources get deployed to specific capabilities, locations and time slots to deliver a class of service. The final decision about the assignment of resources to deliver services to particular customers is left to the operational planning stage. Section 5.5 presents a case study of a typical medium-term planning scenario.

The results of the tactical resource planning process can be presented in various forms and shapes which often depend on the specific application context. The main outputs, however, can be generally described and classified as either capacity or deployment plans:

- *Capacity plans* allow resource managers to easily review the current state of service delivery. Such plans are coarse-grain in their nature, meaning they only present a summary of how well the available resources can deliver the expected customer demand for services. Findings are only expressed in terms of volumes and thus do not contain references to individual resources or specific demand. Using long-term capacity plans as direct input, tactical resource planning produces more detailed, more specific medium-term capacity plans as intermediate output.
- *Deployment plans* refine the information encapsulated in tactical capacity plans further by explicitly specifying the capabilities, locations and time slots to be used by individual resources, i. e., they describe individual resource deployments. Such plans constitute action plans which can be directly fed into subsequent scheduling components.

5.3 Challenges in Engineering a Tactical Resource Planning System

Having discussed the fundamentals of medium-term planning in the last section, this section looks at the major challenges which a tactical resource planning system has to address in order to be successfully deployed and used in a service environment. We begin by outlining the flow of information and decision making in tactical resource planning. We then use the description of the process to highlight the challenges.

5.3.1 Decision Making in Tactical Resource Planning

Figure 5.3 outlines the structure of a standard approach for tactical resource planning and deployment. The depicted basic building blocks can be found in the vast majority of planning systems.

The first phase of the planning algorithm is the *demand aggregation*. During this step, both actual customer demand and forecasted work are combined. In addition, single jobs or tasks are aggregated into demand volumes: jobs with common characteristics are added together. Rather than dealing with 20 individual maintenance jobs, for instance, the planning can be based on a single maintenance volume of 20. This technique reduces complexity and thus improves overall performance. It is made possible by the fact that tactical planning is not concerned with the assignment of resources to specific work as that is the objective of operational planning (scheduling), but is rather concerned with the deployment of resources to service volumes.

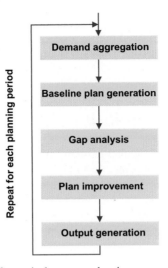

Fig. 5.3 A standard approach for tactical resource planning

The *baseline plan generation*, the next step of the planning process, sees the compilation of an initial resource deployment. All resources are deployed to their default values with regard to their capabilities, their location choices and their availability, and the demand volumes they are expected to clear are approximated. In a baseline plan, resource flexibility, such as the ability to work in various locations with multiple skills, remains unused.

The main aim of the *gap analysis* stage is the identification of any cases of under- or over-resourcing in the baseline plan. While under-resourcing refers to scenarios where customer demand cannot be satisfied on time, over-resourcing manifests itself in under-utilised or even surplus resources. In a typical example, a certain amount of maintenance work might be expected to fail in an area during a week while, at the same time, the neighbouring area has a contingent of surplus engineers, i. e., has unused engineers with maintenance skills.

The *plan improvement* uses the gap analysis to determine plan alterations. It aims to reduce both under- and over-resourcing by shifting and reassigning resources to different skills, locations and even availability slots. In the above example, moving under-utilised maintenance engineers into the neighbouring under-resourced area would lead to a vastly improved service delivery for the customers. In Sect. 5.4.2, this optimisation phase is examined in more detail.

The final step of the tactical resource planning cycle is the *generation of output*. The optimised plans are analysed from different perspectives and the compiled results are exposed to resource managers and to other components of the service chain management system. Beside the standard capacity and deployment plan results, typical outputs include reports on under-utilised resources to facilitate loaning procedures, reports on under-resourced capabilities as inputs for training plans, and summaries of spare resource capacity which can be fed into customer appointment booking systems.

The tactical resource planning approach described above highlights three main challenges that must be addressed before a useful tactical planning system can be deployed in service organisations. They are challenges in the areas of optimisation, visibility and integration.

5.3.2 Automation and Optimisation

The need for automating the tactical planning process can not be overstated. With automation, plan generation becomes faster and plans adhere better to complex business rules, thus limiting errors. Rather than dealing with the planning fundamentals themselves, resource managers are presented with computer generated plans which adhere to well-defined rules and principles, and thus resource managers can concentrate on exceptions and potential problems. For this, plans have to be efficiently, i. e., quickly and frequently, produced and have to constitute effective utilisations of the workforce. This means, for instance, for a medium-term planning module; it has to be capable of compiling optimised resource plans for large numbers of possible permutations of capability, geography and availability with a click of a button.

The automated generation of a tactical plan involves establishing a good or even the best possible resource deployment. Potentially, a huge number of plans could be considered. As an example, if there are n engineers available and each engineer can work in two different geographical areas, then there are a total of 2^n different possible area deployments. For 10 engineers, there are 1,024 different deployments, but for 20 engineers this number grows to more than a million plans. Scenarios (i. e., class of problems) where the number of deployments (i. e., solution space) grows exponentially with the number of engineers (i. e., problem size), are called combinatorial optimisation problems.

The "combinatorial explosion" of the size of the solution space makes this class of problems particularly hard to solve as it is often not feasible to search through all candidate solutions in order to establish the best one. Solution approaches have to employ strategies that restrict the search to promising areas of the solution space. Furthermore, special consideration has to be given to the overall running time of the planning process as resource planning tools are often used interactively. Clearly, generating optimal or near-optimal resource plans is a highly complex and thus challenging task for an optimisation system.

5.3.3 Visibility and Control

A modern system for the tactical deployment of resources has to provide resource managers with full visibility of demand and supply at all abstraction levels at any given time, usually both in graphical and numeric form. Furthermore, it has to offer control over all aspects of the planning mechanism itself, i. e., it must allow for situation-specific tailoring of the planning objectives and rules. This should include the capability to analyse what-if scenarios. Control mechanisms, such as the ability to focus service provision on new products during marketing campaigns or restrict service provision at certain locations during construction work, are typical examples. The challenge here is to provide demand and resource visibility, and full control over the planning process.

5.3.4 Integration in the Service Chain

The data rich environment of service organisations poses a two-fold challenge for tactical resource planning. Firstly, the exact nature of the data to be captured has to be chosen carefully. For instance, resources such as field engineers or call centre agents are all unique, and possess different experiences, productivities and preferences. The data should be chosen in such a way that it reflects this level of detail for tactical planning. Secondly, the sheer amount of information is an engineering challenge itself which should not be underestimated. Large service businesses often have to tactically deploy tens of thousands of resources to service hundreds of thousands of jobs each week, and thus the data warehouse maintaining all this data is a critical link. For example, customer demand in tactical scenarios often includes both actual and forecasted components, as opposed to only actual components used in operational scenarios and forecasted components used in strategic scenarios. Also, the functionalities offered during the tactical stages have to seamlessly integrate with both long-term capacity- and short-term deployment- planning. In addition, tactical resource planning is only one of the many elements in an integrated service chain system. With many different providers active in this market, such systems are usually heterogeneous in their nature. It is often a complex task to fully interlink a tactical resource planning and deployment module with all other service chain components such as long-term forecasting, scheduling, resource attendance management and service reservation. Thus, well defined, modular interfaces have to be provided to achieve seamless integration. The integration of tactical resource planning, both with regard to data and functionality, is a key enabler for successful service chain management.

5.4 Optimising the Tactical Resource Planning Process

The previous section outlined the three main challenges that should be addressed before automating the tactical resource planning process. This section presents the techniques that must be employed to engineer an automated system with emphasis on one of the challenges, optimising the resource plans.

5.4.1 Fundamental Decisions

A fundamental question to answer before deciding on a specific approach for tactical resource planning and deployment is on the required result of the planning:

Does one simply want to generate a plan that fulfils all conditions and constraints[2], or does one want to find a very good or even the best plan among the set of all possible plans? In the former case, the planning task can be seen as a constraint satisfaction problem (Tsang 1983), and planning can stop as soon as a single valid plan has been established. In the latter case, planning is interpreted as optimisation (Russell and Norvig 2003), and one usually has to iterate through a sequence of acceptable plans, compare them to one another and establish the best plan. The optimisation approach is more widely used, and we limit our discussion here to this setting.

Another important decision that needs to be made is whether the plan generation should look at the planning time window as a whole or whether the overall plan should be iteratively composed of partial plans for each time period within the planning horizon. For example, a seven-day plan for 100 resources could be generated in one step and thus would consider 700 deployments, or it could be decomposed into seven one-day plans with 100 deployments each. While the former allows a more complete judgment of the resource situation over the entire planning horizon as it considers dependencies between different planning periods, it also adds significant complexity to the planning task. Therefore, real-life planning systems tend to adopt the "divide-and-conquer", i. e., iterative, approach meaning they generate seven-day plans by first planning for day one, then for day two, and so on.

5.4.2 Plan Optimisation Techniques

The plan improvement phase of the previously discussed resource planning approach consists of translating the findings of the gap analysis into plan modifications in order to enhance the quality of the initially generated baseline plan. Central to this stage is the question of what actually constitutes a plan improvement. The key instrument to answer this question, i. e., to judge the quality of a plan, is the objective function (Russell and Norvig 2003). This function allows the evaluation of a particular resource deployment by assigning a fitness value to it. A plan improvement is thus an alteration that leads to a plan with a better objective score. Scenarios in which several objectives exist in parallel are referred to as multi-objective optimisation. In the tactical resource planning arena, objective functions usually include quality of service and cost based factors as illustrated in (5.1) for the single-objective case (λ allows the adjustment of the importance of both contributing factors) and (5.2) for the multi-objective case. They therefore present a balanced evaluation of resource plans with regard to these two main objectives. The quality of service is typically measured by the amount and type of services provided to customers on time. On the cost side, properties such as skill, location or availability changes are considered.

---

[2] Such constraints include, for instance, thresholds on the available capacity and limitations on the capabilities, locations and availability for each resource.

$$\text{Objective} = \lambda * \text{Quality\_of\_Service} + (1 - \lambda) * \text{Cost} \qquad (5.1)$$

$$\text{Objective}_1 = \text{Quality\_of\_Service} \qquad (5.2)$$

$$\text{Objective}_2 = \text{Cost}$$

Due to the combinatorial nature of tactical resource planning problems, it is usually not feasible to compute and evaluate all potential plans in order to pick the best. Due to this characteristic, optimisation approaches can only look at a sub-set of promising plans and overall optimality of the best solution found can usually not be guaranteed. Only limited research on the optimisation aspect of tactical resource planning specifically in the service chain has been carried out so far. Figure 5.4 presents an overview of applicable optimisation approaches.

Local search techniques are a well-known class of such optimisation algorithms. Their aim is to iteratively improve the initial baseline plan in small steps. By searching a limited set of plans similar to the current plan, only a small number of plans have to be evaluated before a plan alteration is carried out, and the process is then repeated. In tactical resource planning, for instance, such a neighbourhood could contain all deployments where only the assigned skills, locations and time slots of a single resource are altered. Examples of this class of optimisation techniques are Hill-Climbing, Simulated Annealing (Kirkpatrick et al. 1983), Tabu Search (Glover 1989) and Guided Local Search (Voudouris and Tsang 1999). A case study of a simple hill climbing setup is presented in Sect. 5.5.

In contrast to local search techniques, global search heuristics tend to look for a global optimum by simultaneously searching through different parts of the solution space. One well-known example is Genetic Algorithm (Holland 1975). There is a nature-inspired technique that could be used to identify favourable characteristics in a set of different resource plans and to subsequently combine them into improved plans.

Linear, non-linear and dynamic programming approaches are widely used industrial optimisation techniques which aim at optimising the objective function subject to a set of constraints (Luenberger (2003) provides an overview of this class of algorithms). However, these approaches are computationally intensive, i. e., they take a long time to run, especially with the complexity of data and constraints found in real-life planning scenarios, and are thus only applicable to a limited extent in practice.

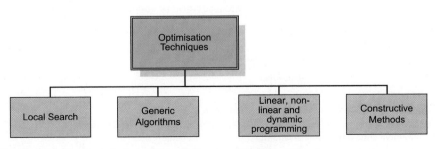

Fig. 5.4 Optimisation techniques for tactical resource planning

Constructive methods follow a different approach altogether. Rather than generating a sequence of plans, only a single plan is constructed following a well defined set of rules and heuristics. In order to derive a high quality plan, problem-specific knowledge must be incorporated in these rules and heuristics. Although successfully applied to classical supply chain problems, the sheer amount of constraints, requirements and conditions to be considered often limits the effectiveness of this approach in real-life resource planning scenarios.

5.5 A Case Study

The main aspects of the resource modelling and resource planning processes are illustrated in this section by means of an example. In this scenario, engineers deliver communication products and services to customers at their premises. This work includes provision of new services, repair of faulty services and ceasing of redundant services. Table 5.1 lists the attributes captured for both jobs and engineers.

Each job is characterised by a unique job number, the location of the customer premise, the skill required for delivering the service, an appointment time window and indicator whether the work is based on an actual job or a forecasted service. To give an example, job no. 1 requires the delivery of a new phone service at an address in East London on Thursday afternoon, and this job represents an actual service commitment. The engineers, on the other hand, are identified by their name. They can work in various areas and have preferences for the different locations, they possess multiple skills with specific productivity rates and preferences, they are potentially available for different shifts, and they can be part of the standard workforce of the communications business or can be brought in as contractors. Engineer *Adam Smith*, for instance, works by default in Central London (preference one) but can also work in East London (preference two) and North London (preference three). He is a provision engineer by default (preference one) but can also do repair work (preference two). For his default skill, he has a high productivity of five jobs per shift but his secondary skill only shows a productivity of three jobs per shift. For Thursday, the afternoon shift is his first preference but he could also work in the morning if required.

Each engineer can work in one area with one skill per shift, and can only work one shift per day. The task is to generate a seven-day capacity and deployment plan

Table 5.1 Job and engineer characteristics

Job	Engineer
Job number	Engineer name
Customer premise	List of locations, with preferences
Required skill	List of skills, with preferences and productivities
Appointment time window	Availability, potential overtime
Type (actual or forecasted)	Type (standard, contractor)

that delivers a high volume of services every day while controlling the incurred costs, i. e., reducing the effects of skill, location and shift changes for the engineers. This objective can be expressed as given in (5.3).

$$\text{Quality\_of\_Service} = \text{Volume\_of\_Service\_Delivery} \qquad (5.3)$$
$$\text{Cost} = -B_1 * \text{Area\_Changes} - B_2 * \text{Skill\_Changes}$$
$$- B_3 * \text{Shift\_Changes}$$
$$\text{Objective} = \lambda * \text{Quality\_of\_Service} + (1 - \lambda) * \text{Cost}$$

While the quality of service is directly linked to the volume of jobs expected to be cleared, the cost is a weighted sum of the number of area, skill and shift changes[3]. The objective function itself depends on the parameter λ which can be shifted between one (purely delivery-focused) and zero (purely cost-focussed).

The seven-day plan from Monday to Sunday is generated iteratively. Following Fig. 5.3, the first step for each daily plan is the aggregation of actual and forecasted work. As an example, East London could show a volume of 20 provision jobs (15 actual, five more forecasted to arrive by then) for Thursday's afternoon shift. In a second step, a baseline plan is established: all engineers get deployed to the areas, skills and shifts with preference one. Consequently, *Adam Smith* will initially be deployed on Thursday to Central London using his provision skills in the afternoon shift. He could, potentially, clear a volume of five according to his productivity.

The subsequent gap analysis identifies any under- and over-resourcing for each combination of area, skill and shift. East London, for instance, might be under-staffed with regard to provision skills on Thursday afternoon as only a volume of 14 out of 20 is expected to be cleared with the baseline deployment. The engineer *Adam Smith*, on the other hand, might be under-utilised, meaning Central London would be over-resourced with regard to provision skills on Thursday afternoon.

In this case study, we consider a simple hill climber for improving the baseline plan. The resource plan is modified in small steps, with each alteration resulting in an improvement, i. e., a plan with a better objective score. Such plan alteration consider moving a single under-utilised engineer to an under-resourced area/skill/shift combination, swapping the deployments of two engineers or shuffling moves where one engineer replaces another one. *Adam Smith*, for instance, can be moved from Central London to East London. This results in an increased quality of service (a higher provision volume is delivered in East London on Thursday afternoon) but also an increased cost (the engineer is deployed to a non-default area). If this, according to the objective outlined in (5.3), constitutes a plan improvement, then the deployment for *Adam Smith* is modified and the resource plan is updated accordingly. This process, a flow chart of which is presented in Fig. 5.5, is repeated until no further moves for any engineers can be found that improve the plan further.

During the final phase, the overall capacity and deployment plans are generated. The capacity plan contains for all area/skill/shift combinations and for all seven days

---

[3] The factors B_1, B_2 and B_3 indicate the weighting of area, skill and shift changes, respectively.

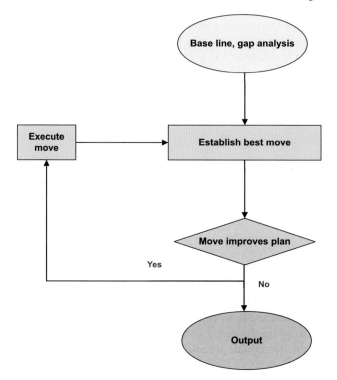

Fig. 5.5 Plan improvement through hill climbing

the total service volume, the service volume anticipated to be cleared and the head count of deployed engineering resources: "East London shows a volume of 20 provision jobs on Thursday afternoon of which 19 are expected to be cleared by four engineers." Aggregate information such as 'East London shows a volume of 150 provision jobs over the whole week of which 130 are expected to be delivered' can be easily extracted. The second output, the engineer deployment plan, lists for each engineer for each weekday the assigned area, skill and shift. Deployment information of the kind '*Adam Smith* will work the Thursday afternoon shift in East London using provision skills' can be directly utilised by a subsequent service scheduling system.

5.6 Summary

This chapter presented an overview of tactical resource planning and deployment in service organisations. The resources in this chapter is people – *field force* or *workforce*. It highlighted the unique characteristics and challenges of such medium-term planning scenarios and outlined a solution approach. The modelling and optimisation process was further illustrated by means of a case study. A recent Gartner report (Maoz and Clark 2007) lists some of the vendors in the resource planning space. This is an indication that the service industry has identified the need for dedicated service chain management systems in general and tactical resource planning systems in particular for field service management. However for utility (water, telecom, gas etc.) based organisations that provide services over networks, there are few commercial tools available for network planning. The next chapter looks at challenges in developing generic network planning systems. In particular it examines the approaches needed to optimally design and plan the utilisation of an organisation's network, thus ensuring that the chain of resources in a service organisation is optimal for service delivery.

Chapter 6
Network Planning for Telecom and Utilities

6.1 Introduction

For network centric businesses such as telecommunication providers and utilities, networks form the core of their business and comprise a very expensive asset that needs careful management to fulfil both present and future requirements of customers. Correctly planning and designing the network is essential to the success of such businesses. The network planning and design process can involve planning and design at different levels of detail from high level strategic or business planning through to low level detailed planning and design. Network planning and design forms part of a wider provisioning process encompassing order handling, job tracking, network design and configuration through to order fulfilment and billing. This chapter focuses on the network planning and design process together with a brief examination of the opportunities provided through use of network optimisation techniques therein improving upon results obtained through use of manual techniques alone.

Enterprises such as Telecommunications Operators, Power Distribution Providers and Water Utilities rely heavily on networks to provide consumers with services and utilities. Networks in general have characteristics such as capacity, performance and cost which affect the distribution of the medium they carry; and so the dimensioning and specification of networks form a major part of the overall design process. For network operators the underlying networks are crucial to their core business and the extension and upgrading of the network is essential in order to address new markets and support the delivery of services/products to the consumer. These services can be telecoms services such as voice, video and data, or for commodities, the networks can deliver energy in the form of gas or electric power or water to the consumer. The planning and design of networks forms a key function within those businesses. Given the high cost associated with planning, building and maintaining those networks it is often critical to the overall success of the business. When a network operator upgrades or extends the network, consideration must be given to

C. Voudouris, G. Owusu, R. Dorne, D. Lesaint, *Service Chain Management*
DOI: 10.1007/978-3-540-75504-3, ©Springer 2008

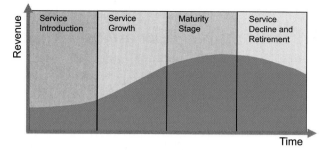

Fig. 6.1 Service/product lifespan

the network's ability to support not only current services/demands but also forecast demand.

For telecoms this forecast demand might be the result of delivering new services or increased usage of existing services. Indeed, as new services are introduced, older services may decline or be retired. Services place a demand on the network that must be well understood so the development of the network can evolve in a cost effective manner to facilitate the delivery of services/commodities to consumers and allow for the resultant revenue streams.

The introduction of new products/services and their resultant revenue typically follow the curve as shown in Fig. 6.1. After the product/service is initially introduced and promoted, there is a period of steady growth as more consumers take up the service. Following this phase the service/product reaches a stage of maturity until it finally starts to decline as the result of competing products and services. Whilst this diagram shows the revenue trend over time for a new product/service, a similar curve could also show the network capacity requirement over the same period of time and the resultant demand on the underlying network.

When we further consider that the network may deliver many such services as shown in Fig. 6.2 (dashed lines representing different services), with each service at varying stages in their lifecycle we can see that the forecasting of demand and mapping this to required network capacity becomes very complex. This can be further complicated by consumer segmentation and competition effects. A prime example of this has been the rollout of broadband in the telecoms marketplace. The take up of Broadband has followed the predicted pattern as shown in the early stages of Fig. 6.1. The increased levels of demand have placed significant demand on existing network which have had to be augmented as a result.

Utility providers tend to deliver commodities such as power or water over their network rather than services. The demand for these commodities again must be well understood when designing the network. The network must not only be capable of providing typical capacity to end users but must also be able to handle surges in demand. For example, during the 2006 World Cup in the UK, demand in the power network rose by the order of several thousand Megawatts as people turned on kettles during half-time intervals during matches. Power companies for example have reserve power generation for such short term demand such as Hydro Electric

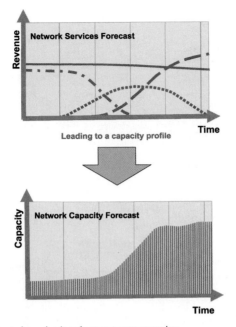

Fig. 6.2 Mapping projected service/product usage to capacity

Power Generation which can provide a significant short term power injection into the power grid. Utility providers also have to match supply with demand. The supply of a commodity may be sourced from a number of suppliers and may involve matching forecast demand with the availability and cost of different supply streams.

The remainder of this chapter is organised as follows. Section 6.2 provides a general overview of the planning and design process. Section 6.3 describes the benefits and application of automation to the planning and design process. A more detailed examination of network optimisation applications for both telecommunications and utilities is presented in Sects. 6.4 and 6.5 respectively. Finally, a summary of the chapter is given in Sect. 6.6.

6.2 The Planning and Design Process

The Network planning and design function within businesses such as Telecoms, Power and Water Utilities defines a complex and labour intensive activity. For large utilities this activity relates to the build and design of new networks, augmentation of existing networks and the configuration of networks (see Fig. 6.3) in order to meet the demands placed upon the network. These demands might be the result of increased network coverage, new services or increased consumer demand.

The construction of networks can be extremely expensive when we consider the significant costs associated with for example the digging up of roads, laying network

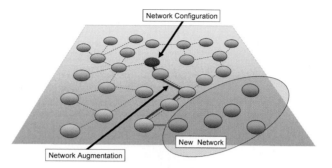

Fig. 6.3 Extending, augmenting and configuring networks

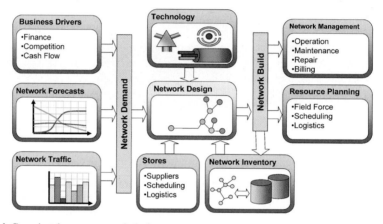

Fig. 6.4 Generic telecoms network design

infrastructure and in-life maintenance. The design and planning of networks can involve considerable effort and is usually carried out by expert network planners. Given the complexity involved in network design especially when dealing with large networks, complex technologies and local planning rules, the network planner is frequently faced with a significant design problem. Often the network planner will strive to use their experience to find a solution that the technology supports and seems reasonable in terms of overall cost.

The network planning and design process shown in Fig. 6.4 usually follows a defined process dependant upon the type of planning and design being undertaken. In general, the planning and design of networks can be either proactive or reactive. In proactive network planning the network is dimensioned and designed to meet anticipated growth in demand. This might, for example, be triggered by demand forecasts indicating the take-up rate of a new service resulting in a network that needs to be upgraded in order to provide that service. In reactive planning the network design function is triggered by increased current demand for new capacity or by extending the network to reach a new customer base. Reactive planning generally involves the reconfiguration or augmentation of an existing network whereas proactive planning typically introduces new network. Growing and extending a network in a proactive manner as opposed to reactive reconfiguration of networks typically depends upon business drivers such as cost reduction and must be weighed against any benefits derived.

6.3 Automating Network Design

Network planning and design can be a very complex activity, especially when we consider the design and planning of very large complex networks using a plethora of design rules and constraints. Often the network designer is driven by the need to produce a design that satisfies the design criteria of the underlying network technology whilst, where possible, attempting to reduce the cost of the design. This, by its very nature, is very difficult and the designer tends to rely on experience to deliver a best effort design. Often, given a design problem, there may exist many possible solutions, each with particular merits and disadvantages. Ideally it would be best to consider all possible solutions and pick the best solution in terms of cost and design validity. This, however, is not possible when design problems become large and many solutions exist. As a result, a designer, in general, will compromise in their attempts to produce a valid design at reasonable cost.

The automated design of networks (see Fig. 6.5) can aid in the design process by allowing many solutions to be generated and evaluated, driven by the requirement to discover low cost, yet valid, solutions (Conway et al. 2001). By capturing the rules for network design and using network design algorithms (including intelligence based algorithms) we can apply computing power to automate the network design process resulting in the discovery of solutions that can be considered 'good'

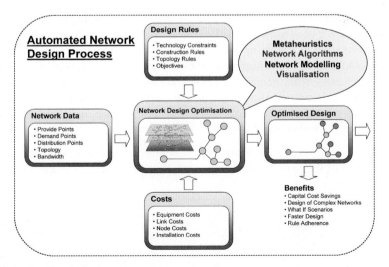

Fig. 6.5 Network optimisation process

whilst at the same time attempting to drive down the cost. In essence, network optimisation applications attempt to capture design expertise and use computing power to discover good solutions. The benefits associated with automated network design are numerous and include low cost designs, rule adherence, and significant improvement in design time. For such applications to function well not only should design expertise be embedded within the tools but also a clear encoding of the problem allowing the various solutions to be traversed.

Many network optimisation applications make use of Intelligent Search algorithms or Metaheuristics (Voudouris et al. 2001) such as Genetic Algorithms, Simulated Annealing and Ant Colony Optimisation to discover solutions to network design problems. These hard problems are part of a wider family of problems for which no algorithms exist which can guarantee the identification of an optimal solution in reasonable time. Intelligent search algorithms use different mechanisms to guide the search for good solutions through a landscape containing many solutions. Typically the number of possible solutions can far exceed the number that could be determined manually in the lifetime of a network designer.

Telecommunication networks and utility networks each have their own characteristics leading to domain specific problems when considering their design. The following sections discuss some of these characteristics and the opportunities for network optimisation.

6.4 Optimisation of Telecommunication Network Design

Consider a nationwide telecommunications network typical of incumbent operators serving millions of customers. From a physical perspective the network can be represented by point to point connections between each customer to the local serving exchange (usually via a copper pair) and a network of cables between these exchanges to form a core trunk network (see Fig. 6.6). Planning and optimisation of such a network could simply be portrayed as a matter of ensuring sufficient bandwidth to each customer and ensuring that the core network provides enough capacity between exchanges while remaining resilient to single cable failures.

However, telecommunication networks are extremely complex and hence design, planning and subsequent optimisation is difficult. There are many reasons for this, which include the following:

- Almost every household and business is connected to the network, making the sheer scale of the network very large with wide variations in terms of customer usage patterns and geographic location.
- Although connections between customer and network are primarily point to point (no sharing), noise and crosstalk effects exist between lines within a cable, which decreases the quality of the connection, placing limits on the services that can be offered.
- Larger businesses and organisations have dedicated fibre optic links connecting to the network, thus demanding extremely large amounts of bandwidth.

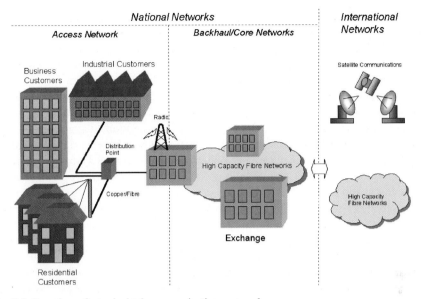

Fig. 6.6 Overview of a typical telecommunications network

- The core of the network consists entirely of optical fibre, allowing a single fibre to carry millions of simultaneous telephone calls, thus requiring that the network must be as reliable as possible.
- The network supports a variety of services, such as telephony, broadband internet and business-oriented services such as virtual private networks and private lines. Such services are carried by different layers in the network thus each of these layers need to be designed and planned with due regard to the others.

The consequential optimisation of such a network needs to address each of these factors. This section describes how planning and design functions can be performed with respect to the above issues.

Any sufficiently large telecommunication network will serve customers that demand a variety of different services across a wide geographic area. As a result the network itself must be able to grow both in size and in capacity as and when required. Building new exchanges is extremely expensive and time-consuming as it requires building the premises as well as laying ducts and cables from the existing network deployment and deploying suitable equipment within. The placement of such an exchange needs to be considered very carefully so that the minimal infrastructure is provisioned both between the exchange and the rest of the network and also between the exchange and the anticipated customers (this includes street furniture such as cabinets). One also needs to ensure that the maximum bandwidth capability is available to customers given the assumed medium between exchange and customer. In the access regime residential customers are predominantly connected on a point to point basis with the local exchange. This means that the (usually) copper line connects the customer with the exchange with no additional sharing of the medium with anyone else. However, given the propagation effects of signal transmission, noise arising from crosstalk from one connection to another in the cable reduces the quality of signals that can be maintained on a given connection. This problem increases both with the number of simultaneous users as well as the associated bandwidth rate of the users. As a result, careful consideration must be given to how services are provided to customers, particularly with respect to guarantees of bandwidth availability. It is customary that an agreed plan is adopted by all service providers that use specific frequencies of signal transmission so as to minimise the crosstalk between adjacent lines. As many exchanges now have equipment installed from a variety of different service providers (known as Local Loop Unbundling), it is important that such a plan is both optimal for all parties as well as policed to ensure that it is properly maintained.

One of most significant advancements in communications in recent times has been the development and deployment of optical fibre and the associated transmission systems. Since its initial deployment in national networks in the early 1980s, fibre optic communication systems have rapidly become the medium of choice for both high bandwidth and long distance communication. Their lightness, thinness and flexibility allow them to be installed in almost any environment and their intrinsic attenuation is such that a kilometre of optical fibre is equivalent to a single pane of ordinary glass. There are a variety of optical fibre types and specifications, each with its own characteristics, benefits and applications. The correct choice of fibre depends on the wavelengths that need to be supported, their maximum bandwidth (or bit rate) as well as the length of transmission before the signals are detected and electrically processed (known as regeneration).

One extremely successful technology that has taken advantage of the vast bandwidth capabilities inherent in optical fibre has been wavelength division multiplexed (WDM) technology (Spirit and O'Mahoney 1996). The basic concept is relatively straightforward: instead of attempting to increase the bit rate of a given signal (which becomes increasingly difficult due to distortion effects), merely send multiple signals along the fibre with each signal being transmitted on a slightly different wavelength. At the far end a specially designed filter splits the signals into their constituent parts (similar to a prism converting white light into a rainbow of colours) and presents each signal to the correct system. With systems operating at 10 Gbit/s (10 billion bits per second) on a wavelength and 160 wavelengths on a fibre, WDM systems today offer over 1 Tbit/s of capacity on a single strand of fibre. The design of such systems is extremely complex, in that the placement of intermediate amplification to overcome the losses in the fibre needs to be carefully planned, along with the method of creating and detecting the optical signals at each end. In addition, methods to counter the presence of distortion effects need to be incorporated in high capacity/long distance systems as well as consideration for error correction methodologies to maintain performance margin. Using all these techniques, WDM systems spanning the world's continents and oceans exist, providing the underlying backbone of the global internet.

The design and optimisation of point to point transmission systems be they copper pairs between an exchange and a customer, or an optical fibre link between two international points of presence for a global internet provider, is usually performed in isolation with the rest of the network. However, the design and optimisation of the network itself cannot be performed in such a way, it needs to take into consideration the specific requirements and characteristics of the equipment and systems that are to be deployed. It is this design, planning and optimisation that the rest of this section shall focus.

6.4.1 Network Tiers

The purpose of introducing tiers in a network is to efficiently aggregate and amalgamate traffic that is incident from the customers in the access regime and place this traffic on bearers that are dimensioned to accept this traffic with minimal contention, yet without extreme overprovision of bandwidth. Traffic becomes more concentrated as it nears the inner core of the network, so larger and more sophisticated systems are required to switch and manage this traffic as well as higher capacity transmission systems to transport this traffic from one part of the network to another. A modern national telecommunications network may contain up to 50 inner core nodes, with hundreds of secondary nodes and thousands of local exchanges. At each stage or tier (shown in Fig. 6.7), traffic that does not need to be sent deeper into the network is switched at the lowest possible tier, thus placing less pressure on the higher tiers.

The architectures of these tiers differ from each other as a result of the function that they are providing and the bandwidth that they accommodate. Lower tiers such as outer core and regional areas tend to be designed as rings, allowing services to be protected as they pass from the access environment to the core. In the event of

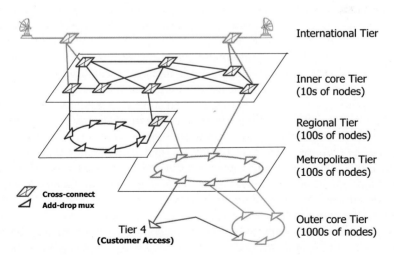

Fig. 6.7 Network tiers

a failure of a section of the ring (for example a cable dig-up) management signalling within the ring itself recognises the fault and re-routes traffic around the other side of the ring automatically (usually within 50 ms) and then raises an alarm via the management systems so that remedial action (i. e., repair) can be carried out. The architecture of the inner core (and pan-continental networks) differs in that a series of direct point to point systems tend to be deployed interlinking large switches. Each switch is connected to a number (usually at least three) of other switches so that in the event of a link failure multiple alternative routes can be used to circumnavigate the problem. Such restoration of service tends to be slower than automatic ring switching, but has the advantage that it requires less bandwidth to be installed for the protection of services, although guaranteeing route separation is absolutely critical to avoid node isolation.

In order to optimise a telecommunications network, one of the first considerations is to associate each node in the network with a particular tier. Putting a node too high in the tier structure would result in too much equipment and infrastructure being deployed at considerable expense, whereas putting it too low would mean that it would be unable to handle all incident and transit traffic effectively. Furthermore, having too many inner core nodes is expensive to provision and maintain, whereas having too few would result in significant issues if such a node to be isolated from the rest of the network (such as a fire or power failure). To help select the correct number and location of inner and outer core nodes, the network planner must understand both the current and future traffic demand as well as the underlying infrastructure on which new capacity can be deployed. A subsequent network optimisation would identify potential physical routes that could accommodate the traffic demand, quantify the amount of equipment required in each node, the bandwidth of the transmission systems required between them and make an assessment of the impact of network failures (link and nodal) and assign a relative penalty for each design.

Given a network with thousands of exchanges and many more cable sections between them, a network optimisation that can examine each and every possible combination of network design and identify the most optimal solution could take longer than is practical even using the fastest computers available. As a result, optimisation techniques that seek 'optimal' solutions using intelligent search algorithms are necessary. Regardless of technique, the algorithms express the network characteristics and constraints as a mathematical function and attempt to minimise (or maximise) this function with respect to the penalties and costs that have been specified as part of the optimisation process. In such a manner although it is never possible to guarantee that any proposed solution is the most optimal of all possible solutions (unless the network is particularly small), provided that sufficient time has been allowed to conduct the search, one can be satisfied that all mandatory rules and criteria have been fulfilled (i. e., the solution is valid) and that it is a 'good' solution (in that it is better than the myriad others examined).

In general, network optimisation tends to be conducted at a particular regime of the network. For example the access network would be optimised in such a way to minimise the amount of cable and duct deployed without regard to the core network. Similarly the inner core network would be optimised in terms of links and switch capacity by taking the overall aggregated traffic demand between nodes as a basis, as opposed to the individual traffic streams from which it was constructed. Furthermore, up until recently much network planning and optimisation has been conducted for geographically separate regions (autonomous regions of a country or individual countries in a pan-continental or world-wide network). Clearly such planning is easier as a result of this simplification. While the resulting network may be very good locally, on a wider scale the overall network tends to be less optimal. New tools and techniques are now becoming available that can address these issues, partly as a result of larger and more powerful computational facilities and partly due to more sophisticated algorithms and approaches. As a result, multi-network analysis and optimisation is becoming increasingly possible, allowing solutions to be found that are more optimal than would have been possible from merely examining each regime in turn.

6.4.2 Network Layers

Another key difference between the telecommunications network of a hundred years ago and today is that fact that our current network can support a multitude of different services and, consequently, service providers. The basic telephony service is quickly becoming subsumed into more advanced services being offered to customers. Today's network offers broadband services, private lines, virtual local area networks (LANs), and a host of other services for particular clients. As a result the telecoms network has to be able to support various network layers over which these services can be provided. Each layer in the network treats the layer beneath in a similar manner that the telecoms designs treated the cable and duct infrastructure – in other words as a constraint that is expensive, time-consuming or simply impossible to alter. Because of this approach, the locations and interconnectivity of these layers may not be as optimal as desired. However, each layer has to consider not only the requirements of the layers above, but also the fact that there may be more than one service provider at that layer (for example multiple internet providers) and as a result the lower layer has to compromise between the requirements of all interested parties. Given the large number of layers in the communications network and particularly the cost of interconnecting, operating and evolving them, it is evident that attempts to rationalise the network to a few well-defined platforms that are able to offer a wide range of services on a flexible and dynamic basis would be advantageous.

The ability to optimise a network with respect to multiple layers is much more difficult than for a single layer. As mentioned above, there may be more than one instance of the layer due to multiple service providers and even without this additional complexity, choosing sites and interconnectivity that provides a global optimum could result in sub-optimal solutions for each of the layers when considered individually. As these layers tend to be managed and operated as commercial entities in their own right, the overall strategic benefit of global optimisation needs to be expressed clearly and appropriately.

6.4.3 Summarising Network Optimisation

We have seen that the term 'network optimisation' could be associated with a variety of different meanings. It could refer to the optimisation of specific equipment functionality or switching system or even transmission medium. Normally it refers to the design and planning of networks assuming a set of characteristics of these inherent elements, but even then can be associated with different contexts. Optimising specific regimes such as access or inner core networks require vastly different modelling requirements and information as they attempt to address very different issues. Most importantly we have shown that optimising local regimes can lead to poorly optimised overall networks, and that modelling specific layers can also lead to sub-optimal solutions. However, attempting to optimise all regimes across all layers represents an extremely large problem, both technically and commercially as it requires communication and co-operation between the operators of each of the layers in question.

6.5 Applications of Network Optimisation Within Network Utilities

The last section was dedicated to the optimisation of telecommunication networks. It discusses many areas of optimisation such as minimisation of cable and duct deployment, network equipment placement, bandwidth allocation and multiple layer optimisation for different service provisioning. In fact, from the optimisation point of view, there are many similarities between telecom networks and utility networks. Minimisation of amount of cables and ducts for a telecom network would be equivalent to the minimisation of power cables for an electricity network, and water pipes for a water network. Equipment placement problem for telecom networks can also be thought of as a transformer or a circuit switch placement problem for an electricity network. Identifying the best route to minimise signalling loss and road dig-up cost by sharing trenches between an exchange and a premise for a telecom network would be very similar to the minimisation of power loss between a sub-station and a premise in an electricity network. This section provides a brief description of power, water and gas networks with possible optimisation areas for those utilities.

Power transmission is typically considered between power plants and substations, whilst electricity distribution is between substations and premises. The high voltage transmission usually takes place at 110 kV (or above), over a long distance through overhead power transmission lines. Each substation serves a particular geographic area by stepping down the voltage to 11 kV (or lower). Due to the high investment cost in the electric energy sector, it is paramount to design transmission networks to transport the energy as efficiently as possible, while taking into account network safety issues, geographical constraints and economic factors.

One of the optimisation areas in power network design is to minimise the cost of reliability of distribution networks by reconfiguring the circuit switches. The reliability of power supply is determined by the occurrence and the duration of interruptions to the affected customers. During an electrical fault, the corresponding circuit breaker opens to disconnect the entire cable from supply of electrical energy. Customers who are on the faulty cable experience an interruption in service. If the interruption is greater than a specific time interval, a monetary compensation by the electricity company is required. For a large radial power distribution network, the number of possible permutations of opening or closing switches to isolate a fault or maintenance area is very large. An efficient search approach is necessary to provide an optimum switch configuration that minimises the cost of reliability within a reasonable time frame.

Another possible optimisation area includes minimising the investment cost in transmission facilities by defining optimal positions of transformers, switches and routings of power lines (see Paatero et al. 2002 and Mithulananthan et al. 2004). Redundant paths or lines can be provided so that power can be routed from other power plant to any load centre based on the economics of the transmission path and the cost of power. By designing the network in different regimes, the entire problem can be decomposed into several sub-problems. The first regime can be related to the optimisation of transmission routes and the positions for substations. The second regime can be related to the identification of network elements between substations and premises. Other possible areas of optimisation include minimisation of active power loss by the use of power factor correction, maximisation of throughput and efficiency of a power system.

A water distribution network consists of pipes, interconnections, pumps, valves, pressure regulators, ground and elevated storages and reservoirs. Design parameters include the flow of water in each pipe, pressure at each interconnection, level in each tank and the concentration of chemical treatment on each time step. A common optimisation problem for water distribution is the reduction of the energy cost to operate water pumps in the system (see Ertin et al. 2001 and Wu et al. 2001). This is due to the fact that supplying water to residential and industrial estates can consume large amounts of electricity. Energy cost for water utilities can consume over 50 percent of water utility's annual operating cost. The cost is a function of the energy rate and usage in different time period. The rates are normally divided into off-peak and peak periods. By carefully scheduling the operations of water pumping (i. e., filling up the storage tanks during off-peak periods and minimising any unnecessary peak hour pumping), the overall energy savings can be significant. To achieve this, the entire water distribution system is first presented as a mathematical model. Parameters required for the calculation include the correct dimensions of water pipes, operational cost for each pump at different period of time, maximum and minimum storage tank levels and the required hydraulic performance at customers' premises. An optimisation process can then be performed to determine a pump scheduling policy with the minimum cost for each pump station. The operational policy indicates when and which set of pumps need to operate over a controlled time period whilst still maintaining the correct pipe velocities, pumped volumes, storage tank levels and nodal pressures. However, there is a trade-off between storage and pumping. In a densely populated area, pumping of water is generally more often due to the high demand and the limited space for storage of water. As a result, energy savings by reduction of water pumping will be less considerable.

Another area of optimising a water network is to determine the sizes of water pipes. As mentioned, a water network design consists of fixed locations of pipes, valves, pumps and water storages. Given a network topology with the pipe cost per unit length, and a required pressure demand at each sink node with multiple sources, an optimisation problem can be constructed by finding the correct diameter of each pipe with the least-cost. Using optimisation search techniques, many network scenarios with different dimension of water pipes can be evaluated to strive for the optimum. Each solution is validated to ensure that all the design engineering criteria are met. If not, penalties will then be assigned to any invalid solutions.

Natural gas is a major source for electricity generation through the use of gas turbines and steam turbines. Natural gas burns cleaner fuel compared with oil and coal fossil fuels. Due to its environmental properties, in some countries natural gas is primarily used for heating and electricity generation. A gas network basically consists of a set of compressors, regulators and valves that are connected by pipes. Gas distribution networks are similar to water distribution networks except that gas can be compressed and liquefied.

A common optimisation problem for a gas network can be the minimisation of the operating costs by scheduling the use of compressors cost-effectively. Given a gas network with the known geographical gas providers and customers, predictable demand with different time usage and operational costs for different compressors, an optimisation process can be employed to generate a minimum-cost operative planning to switch the compressors on and off. However, switching off compressor(s) can have an impact on the pressure drop in the system. Constant monitoring of the system is required to ensure the minimum flow of the gas is always maintained.

On the other hand, transportation of natural gas can be thought of a scheduling problem. Scheduling is concerned with the allocation of limited resources over time among both parallel and sequential activities. Transporting the liquefied natural gas (LNG) across oceans is usually done by LNG ocean carriers as natural gas pipelines are impractical across oceans. Tank trucks are then used to transport liquefied or compressed gas to the distribution points such as pipelines for onward gas delivery or end users such as electricity companies. An additional process for gasification or decompression at end users or into a pipeline is generally required. Maximising the usage of tank trucks to deliver the gas to cover the required destinations at the right time and right cost can be considered as a distributed scheduling problem. Many existing techniques such as rule-based, heuristic or stochastic approach (Voudouris et al. 2001) can be applied to generate an optimal or near optimal solution.

6.6 Summary

This chapter discussed an overview of the network planning and design processes within large telecom providers and utilities. Network planning and design is a complex process especially when the multitude of possible design requirements and constraints are considered. Many of these requirements may conflict with each other, leading to a network design problem that is very difficult to optimise if designed manually. Network optimisation provides a means whereby difficult network problems can be addressed to produce valid designs whilst doing so at minimal cost. Network optimisation has evolved alongside the evolution of the telecommunications and utility networks themselves, but now as computational capability and intelligent search algorithms become increasingly powerful and sophisticated it is likely that the networks of tomorrow will be much more flexible, resilient and cost effective than has been possible until now.

Part II
Reservation Management and Resource Scheduling

The focus in Part 1 was on the planning phase of a service organisation. In this part, our focus shifts to the execution phase. By *execution*, we refer to the operational activities that are executed daily. These activities range from customers contacting an organisation to placing orders, reporting faults, or making enquiries; through determining how to price a service; to delivering the service. Customer perceptions of an organisation will be strongly influenced by the experiences arising from executing these activities. A poor execution of these activities will inevitably lead to a loss in quality of service and, in the worst case, a discontinuity in service delivery and loss of revenue. The question then is how does one optimise these operational activities? We provide answers to this question in this part. A prerequisite for optimisation is automation. In this vein we first examine the challenges that must be addressed in order to automate the ways organisations engage with their customers. We then describe the approaches required to optimise the aforementioned operational activities.

In Chap. 7 we make the case for an efficient capacity reservation system that will ensure an organisation delivers what it promises to customers. Related to offering appointments that can be kept, service organisations use pricing techniques to manage the finite capacity they have by encouraging appointments on days with low demand. We discuss demand pricing and revenue management in Chap. 8. The remaining chapters in this part focus on how to manage an organisation's resources on an operational basis in order to deliver optimal services to customers. Chapter 9 is about automating and optimising the design and use of shifts. In Chap. 10 we discuss the use of resource scheduling systems for optimising work allocation – i.e., ensuring that the right level of resources is matched with demand. The last chapter describes the practical aspects of managing the attendance of resources – a basic tenet in getting the right resources to deliver to right customer on the right day.

Chapter 7
Reservation Management and Resource CRM

7.1 Introduction

The increasing sophistication of today's customers poses certain challenges such as responsiveness, accuracy, predictability and the reliability of service appointing to service providers in both private and public sectors. Reservation management technology is rapidly evolving to address these challenges.

A reservation is an agreement between the customer and the business on the commitment of business resources to meet customer demand. Prior to reaching the agreement, both parties need to check their own policies and availabilities to make sure such an agreement is fair, reflecting their respective and mutual interests. Reservation management refers to a bunch of integral activities that normally occur between the customer and the business that aim to enforce business policies to achieve or maintain a desired state of resources and demands. In a broader context, we also term reservation management as resource customer relationship management (CRM)[1], where resource is gathered, consolidated, regulated by the business and consumed by the customer, to emphasise the crucial interplay between the customer and the business resource. Reservation management is an integral part of a service chain network in which business partners are chained together to provide services or require services from one another. The provision of such services covers any activity that involves resource capacity transaction.

This chapter is about reservation management. It has the twin objectives of, firstly, examining the challenges in implementing a reservation management system and secondly, outlining the technologies needed to address the identified challenges. The rest of the chapter is organised as follows. Section 7.2 provides a quick overview of the use of reservation management systems in five sectors of the service industry – airlines, hotels, transportation, health and telecommunications. The choice of these five sectors is deliberate. They are complex, cover a wide variety of customer types, tend to be regulated and cover the objective of service organisations, i. e., maximising revenue whilst minimising operational cost. Section 7.3 identifies

---

[1] We use Reservation Management and Resource CRM interchangeably.

C. Voudouris, G. Owusu, R. Dorne, D. Lesaint, *Service Chain Management*
DOI: 10.1007/978-3-540-75504-3, ©Springer 2008

typical challenges in implementing reservation management solutions. Section 7.4 discusses the strategies to address the challenges. Section 7.5 lists some key technologies that underpin the realisation of the strategies outlined in Sect. 7.4, and also analyses some commercial reservation management systems, notably resource CRM systems.

7.2 A Brief Overview of the Use of Reservation Management Systems

A service represents a special product that can be sold against a specified time period. During this time period, material, equipment, energy, information and/or labour are combined in an organic way to fulfil certain tasks. Examples of such services include airline seats (Littlewood 1972), hotel rooms (Bitran and Gilbert 1996), passenger railways (Ciancimino et al. 1999), hospital beds (Harper and Shahani 2002) and telecommunications lines (Li et al. 2006). Although there are some common characteristics with regard to service across all the service sectors, such as perishable products and stochastic demand, there are also some other characteristics such as urgency, booking mechanisms, resource flexibility and primary business objectives that vary sector by sector.

Urgency characterises whether or not the customer requires instantaneous access to the service. Urgency is used for analysing the periods that customers compete with each other for acquiring services and refers to the severity of such competitions. For airline seats, hotel rooms or passenger railways, there is generally no urgency in acquiring these services, as these bookings could be part of a scheduled trip for the customer. The scenario is different for hospital beds and telecommunication lines – e. g., customers might be struggling to cope with illnesses or may require instantaneous broadband access.

The booking mechanism characterises modes of interplay between the customer and the business. Reservation is a straight-forward way to define the commitment between the customer and the business. However, a reservation is only possible when there is a defined or predictable time duration for the required service, such as in the cases of airline seats, hotel rooms, passenger railways and telecommunication lines. The time duration of medical treatment, in contrast, varies from patient to patient and it is dependent on individual conditions. As a result, queues are used to allocate patients to hospital beds. It should be noted that "hospital bed" is different from General Practice (GP). In GP, doctors only perform the initial screening of patients and would refer them to hospital for further treatment if their medical cases appear to be complicated. In this way, the time period for GP service is more controllable, which makes GP appointments quite achievable.

Resource flexibility is a key factor that determines the scope of business policies. The airline seat is an example of a flexible resource, i. e., the number of seats will increase if more airplanes are added. The increased resource capacity could lead to the drop of service price if enough time is given for resource planning and dispatching. Telecommunication line provision is also regarded as a flexible resource, where re-dispatching technicians from A to B will reshape the resource distribution that in turn impacts lead times. A hotel room is, on the other hand, a kind of resource with a fixed capacity. The seasonal fluctuation of room price is dependent on the changes in the volume of hotel bookings.

Business objectives vary across service sectors. For public sector organisations the emphasis is on minimising operational costs, whilst in private sector organisations, the objective is to maximise revenue whilst reducing operational costs. Examples of private industries include airlines, hotels and transportation. Industries in the public sector include health and the primary focus here is in minimising the lead time.

7.3 Business and Technical Challenges in Implementing a Reservation Management System

There are four major stakeholders with regards to reservation management: namely customer, business, employee and regulator. Figure 7.1 shows the relationships among these stakeholders. The customer requests service from the business; the business organises the employee to fulfil the service; and the regulator oversees all the customers, businesses and employees to make sure they are regulation-compliant.

For the business, the inability to provide a reservation management solution exposes it immediately to the following challenges:

- *Customer dissatisfaction*: All the customers have personal preferences and expectations from the business. It could be an earliest service slot, a cheapest deal, or simply an achievable commitment or a quicker response from the business.

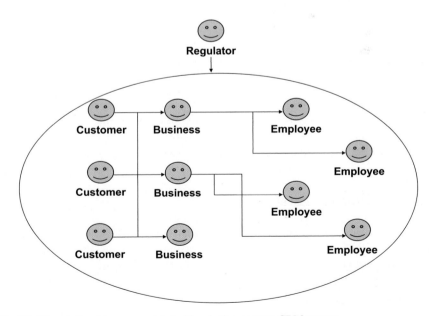

Fig. 7.1 The relationship among stakeholders in the resource CRM system

Failing to accommodate such requirements could lead to dissatisfied customers or in some cases loss of customers.

- *Eroded business bottom-line*: The business operates to achieve maximised revenue and minimised cost. A poor reservation management implementation that misaligns customer demand and business resources could generate considerably idle or under-utilised resources and fail to reap the revenue at the right level, in the right place, or at the right time.
- *Employee dissatisfaction*: Employees dislike an overload of work with peaks and troughs. They prefer customer demand to be evenly balanced across all employees. Existing reservation management solutions often neglect employee interests, which is one of the key reasons underpinning reduced employee productivity and loss of skilled workers.
- *Regulation incompliance*: Regulators dictate many aspects of how businesses operate. For instance, they may ask the service organisations to provide equivalence of access or full service coverage to all the customers. A poorly-implemented reservation management solution would certainly aid non-compliance, thus making it an easy prey to severe penalties by the regulators and, in the worst case, going out of business.
- *A dilemma in achieving balanced objectives*: Customers, businesses, employees and regulators have conflicting interests. For instance, improving customer and employee satisfaction may be at the expense of businesses' bottom-line. Another key challenge is to balance these factors and implement them in a coherent way such that an overall satisfactory result can be achieved.

To fully implement a reservation management system, one has to address other technical challenges. Operating an integrated service chain requires continuous information flows, based upon the best product or service flows that can be achieved.

7.4 Strategies for Implementing a Reservation Management System

This section provides guidelines to those readers who are interested in implementing reservation management or resource CRM solutions. To this end, we scope the key issues and decision points related to resource CRM into three levels: the strategic level, the tactical level and the operational level.

7.4.1 The Strategic Level

At the strategic level, there are some fundamental, long-term issues related to setting up resource CRM, often requiring top-level business approval. Prudent decisions need to be made on:

- Resource network configuration
- Information sharing

- Distribution channels
- Capacity currencies

Resource network configuration establishes the basic business resource structure, normally attributed to the geographical location, the type of resource, the capacity of resource, and the time period. In the telecommunication sector, this could be grounded to exchange the building location, technician skills, man-hours and dates. In passenger railways, this could refer to station-to-station, the class of passenger carriage, the number of seats and the date-time.

Information sharing is a pre-requisite to configuring a resource network, which requires integrated systems and processes through the service chain network. In the hotel business, the information that needs to be shared could be as simple as the number of rooms that have been booked or in occupation over the total number of rooms. In the telecommunication business, such information could be more complex, spanning across both the customer service system (e. g., demand signals, how many reservations have been made) and the operation support system (the exchange lock-down period, the technician deployment plan, the back-end job status, etc.).

Distribution channels refer to the manner in which service can reach end-customers. For example, channels include direct sales and agency sales. Agency sales is applicable when there are a plural of choices in services and a dedicated sales force can best facilitate customers in selecting services. Direct sales are usually applicable where they do not complicate choices in service selection. Airline seats, hotel rooms and telecommunication products are all examples of agency sales. Hospital beds and passenger railways are examples for direct sales.

Capacity currency indicates the sellable unit of service. In passenger railway, this could be in the number of seats. In hospitals, this could be in the number of beds. In telecommunications, this could be either in man-hours or in numbers of jobs, depending on whether it is possible to estimate the time duration of a job.

7.4.2 The Tactical Level

At the tactical level, there are some mid-term issues for which effective solutions need to be devised. These include:

- The pricing policy
- The alignment between business resources and customer demands
- A generic, flexible resource CRM
- An open standard based implementation

The pricing policy is related to the revenue management that originated in the airline sector (Littlewood 1972) and was later spread to other service sectors, such as hotels (Bitran and Gilbert 1996), passenger railways (Ciancimino et al. 1999) and Internet service providers (Nair and Bapna 2001). Kimse and Chase (1998) reported that the most effective applications of revenue management are generally found in service

sectors, such as hotels, airlines, and cruises, in which there exist controlled service duration and variable service prices. Bitran and Mondschein (1995) developed
a stochastic and dynamic programming model that characterises an optimal pricing
policy as functions of the remaining resource capacity and the time left before the
end of resource planning. As the remaining time for resource planning reduces, the
cost for implementing the plan increases, which needs to be reflected in the service
price to balance the profit (for more detail on dynamic pricing and revenue management, see Chap. 8).

A fine alignment between customer demands and business resources is key
to maximising resource utilisation, fulfilling commitments to customers, resolv-
ing conflict among customers, and enforcing business policies and regulations, as
well as maximising business profits. The customer demand pattern is determined by
many factors, such as seasonal adjustment, new technology, new government policy,
etc. There is a limited scope in which the business can manipulate the customer demand pattern. More often, the business simply observes and follows those projected
demand patterns. There may be restrictions on adjustments that can be made to an
organisation's resources. For example in the airline, railways, and telecommunication sectors, where resource is fluid, there are more opportunities to shift business
resources around to align with actual or projected customer demand. For the hotel
or hospital sectors, where the shifting of resource is highly restricted, there is little
scope to align business resource with customer demand.

Like most CRM systems, a resource CRM system is typically linked to multiple
B2B or B2C portals that could require different formats or protocols for resource
booking. A resource CRM system could also be integrated with an enterprise re-

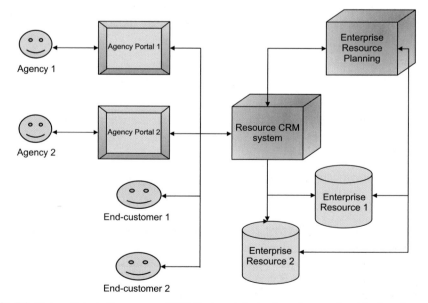

Fig. 7.2 Various links to the resource CRM System at the business front-end and back-end

source planning module that takes these enterprise resources as inputs and produces a projected resource plan as output. Figure 7.2 shows such possible scenarios. It is thereby critical that the resource CRM systems have a generic, flexible architecture that is capable of handling system integration at both the front-end and the back-end.

Open standard based implementation is another measure of achieving flexible integration with external systems. For instance, web services (Christensen 2001) have become one of the standard ways to define component interface APIs, which increases the portability, the reusability, and the potential value of the resource CRM systems.

7.4.3 The Operational Level

At the operational level, concerns are given to the real-time performance, the efficiency and the integrity of the resource CRM system. In particular, efficient algorithms need to be implemented for the following key tasks in reservation management:

- *Mapping the customer request to the business service*: The first step in implementing a resource CRM is to establish the services that customers may require. In certain service sectors, such as airlines, railways, and hotels, it is straight-forward to map customer requests to related services. In other sectors, such as telecommunications, where there is a requirement for fine-grained service codes, locating the right service is not an easy task for the customer who is not familiar with the service codes. More often than not, customers have to interact with agents at customer contact centres to clarify the services they require. Supporting customers via call centre agents is costly; as a result, businesses have also been looking at either offshoring call centre businesses or providing automated service access via the Internet. Existing service description standards, such as WSDL (W3C 2001), UDDI (OASIS 2002), OWL-S (W3C 2006), and service classification codes aim at automating service lookup and matchmaking in B2B domain. However, these standards lack the capabilities for flexibly describing services within the B2C domain. There is some research work, such as in Li (2006) that attempts to address this challenge.
- *Mapping the customer location to the business area code*: There are well-established public area coding systems, such as postal codes, that are familiar to customers; the mapping from customer selected location into business area code is straight-forward, which is usually conducted by automated software programs, e. g., Geographical Information System packages (GIS) like Multimap, ESRI or Autodesk.
- *Mapping between the reservable capacity and the actual resource capacity of various sources*: The former represents the customer view of the business capacity, whereas the latter represents the business view of the capacity for needed resources. There are two basic operations related to this mapping. One is to de-

rive reservable capacity from various resource sources; the other is to map customer orders into capacity bookings for specific resources. It should be noted that different resources could be managed under different policies, e. g., geography granularity.

- *Coping with workflow and allocating resource capacity against workflow:* Workflow represents the business process logic. It defines a sequence of and/or parallel actions that need to be conducted to fulfil an order requirement under certain conditions. Efficient solutions are needed for:

  - a proper workflow language, such as BPEL (IBM et al. 2002), that is capable of describing the business process
  - generating a reservable portion of the workflow at runtime
  - conducting workflow scheduling and interactive fine-tuning of the scheduled workflow.

- *Detecting and responding to resource or reservation abnormality.* This is especially applicable to the sectors, such as airlines, passenger trains or telecommunications, where resource is fluid and last-minute change could affect the fulfilment of committed services. In the cases where reserved services cannot be fulfilled due to resource scarceness, notifications and proposed new appointments will normally be sent to customers.

- *Featured reporting that empowers operation managers or resource managers to make strategic, tactical and operational decisions.* These reports could cover specific resource utilisation at various geography granularities. In certain industries such as in the telecommunications sector, this could also include lead times reports. As the computation of detailed report is time-consuming, concerns are normally given to strike a balance between the accuracy and the responsiveness of these reports. In most cases, reports are computed periodically and stored into database tables. Users of these reports can simply view the stored information instead of the data generated at runtime.

- *High configurability for managed service appointing.* This allows either frequent updates on existing services or the fast loading of new services. Examples of configurable information include business geographical topology updates, geography granularity, the reservation time window length, the time slot and the capacity limit of managed resources, the business rules for exception handling, etc.

- *The scalability of all functional components that can handle huge and growing volumes of data stored in the system.* The key is to identify the independency of functional and data elements, where computational efficiency can be achieved through parallelism. For instance, if a resource is self-contained in a specific geographical domain, then all the data operation can be constrained within this domain.

7.5 Key Technologies

To tackle the issues mentioned in the previous sections, the implementation of useful reservation management systems could benefit from three major disciplines: operation research (OR), artificial intelligence (AI) and software engineering. OR (Constable 1976) is concerned with setting up business policies, examining business processes and dealing with concrete workflow. AI (Barr and Feigenbaum 1986) helps with knowledge representation (such as service ontology) and reasoning, heuristic searches and optimisation. Software engineering (Chang 2002) provides solutions for robust system implementation, software reuse (such as Service Oriented Architecture or SOA), and configuration management that leads to generic systems and software that is easy to maintain. Systems that are built with techniques from these three disciplines provide flexible knowledge representation capabilities, and flexible reasoning capabilities which lead to optimised solutions. They also ensure interoperability with legacy systems.

7.6 Summary

Reservation management and resource CRM play an important role in the service economy, where the responsiveness, accuracy, predictability and reliability of service provision ensures the profitability of the service providers (i. e., the service organisations). In this chapter, we analysed some features of resource CRM within several service sectors, and provided general guidelines for implementing a resource CRM solution.

Besides reservation management, the right strategy for pricing services to the end-customer is critical to a service provisioning company as well. In the next chapter, we will focus on the domain of dynamic pricing and revenue management that has lead in the recent years to the emergence of new companies such as low cost airlines.

Chapter 8
Demand Pricing and Revenue Management

8.1 Introduction

What does Revenue Management (RM) mean and how does it work? In which industries is it being practised already? What is the theory underlying RM[1]? One might have heard the term applied in the context of the airline industry, but how could it be used in other service industries such as telecommunications? Can it be used in organisations of any size? How much effort would be needed to implement it and how complex is the required technology?

This chapter addresses those questions, giving the reader a basic understanding of the underlying techniques and technologies and providing an impression of the different areas in which RM is utilised. We will keep the level of mathematical sophistication to a minimum because the emphasis is on providing a general picture supplemented by insights into current practice.

The purpose of RM is to manage demand by controlling capacity and price in order to maximise expected revenue. In this sense, we can regard it as the counterpart to Supply Chain Management, which is concerned with the supply side of the enterprise. The term yield originates from the airline business and refers to revenue per available seat mile. In other industries it may refer to revenue per available time unit. In recent times, the name RM has increasingly been used in order to reduce the impression that these methods are for airlines only. Actually, the potential fields of application have constantly been extended from transportation-related services and hospitality to subscription services such as recently on-demand information technology services, for an overview see Dube et al. (2005). It is applied in areas where short-term costs are mostly fixed and variable cost is small. For that reason we can discuss maximising revenue rather than profit. But before we dive into the vast field of techniques and applications that constitute RM, we take a brief look at its origins, much of which is still applicable today. In the literature, its birth is usually dated back to the 1980s, when, as a result of the Airline Deregulation Act 1978, price controls in the USA were lifted and free entry and exit from the markets per-

---

[1] We use Revenue Management and Yield Management interchangeably.

C. Voudouris, G. Owusu, R. Dorne, D. Lesaint, *Service Chain Management*
DOI: 10.1007/978-3-540-75504-3, ©Springer 2008

mitted. This resulted in the emergence of the first low-cost carriers, among them PEOPLExpress. Traditional airlines such as American were caught unprepared and PEOPLExpress achieved record profits. Although it could not afford to carry out a price war, American came up with an innovative new concept: Exploiting the different price sensitivities of customers by creating new restricted discount products and controlling the availability of these fares by capacity controls. The latter was supported by a sophisticated system, DINAMO, that made it possible to match or undercut the competitor's prices in all of American's markets. The consequences were stunning: American could under-price PEOPLExpress with its discount fares and still keep high revenue fares in place, eventually resulting in the bankruptcy of PEOPLExpress only one year after the launch of DINAMO. This impressive success of a yield management system, as it was called in that time, was the reason for growing interest of both researchers and practitioners in how to advance and improve this promising approach.

8.1.1 Old Ideas – New Methodologies

Many of the ideas that underlie RM are indeed quite well known and can be found in areas such as marketing or general economic theory. There is however a crucial new side to it: The combination of classic pricing and economic theory with scientific advancements in management science, operations research and especially optimisation on the one hand, and sophisticated information technology systems on the other. American's DINAMO system clearly demonstrated the power of this confluence.

Following Talluri and van Ryzin (2004), RM addresses three types of demand management decisions: structural, price, and quantity. Structural decisions include for example, the selling format, is the price found by auctions, prescribed by the company or subject to negotiation, and the terms of sale. The latter include in particular the conditions linked with selling the product. The structural decisions, strategic in nature, are changed relatively infrequently. In contrast, price and quantity decisions are tactical, involving e. g., optimal markdowns and initial prices on the price side, and optimal rationing by channel, location and time on the quantity side. In other words, RM overlaps substantially with areas of classic marketing and pricing theory as e. g., the customer segmentation, but with the difference that these well-known principles are coupled with elaborate optimisation systems.

RM draws on both scientific decision making and information technology (IT) including the wealth of data in transactional databases like Enterprise Resource Planning Systems and the Internet. It should come as no surprise that organisations are collecting a steadily increasing amount of data, developing the foundations for RM systems. The rapidly improving capabilities of IT and the development of more software applications indicate that such an RM system will in the future most likely be found in most companies where the conditions for effective RM are favourable. The nature of these conditions and how such RM systems are designed is discussed in the next section.

8.2 Revenue Management – Techniques and Technology

In this section we first outline the fundamental ingredients of RM, i. e., some pricing techniques, tactical aspects such as capacity allocation, overbooking and price management. Next, we discuss the structure and implementation issues of RM systems. Particular attention is given to distinction between the basic principles of RM and the supporting information technology (IT). The use of the former without sophisticated IT support is possible and is called low-level RM in contrast to the high level degree to which it is implemented by, e. g., large cruise lines. Depending on the size of capacity that is to be managed, a non-automated use of the principles may indeed suffice to improve revenue, as exemplified by the hotel case.

8.2.1 Basic Principles

RM is not a magic wand that can be applied to any kind of business to increase revenue. For example, if an enterprise faces no capacity constraint they can compensate for fluctuations in demand by creating inventory buffers. As described in Kimes (2000), there are several conditions that help identify potential industry adopters of RM:

- *Relatively fixed capacity*: Service providers constrained to a certain capacity have to balance potential high and low revenue demand in order to attempt to not allow too much low revenue demand that might displace future high revenue demand. Capacity may not necessarily be tangible but could also refer to time-based unit in which a certain service is used. A hotel's capacity is its total number of rooms as for a telecommunications company's is phone minutes. Sometimes capacity is only relatively constrained. For instance, car rental companies could purchase additional cars. The point is that capacity should be fixed in the short run.
- *Predictable demand*: Every proper RM system relies heavily on the quality of demand forecasts. This is easily seen when considering the case of a hotel: Assume that today is Wednesday and that many high-paying business customers will arrive at the hotel next Monday. We will certainly try to ensure that enough rooms are available at this time and hence possibly reject early discount requests for Monday that arrive if it appears that the hotel could be booked on Monday.
- *Perishable inventory*: For the application to the service industry inventory relates to time periods in which a unit of capacity can be used. Thus, a hotel has an inventory of room nights and each day the telecommunications company has an inventory of bandwidth per minute. If the service is not used during a given time period it is worthless; an empty airline seat is worth nothing.
- *Appropriate cost and pricing structure*: The business should have the characteristics of relatively high fixed cost and low variable cost. This condition stems from pricing theory and provides the revenue manager with the needed flexibility to discount prices fairly deeply while still ensuring a positive profit margin. Internet cafés need to invest in their equipment and to pay their monthly flat rate,

but allowing a customer to surf the web for a while incurs no variable cost at all. Building an UMTS network requires large investments, but again variable costs are very low.

- *Time-variable demand*: The realised demand changes over time and must be predicted. In particular for service providers, the duration that the service is used also needs to be forecasted in order to utilise the given capacity optimally.

Suppose we have a certain industry in mind for which these conditions apply, say a hotel. What are the basic principles that RM makes use of? In a study for the European Commission, Arthur Andersen (1997) lists five 'functional aspects of yield management':

- *Market segmentation*: Identifying distinct groups of customers that behave differently from one another and that are relevant to a company's marketing activities, pricing and other business decisions.
- *Price management*: Systematically offering different prices to different customer segments, in response to changes in demand.
- *Demand forecasting*: Forecasting future demand on the basis of past sales and known future events; a business can more rationally and accurately anticipate the size of different market segments and the prices that each segment will accept.
- *Availability and/or capacity management*: Limiting or shifting the availability of certain products or services according to customer demand.
- *Reservation negotiation*: It is in the reservation or sale process that management must implement its decisions about pricing and availability. Where the opportunity to negotiate exists, 'up-selling' to a more expensive product or 'cross-selling' to an alternative product may be attempted.

Let us elaborate on that using the hotel industry as an example: If we intend to use RM concepts, first we need efficient *market segmentation*. A potential segmentation should reflect the estimated price sensitivity of the corresponding customer group, but should only be detailed to the extent to which so-called cannibalisation and arbitrage can be excluded (or at least kept at a low level). Cannibalisation refers to the problem of customers in the high rate segment trying to find ways of buying at the lower rate which was not intended for them. Since there are different prices for the same product, there would be an incentive for arbitrageurs to buy the product at the low rate and resell it at the high rate. For example, a small hotel might use the following segmentation:

- Individuals
  - Individual
  - Special events (Wedding, etc.)
- Business
  - Conferences
  - With Local Company Rate (LCR) contract
  - Without LCR contract

- Travel industry

  - Travel parties
  - Organiser

- Others

  - Airline Crews
  - Exhibitions

Since cannibalisation and arbitrage can completely undermine all benefits from price differentiation, the design of the price differentiation is important. Possible strategies include choosing unambiguous group affiliations (children, students), imposing restrictions on the product (2-day minimum stay), and using specific channels, among others. For an in-depth treatment of market segmentation, see McDonald and Dunbar (1998); for a more quantitative treatment, see Wedel and Kamakura (2000).

Finding a price for each segment first requires the calculation of the lower price bound, i. e., the variable cost for providing service to a customer. This will be the crucial element to providing pricing flexibility with a guarantee that the customer at least contributes to covering the fixed costs. Based on the observed current and historical demand patterns, the competition's prices as well as the knowledge of future events like a trade fair, the appropriate price can be found.

Early anticipation of higher willingness to pay in higher prices is based on effective demand forecasting. The principles discussed so far are all fundamental pricing concepts that can be used without sophisticated IT systems and are therefore already widely practised, although some small companies might not have yet implemented even these principles. For example, one of the authors recently met an hotelier owning a small house of about 40 rooms who stated that he offers all his rooms at the same rate throughout the year.

Forecasting, however, usually needs IT support and hence should be counted among the high-level RM functions. It is concerned with forecasting important inputs to a RM system such as the future quantity of demand and probabilities of cancellations. If cancellations of the sold service are possible, the latter input is crucial in calculating the optimal level of overbooking. In small companies, often no real forecasts are being used, instead an intuitive approach is chosen by maintaining pick-up statistics, i. e., the number of bookings for every day of the next month for example is fed into a spreadsheet and being prescribed every day. Combined with the knowledge of future events that will affect demand – like e. g., a soccer game – are also entered. In this way potential bottlenecks can be anticipated early without sophisticated software and may be indeed satisfy the needs of small companies.

Suppose that we segmented the market efficiently, the prices are defined, and the forecasting system is in place. Service requests from customers of different segments are coming in; but here the question arises how to optimally allocate the available capacity. That is, when should we deny service to a low revenue customer although still having unused capacity in favour of waiting for a potential future high revenue customer? This question is addressed by the functional aspect *capac-*

ity management, which will be explained in Sect. 8.3. A large body of literature exists on this topic, mainly based on airline and hotel applications. Some comprehensive overviews are listed in Table 8.3 at the end of the chapter. For many other industries these techniques also apply; Roland Berger (2003) proposed applications for telecommunication providers for the General Packet Radio Service (GPRS) market. Capacity for this mobile phone data service is the corresponding available base transceiver station (BTS) capacity. Splitting up the market into high-end business users and low-end private users, one defines products for each segment meeting their corresponding needs. The product for the business user might include a guaranteed transmission bandwidth and a certain amount of capacity would be allocated to these users in order to uphold this guarantee.

Finally, *reservation negotiation* comes into play for example if a customer calls the reception to enquire about the room rates. The receptionist might start to quote prices in the middle rates and then try to up-sell to higher priced rooms by highlighting corresponding characteristics like quieter location or more luxury features of some sort.

To sum up, the basic principles market segmentation, price management, forecasting, capacity management and reservation negotiation can be applied to every business that meets the conditions described above. Independent of the company's size, RM principles can be and often are already applied on a low level. When the capacity to be managed is large, the company should also consider usage of IT systems that take over the tasks of forecasting and optimisation of capacity allocation decisions. To give an impression of its potential impact, here exemplified for the hotel business, we quote from Jones (2000): "Emerging evidence suggests that Yield Management leads to 1–8 per cent performance improvement."

8.2.2 Revenue Management Systems

Let us investigate what a RM system could look like for an organisation that is too large to handle the forecasting and optimisation processes manually – excluding the possibility of hiring an impressive army of analysts.

Most managers are obviously reluctant to invest in IT systems if they face high implementation cost and uncertain payoff; the risk of becoming dependent on the consultancy of the software vendors is a particularly strong deterrent. The good news is that there is often no need for large investments in the infrastructure since most required components are already present in the form of the company's Enterprise Resource Planning System (ERP), Property Management System (PMS), or the like. Their databases comprise a vast amount of organisation-related data, often including customer purchase history as well as product and pricing information. This constitutes already the basic foundation for an RM system providing necessary information for the forecasting and optimisation modules. For example, hotels have a PMS that can provide data on bookings and cancellations, prices and product specifications. For some of the PMS that are usually used in the market, the corresponding software vendors offer additional RM modules. So in this case the technical implementation is relatively easy although there is of course still the need to have specifically trained analysts to work with the system.

RM systems differ from the manual calculation of the optimal controls by their higher speeds, ability to process larger amount of data, and the use of sophisticated mathematical procedures that attempt to capture most of the problem's complexity. The latter is indeed remarkable if we wish to incorporate information on the competition's prices, their anticipated strategy, future customer purchase behaviour etc. Despite its capabilities, the system can obviously only work with the information given. Human decision makers are thus needed e. g., to insert information not included in the database and to adjust the recommendation of the system according to their experience. In particular the analysts should be able to influence the forecasts if information about certain events or changes in the market would otherwise not be included. The RM system is hence a decision support system that helps to process a large amount of data into a clear recommendation that can then be used by the manager as the basis for the final decision.

An RM system typically consists of the following components: The ERP (or some other data source) provides the data input needed for the core processes, forecasting and optimisation. Next one needs to estimate the demand model (see van Ryzin (2005)) for a discussion of current and future demand models), then the system forecasts demand based on these model parameters as well as other required figures based on the provided data. This might be, for example, cancellations for later calculations of the optimal overbooking level. The forecasted information is then used in the optimisation process to find the optimal controls.

For the purpose of better illustration consider again the case of a telecommunications company providing GPRS. Along the lines of Roland Berger (2003), in this simplified application example, we simply split up the market into high-yield and low-yield customers. Two corresponding products aim for these segments:

- *For high-yield customers*: Guaranteed bandwidth, at a high fixed monthly price, low volume price.
- *For low-yield customers*: No bandwidth guarantee, low fixed monthly price, higher volume price.

It is known how many customers are currently under contract for the high- and the low-yield product, the historical demand patterns and all prices as well. The RM system uses this data to forecast demand for those two products for time periods within the upcoming day (or week). The optimisation module has then the task of computing the optimal capacity allocation to the potential customers in order to ensure that on the one hand the high-yield users are guaranteed their bandwidth but on the other hand to minimise the expected amount of reserved capacity for high-yield users that will be left unused and thus could be used to accommodate demand from low-yield customers.

8.3 RM – Theory and Practice

Having depicted the basic aspects of RM in the last section, we devote ourselves now to its finer nuances. Of the five functionalities of RM, three in particular stick out because they require profound mathematical procedures: forecasting, price and capacity management. These constitute the core processes of a RM system. In what follows, we describe the major fields of research, give an example for a capacity control model formulation, and outline the current extent of industry adoption.

8.3.1 Theory Outline

The problem lying at the heart of high-level RM is how to make the decision of accepting or denying an arriving service request. Generally, this problem is approached by finding booking policies that accept the request only if its revenue exceeds the *expected opportunity cost* associated with the acceptance of the request. In other words, we face the trade-off between accepting immediate revenue on the one hand and reserving the capacity for later potentially higher revenue demand to realise.

Researchers have been working on this simply stated problem for over 30 years and have proposed a multitude of different models and methods. The actual complexity stems from the uncertainty and the nature of the displacement cost, because in order to compute the displacement cost from accepting a booking, one would have to take into account all possible implications for the booking process as well as many factors like network effects, cancellations, up-selling, strategic customer behaviour, etc. For that reason it is not feasible to model the problem to its full extent but rather models are being used that confine themselves to some selected aspects.

RM theory can be roughly categorised by the research areas Forecasting/Estimation, Capacity Management, Overbooking and Price Management (see Fig. 8.1).

8.3.1.1 Forecasting and Estimation

The term *expected* opportunity cost already implies that there is uncertain information which we need to quantify. Two fields deal with this task: forecasting and estimation. The latter relates to finding parameters, e. g., for a demand model, that best fits some given set of data. Forecasting, however, is concerned with finding future, unknown data. The areas are intimately connected with each other as estimation of demand model parameters is often used to calibrate the forecast.

The specific data we are aiming for depends on the optimisation module of the RM system. We distinguish between quantity- and price-based RM, where the former uses capacity controls and the latter price controls. Which controls are being used by a given company depends on its ability to adjust the prices and quantity.

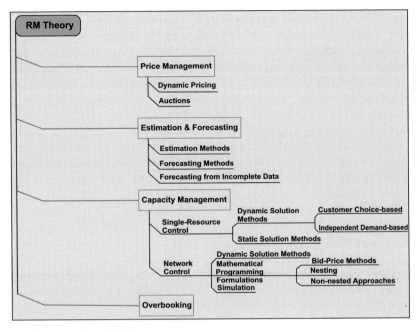

Fig. 8.1 Categorisation of RM theory

Airlines have large quantity flexibility because their products are using the same homogeneous seat capacity, therefore they mostly use quantity controls. The optimisation procedures are quite different depending on the controls used, and so are the required forecasts.

As described in Talluri and van Ryzin (2004), *quantity-based RM* relies on forecasts for demand data, cancellation, and no-show[2] probabilities, cross-selling and up-selling probabilities, and for some models on arrival patterns of the service requests. Furthermore, predictions of the number of customers that are turned away by not offering a certain product any more as well as the number of customers that then will buy substitute products might be needed. Even the future revenue of the products might have to be predicted because, e. g., price wars could force the management to unplanned price changes.

Price-based RM usually needs estimates of demand function parameters and cross-price elasticity. We may also require forecasts of the potential market size, demand and purchase behaviour if the inventory is nearly depleted.

Forecasting methodologies can be characterized by the aggregation level on which data is forecasted, if the forecast is itself aggregated from other forecasts and if we estimate the parameters of the demand model on the basis of a given functional form (parametric forecasts) or if the function itself is being estimated (nonparametric forecasts). The aggregation level depends on the available data and

---

[2] A show/no-show corresponds to an expected customer who finally does/does not turn up to require the service.

the needed input for the optimisation routine. There are two basic forecasting strategies for aggregated forecasts, namely the Bottom-Up and the Top-Down approach. In the case of availability of data at a very detailed level, the Bottom-Up approach can be used to obtain first sub-forecasts on a detail level to be later aggregated to the desired level. The opposite way of starting the forecast on a highly aggregate level and disaggregating it to the desired lower level is accordingly call Top-Down forecasting.

There exits a wealth of literature on forecasting issues as this field has been active long before the dawn of RM. It would be beyond the scope of this chapter to delve into the mathematical models that stand behind forecasting software packages; the interested reader is referred to Chap. 4 as well as the cited literature in the last section of this chapter.

8.3.1.2 Capacity Management

In our quest for accurate and efficient calculation of the expected opportunity cost, we need to model the decision problem in such a way that it can be computed within the given time frame. By means of assuming away dispensable aspects of the problem one can find many potential ways of computing the expected opportunity cost in a reasonable time. Capacity management is concerned with finding a (sub-)optimal booking policy given the forecast information, i. e., a policy that indicates when to accept or to deny a service request in order to maximise revenue. Research areas include *Single-Resource Control* and *Network Control.*

Single-Resource Control refers to techniques of how to optimally choose a booking policy if the product uses only one resource. For the airlines, this corresponds to single-leg flights and most research has been carried out with this application in mind though it can be similarly applied to other service industries. As seen in Fig. 8.1, Single-Resource Control consists of dynamic and static solution methods. In contrast to the static ones, dynamic solution methods do not assume a specific arrival order of the booking requests and an accept/deny decision is made upon each service request arrival. Static methods and possibly also dynamic methods use the so-called independent demand assumption, i. e., assume that demand between the different booking classes is independent. Dynamic methods also offer the possibility of incorporating models of customer choice that reflect the decision between a number of offered products, rather than assuming that service requests arrive product-wise, i. e., a customer considers only one product and the non-purchase option. In recent times, most research endeavours have been devoted to dynamic solution methods for single-resource problems and to network problems in general.

Network problems are the extension of single-resource problems to the multi-resource case. Consider for example a hotel; the products it offers are all possible combinations of arrival date, length of stay, and room rate. Each product uses one or more resources, in this case the days that a guest occupies a room. Each resource has a capacity equal to the total number of rooms. Network problems like this one have the property that the products are interconnected since renting a room for a longer time at low rate prohibits from using the room to satisfy potential future high revenue demand. Hence it is no longer possible to maximise revenue for each resource independently, but rather the implications for other products must be taken into account.

Following the classification of Pak and Piersma (2002), network problem approaches can be distinguished as either dynamic solution methods, mathematical programming formulations or simulations. *Dynamic solution methods* adjust the booking control policy continuously in contrast to the prior examined mathematical programming ones. Policies can also be obtained from running *simulations* repeatedly. *Mathematical programming methods*, however, are constructing a solution at a given point in time for the complete booking period. This solution is usually adjusted a multitude of times during the booking period by re-optimising the underlying models.

Let us exemplify the latter methodology by formulating a simple model for the hotel case: For sake of simplicity suppose we have only three room rates, each guest is staying a maximum of three days and we are interested in an optimal room allocation for the next five days as possible arrival dates. Totally we have then $3 \cdot 3 \cdot 5 = 45$ products denoted by j, where j is in the set $\{1, 2, ..., 45\}$. The associated revenue r_j is defined by summing up the corresponding room rate for the length of stay. Assuming the hotel has 300 rooms, this leads to a capacity $c_i = 300$ for all resources i. The forecast module provides two forecasts:

Table 8.1 Demand forecast by rate and length-of-stay distribution

	Price categories			Length of stay		
	$79	$99	$129	1-night	2-night	3-night
Monday	90	40	30	50%	40%	10%
Tuesday	120	70	40	60%	20%	20%
Wednesday	110	80	60	70%	20%	10%
Thursday	80	60	30	90%	10%	0%
Friday	100	30	10	50%	40%	10%

By aggregating these two forecasts we easily obtain a forecast giving us the expected demand d_j for each product j. For example, 10% of Monday's 40 expected customers for room rate $99 intend to stay three nights giving us an expected demand of 4 for the product "arrival on Monday and staying three nights at $99 per night." This information can then be used as constraint in the optimisation problem, i. e., the demand constraints on what we can possibly sell. Hence we allocate at most d_j units of capacity for each product j. We can only rent the rooms that we have, hence the capacity c_i constraints the sum of all allocations for each day i. Finally, allocations should be positive, and we seek to maximise the revenue over all offered products simultaneously. Thus we have the following linear programme:

$$\max_x \sum_{j=1}^{n} r_j x_j$$

$$s.t. \sum_{j=1}^{n} b_{ij} x_j \leq c_i , \quad \forall i ,$$

$$x_j \leq d_j , \quad \forall j ,$$

$$x_j \geq 0 , \quad \forall j .$$

The variable b_{ij} is defined as 1 if resource i is used in product j, and 0 otherwise. As explained above, we intend to calculate the expected opportunity cost in order to define the optimal booking policy. In this case, the opportunity cost can be found computationally by solving this linear programme and obtaining with the sensitivity analysis the so-called shadow costs λ_i associated with the capacity constraints for each resource. The shadow cost λ_i reflects the additional revenue that could be realised if the resource i had an additional unit of capacity. Hence they can also be seen to be the opportunity cost of using this resource. Overall, the opportunity cost of a product is the sum of shadow prices of the resources it uses.

In our case, the problem is deterministic so that these are also the expected opportunity costs. The optimal policy consists then of accepting requests only if their revenue exceeds the sum of shadow costs of the resources the requested product is using. As mentioned before, the policy is defined for the whole time. However, the system should be re-optimised to account for changes in the forecast and for revealed booking information. Note that the problem dimension grows with the number of products, so this approach would in practice be computationally intensive. Excluded was also the effect of demand uncertainty; useful demand forecasts do not predict single numbers but rather demand distributions. Many more features depending on the specific industry might be needed; this discussion just gives an impression of the complexity of this problem.

Overall, network problems arise in most service industries and are as important as they are complex. As it is easily seen from the example above, the amount of products that must be managed in practice is usually very large. This results in the need to surrender some degree of optimality for the benefit of faster algorithms. This is accomplished by making use of heuristics which provides (near-)optimal solutions in a faster processing time.

8.3.1.3 Overbooking

Overbooking is important if customers have the right to cancel their service request or may not show, and if the cost of denying service to a booked customer is relatively low. It is insurance for the company against the risk of losing revenue opportunities due to unused capacity caused by cancellations and no-shows. However, it must be applied with great care because bumped customers might not only incur direct cost but also cost in terms of bad will. Overbooking is widely accepted for airlines and car rentals, but this does not necessarily transfer to other service industries. For example, resort hotels should be very cautious when using overbooking. The bad will of customers arriving at their hotel for a three-week dream holiday at Palm Beach only to find that they cannot be accommodated, might considerably damage their business. As stated in Phillips (2005), most companies follow one of four overbooking policies:

- A simple *deterministic heuristic* that calculates a booking limit based only on capacity and expected no-show rate.
- A *risk-based policy* involves explicitly estimating the cost of denied service and weighing those costs against the potential revenue to determine the booking levels that maximise expected total revenue minus expected overbooking costs.
- A *service-level policy* involves managing to a specific target – for example, targeting no more than one instance of denied service for every 5,000 shows.
- A *hybrid policy* is one in which risk-based limits are calculated but constrained by service-level consideration.

8.3.1.4 Price Management

Strategic pricing sets the limits within which RM operates, so Price Management is here considered on the operational level. As discussed before, RM systems can use either price or quantity controls to maximise profitability. The controls can also

Table 8.2 RM practices in different industries, quoted from Chiang et al. (2007)

Industries	Example of practices
Hospitality organisations	
Hotels	Provide special rate packages for periods of low occupancy; use over-booking policy to compensate for cancellation, no-shows
Restaurants	Move customers to off-peak periods by offering discount coupons, or charging reservation fees and higher meal prices on Friday and Saturday nights
Golf	Use different prices to reflect the value of different times of the golf course
Resort	Provide different resort packages to attract different customers
Transportation-related industries	
Boat	Provide discount to stimulate demand
Railways	Divide customers into standard class and first class; provide different prices based on the day of travel and the time of the day
Subscription services	
IT services and Internet services	Allocate resources such as human resource, computing capacity, storage and network capacity among segments of customers and determine appropriate price for each segment, high class customers will be served with priority
Mobile phone network services	Control call admission based on customer priority, higher class customers will be served with priority
Miscellaneous	
Project management	Use capacity planning and scheduling to reserve specific capacity for customers willing to pay higher prices to have critical activities
Natural gas, petroleum storage and transmission	Make the right price for the transportation services so that the pipelines stay full

be used together, see e. g., Weatherford (1994) for a simultaneous pricing and allocation formulation. Particular importance is attached to the single-period pricing problem for a finite time period with perishable, non-renewable resources that are used to accommodate price-sensitive, stochastic demand processes. This problem is essentially equivalent to the single resource capacity control problem and therefore the related theory applies to the RM context. Extensive overviews of dynamic pricing methods are given in Table 8.2.

8.3.2 Industry Adopters

Today, most RM research is still devoted to the traditional fields of application: airlines, hotels and car rentals. Within the last years, however, the research has extended its focus to many other service-related industries such as restaurants, casinos, saunas, golf, conference, boat charter, railways, IT services and Internet services, mobile phone network services, sales management and project management, among many others.

In their recent paper, Chiang et al. (2007) review related work published after 1998, and their overview of RM practice in different industries as quoted in Table 8.2 clearly demonstrates the generality and flexibility of the RM approach.

8.4 Summary

RM has seen a notable boost in both research and industrial acceptance within the last years. Scientists and practitioners are working feverishly on further fields of application and are constantly driving the frontiers forward. This chapter aims at creating a general understanding and feeling for the basic concepts and importance of RM. Its application on a high level includes technologies and systems for demand forecasting and optimisation that can significantly augment revenue. We therefore consider that RM constitutes a crucial element in Service Chain Management and, with regard to the observable increase in fields of application, that it will continue its penetration of management practice in the service industries.

Behind any RM system, there are people and employees in the service chain that enable the service to be provided to the end-customer. Providing the right pricing strategy for maximising revenue means inevitably to have in place an efficient management of the personnel. Next two chapters look at the challenge of personnel shift scheduling and work allocation that help to control the cost of service provisioning while maintaining a certain level of service to customers.

8.5 Further Reading

In Table 8.3, we list several books and journal papers that provide a widespread treatment of RM. They form a good starting point for the interested reader to delve into the subject.

Table 8.3 Recommended further reading on RM

RM overviews	
General RM	The recently published books by Talluri and van Ryzin (2004) and Phillips (2005) constitute good introductions to RM, the former one also introducing forecasting and estimation methods. Yeoman and McMahon-Beattie (2004) provides insight of how RM is practised in form of case studies. It is an extension of Ingold et al. (2000) that focuses on both service sector studies as well as some theoretical aspects. Research is reviewed by McGill and van Ryzin (1999) and more recent research by Chiang et al. (2007). The latter also specifies references to recent RM applications for numerous service industries
Overviews of pricing research in RM context	Bitran and Caldentey (2003) review pricing for inventory problems over a finite time horizon, Elmaghraby and Keskinocak (2003) focus on dynamic pricing literature for inventory problems and categorise related literature. Yano and Gilbert (2004) devote their paper to joint pricing and production decision models. Fleischmann et al. (2004) review recent work linking pricing decisions with operational insights
Specific industry reviews	Kimes (2003) is mainly concerned with RM for the hotel and restaurant industry, Boyd and Bilegan (2003) for e-commerce and Pak and Piersma (2002) provide a research overview for the airline business

Chapter 9
Personnel Shift Scheduling and Rostering

9.1 Introduction

Personnel Shift Scheduling and Rostering problems are found in many different types of organisations and industries including manufacturing, call centres, the airline industry, health services, utilities and the transportation industry. More generally, the importance of an efficient shift scheduling system is critical to any large organisation especially in the service economy where production and consumption normally coincide. The generation of optimised shift and roster patterns is, undeniably, a key instrument for making best use of the resources of a service enterprise. The efficiency of such a system leads to *maximisation of the customer experience* by matching the demand with the appropriate staffing level and *minimisation of the cost* by reducing idle time of the resources.

A service enterprise is usually resource rich, having a large workforce; its overall performance is therefore strongly related to the efficiency of its personnel scheduling systems. These latters determine the enterprise's capability to maximise the use of its resources and hence the total number of resources required to run the business. Less people for the same service level means inevitably higher margins and benefits for a service enterprise. This is particularly true for large organisations with thousands of employees; a 2% productivity increase may be negligible for small companies, while this becomes significant cost savings to large organisations. On the other hand, a badly resourced service company implies that either the quality of the service will be poor because of discontinuity due to lack of resources or expensive because of surpluses.

Furthermore, nowadays a service enterprise needs to be more agile to stay competitive requiring the ability to flex its resources according to the demand. Thus it becomes critical to understand sooner rather than later the impact of a change whether it comes from new regulations, working practice forced by a new offering of the competition, for example, or any other organisational change. Automated shift scheduling systems can help assess this impact better and faster, even allowing for the running of what-if scenarios. For example, what is the impact on the workforce if the company would like to launch a new service?

However, the problem of allocating rosters/shifts to employees is both difficult and time consuming; for any (automated) personnel scheduling system it is critical to bear in mind that such a system will, inevitably, have a significant (positive or negative) impact on the organisation's overall performance and, very likely, on its customers' perception as well. It is important not to underestimate the complexity of shift scheduling problems. Personnel scheduling is a very complex and time consuming activity for a number of reasons: firstly, shift scheduling problems are difficult because of having to satisfy operational requirements, complex employment laws and staff preferences; secondly, they are organisation-dependent with specific definitions for staff skill, shift types, planning periods and operational requirements; thirdly, there are numerous ways to design and allocate shifts to people and the number increases exponentially with the number of staff, shift types and the length of the planning horizon; finally, many of the decisions made by the rostering experts of the company are of a subjective nature, drawing on personal experience, and are therefore difficult to model systematically leading to problems of knowledge acquisition.

Section 9.2 proposes a general description of shift scheduling and rostering problems along with some examples from different sectors. Following this, we then discuss the different families of approaches that can be found in the literature for tackling this difficult family of resourcing problems and finally we provide a summary of this chapter.

9.2 General Description

Personnel shift scheduling and rostering is usually an operation with a time horizon from one day to a few weeks depending on the sector of activity. It is common to distinguish three main phases in the process of personnel scheduling: staffing, shift/roster design and shift/roster allocation.

Staffing is concerned with the prediction of the future amount of work to be carried out and the translation of this work into required resources in order to meet some service levels. Shift and roster design relates to the creation of shifts and rosters, while shift and roster allocation focuses on allocating (groups of) people to rosters to ensure some staffing levels are met. As shown in Fig. 9.1 some of these steps may not be required depending on the industrial sector and/or company. In the same manner, we may loop several times between these different steps until certain business objectives are met. By means of example, one may want to loop between the shift/roster design phase and the shift/roster allocation phase until minimum staffing levels are met. In other words, once a shift allocation has been produced, one may consider again the shift/roster design phase to improve the overall quality of the shift allocation and so on.

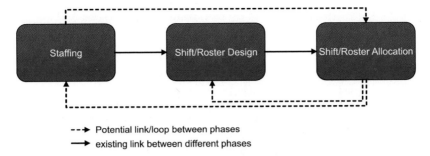

Fig. 9.1 Process overview for personnel shift scheduling and rostering

As another example, shifts and rosters may have been already created and cannot be changed before considering allocating shifts/rosters. In such a case the shift/roster design phase is ignored and the shifts/rosters directly allocated using existing shifts/rosters to meet the staffing requirements (cf. Fig. 9.1).

9.2.1 Staffing

Usually a workload prediction is expressed in terms of the number of activities to be performed by the company over the time horizon. The time horizon and workload are defined according to the service enterprise. For example, when considering a nurse staffing problem, the number of expected patients per ward over the time horizon and seriousness of illnesses are commonly used, while for call centres the number of incoming calls per time unit is more appropriate.

However, we can distinguish three distinct cases: firstly, the workload can be fully forecasted, as in call centres where the number of incoming calls is totally unknown at the beginning of the day; secondly, the workload is partly forecasted, as in the utility sector where some of the workload is known before the shift scheduling phase (some customers may have notified that they are having problems with their service); and thirdly, the workload is fully known, as in the airline industry where flight timetables are known in advance and the number of crews required can be fully determined. With regard to the second case, it is important to note that the further we look in the future the more uncertain the demand becomes. This is due to there being fewer known events and, consequently, an increase in the forecasted element of the workload. By way of example, Fig. 9.2 shows the forecasted hourly demand for a call centre. The number of incoming calls/services, from two different telephone numbers (customer service and helpdesk), which are expected to hit the call centre are displayed in a bar chart.

From a more general point of view, in the context of a service enterprise we can define the demand as a number of services that will have to be performed by the company's workforce over the scheduling horizon.

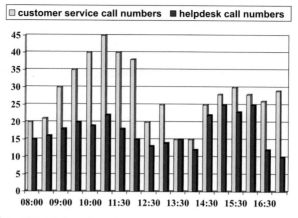

Fig. 9.2 Daily demand graph for call centres

The problem of staffing comes down to the translation of a given workload into a number of resources (usually people, possibly assets) required to meet a given service level over the time horizon. Usually a service is broken down into a subset of activities and for a particular activity we can then deduce how many people, assets (this may require the system to be connected to an inventory system) and particular skills are required. For example, it will be known by a hospital's surgery manager that for a particular intervention/surgery how many surgeons, doctors and nurses will be required and for how long. With regard to call centres, the number of staff required is usually deduced directly from the number of incoming calls per time slot using some queuing theory models or more simply from operations statistics (see Sect. 9.3).

Service levels are commonly expressed in terms of three parameters, and as either per time unit, per skill or in some cases per area (e. g., for field force deployment) over the time horizon. These are:

- *the minimum requirement*: the minimum number of resources required to run the business,
- *the target requirement*: the ideal number to match the demand at this service level requirement,
- *the maximum requirement*: the maximum limit for the number of resources to be allocated. Typically this parameter may define operation limits such as maximum number of seats to answer *new service subscription* calls in a call centre.

Figure 9.3 exhibits a typical report obtained by the manager of a call centre after the staffing phase has been completed. In this example, the call centre personnel have different skills for handling three types of calls: *new services, help desk* and *technical support*. For each time slot of the day, minimum, ideal and maximum requirements in the number of employees are provided. For example, the first three cells of line 1 in Fig. 9.3 show that a minimum of 2.7 employees having *new services* skill are required to be at work between 8 and 9 a.m., the ideal number being 3 operators and the maximum 6 (possibly due to a maximum number of available desks).

Hours / Skills	8:00-9:00			9:00-10:00			10:00-11:00			11:00-12:00			12:00-13:00			13:00-14:00			14:00-15:00			15:00-16:00			16:00-17:00		
	Min	Best	Max	Min	Best	Max	Min	Best	Max	Min	Best	Max	Min	Best	Max	Min	Best	Max	Min	Best	Max	Min	Best	Max	Min	Best	Max
new services	2.7	3	6	3.3	4	7	4.1	5	7	4.6	5	8	5.2	6	10	5.2	6	10	4.5	5	9	3.4	4	6	2.7	3	6
helpdesk	1.5	2	6	2.0	2	8	2.6	3	5	3.0	4	6	3.5	4	6	3.5	4	7	3.1	4	8	2.3	3	8	1.7	2	6
technical support	3.5	4	8	4.0	5	7	4.7	5	9	5.0	6	9	5.4	6	9	5.2	6	10	4.8	5	7	3.9	4	7	3.4	4	8

Fig. 9.3 Example of staffing for call centres

Once the staffing phase has been completed, it is expected that some prediction of the number and type of resources (skills, experience, role, area, etc.) required per time unit to meet different levels of operation will be made. Now we need to consider the phases of designing shifts/rosters and assigning people to those shifts/rosters to meet the required staffing level.

9.2.2 Shift and Roster Design

In this section, we start by giving some general definitions and describe the different challenges encountered in shift and roster design.

9.2.2.1 The People

Commonly, employees are aggregated in functional and/or organisational units or groups. A certain hierarchy of grouping is usually defined with two or more levels; the top level is commonly called the "unit," which can be sub-divided into groups and subgroups, and the bottom level usually refers to a single employee. For each unit/group there may be several skills (preferred and potential) and availabilities (working time, overtime, rosters) defined. We will see later that, for management and automation of allocation of people to shifts and/or rosters, it is always a good approach to arrange people into groups rather than as individuals as this significantly simplifies the generation of shift allocations.

9.2.2.2 The Shift

A shift is represented by a time interval that can apply to one or several days of the week. Different shifts can be defined for specific days of the week, such as weekends, or for specific times of the day such as morning, afternoon and night shifts. Two or more shifts may overlap, and they may have the possibility of being allocated to the same person or group of people. This allows us to represent a morning

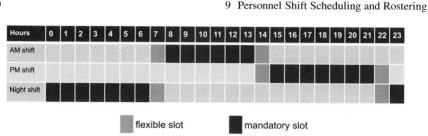

Fig. 9.4 Typical daily shifts for nurses

shift finishing after the beginning of an afternoon shift with some people doing both consecutively. In addition, it is commonplace to allow flexible start and end times at the beginning and end of a shift so that the company has some means of increasing or decreasing the size of its personnel at some point of time during the day or the week.

Figure 9.4 displays three shifts for nurses, i. e., morning shift, late afternoon shift and night shift with flexible start and end times.

9.2.2.3 The Roster

A roster is a set of shifts for a certain period of time. In real-world applications, rosters can be very complex and have long durations over several weeks. Figure 9.5 shows an example of a two week roster for different groups of nurses.

Usually rosters are allocated to groups and in the example of Fig. 9.5, a nurse being allocated to one of these groups means she follows this general pattern but may still have some other personal requirements that will need to be dealt with as well.

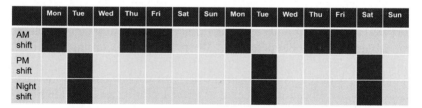

Fig. 9.5 Typical two week roster for a group of nurses

9.2.2.4 Shift and Roster Requirements

Personal Shift Scheduling and Rostering problems cover a variety of sectors each with a different set of requirements. There are, however, a number of operational requirements that are common to all sectors. These will be described first, before we give an insight into some of the more complex requirements that can be found in real-world problems.

- *Working hours*: the minimum/maximum number of hours worked over different periods of time. Flexibility can sometimes be added with the possibility of overtime or flexible start/end times. Similar limits over the number of working hours can be defined per week, month and/or even year.
- *Rest periods*: the minimum/maximum number of hours before a staff needs to have a break or the minimum free time between two shift assignments.
- *Free days*: the minimum/maximum/consecutive free days to be given over different periods of time.
- *Holidays and vacations*: specifies when employees take their holidays according to business policies, ensures holidays are fairly attributed amongst the staff and according to their preferences when possible.
- *Shift compatibility*: defines compatibilities between shifts and staff. For example, a group of employees can be allowed to work on morning and afternoon shifts within the same week or to define the minimum/maximum/exact number of consecutive shifts that can be allocated to the same person over different periods of time.
- *Individual preferences*: any requirement specific to the individual due to personal reasons: disability, preferred shift end times due to family constraints, etc.
- *Skill level*: the minimum/maximum/optimal number of (different skills or types of) staff to be rostered in per time slot.
- *Service level*: the minimum/maximum/optimal service level expected per time unit or over different periods of time (week, month, year) or groups of people (service level per team, unit, overall company)
- *Overtime*: the minimum/maximum hours in overtime allowed per staff over different periods of time.

The large number of variants that these requirements can have gives rise to the complexity within rostering problems. As an example, some of the complicated requirements that can be found in the literature for nurse rostering (Cheang et al. 2003) are listed:

1. constraints among groups/types of nurses, e. g., nurses not allowed to work together or nurses who must work together,
2. historical record, e. g., previous assignments,
3. preferred skill amongst a set of potential skills or alternative skills,
4. different terms in contracts depending on the employee,
5. tutorship (both tutor and a personnel member will have to work together).

9.2.2.5 Challenges in Shift and Roster Design

Shift and roster design aims at defining the shifts and rosters for an organisation and its functional/organisational units (e. g., should there be shifts in the morning, afternoon, overnight, at week-ends). Obviously, the definition of shifts depends strongly on the nature of the operations. When creating shifts, one has to consider various aspects such as operation time, regulations (breaks, maximum working time before a break), the physical difficulty of work, etc. The process of creating shifts and rosters is a very complex activity that usually requires a deep analysis of the organisational environment. It is a serious mistake to separate this phase from its context. The construction of shifts/rosters is traditionally seen as a tactical decision rather than an operational activity because the introduction of a new shift/roster cannot be repeated too frequently since the switch from one roster to another is costly and time consuming. However a computer-based system can still help here to optimise the generation of shifts by simulating the impact of shift changes on the quality of service (customer experience, employee happiness, etc.) and costs (productivity, etc.). This would be even more relevant to companies changing their operations frequently, i. e., continually providing new services, as they require to optimise rosters accordingly. But usually most personnel scheduling systems are differentiating the design of shifts/rosters from the allocation of shifts to people.

9.2.3 Shift and Roster Allocation

The problem of shift and roster allocation is defined as the problem of allocating resources to rosters in order to meet a demand. In many cases, this demand is expressed by a minimum service level to be achieved for each time slot over the planning horizon.

For an organisation, the complexity of shift allocation problems leads personnel managers to spend a large amount of their time constructing rosters. Due to the complexity of the requirements and their antagonistic natures (employee preferences vs. business objectives), in the majority of cases personnel managers do not succeed in generating rosters which satisfy both operational requirements and staff preferences. Conflicting legal, management and staff requirements must be considered when making rostering decisions. For example, management requirements for the cover and skill mix needed for a particular task often conflict with the maximum working hours allowed (by law and contract) as well as with individual staff preferences.

For this reason, we divide the constraints in two categories: hard and soft. A hard constraint corresponds to an operational requirement that must be satisfied. Typically we find governmental or contractual requirements in this category. Soft constraints cover requirements that, if satisfied, would improve the quality of the shift scheduling but that will not compromise its validity. Here we find personnel preferences such as balancing the workload among them or preferred working skill(s) for an employee.

Figure 9.6 exhibits a general view of a typical shift allocation process with multi-skilled people. Decisions can be made at two different levels; firstly groups are created with people sharing some common capabilities or objectives and secondly, rosters are allocated to groups. The creation of groups is typically based on skills,

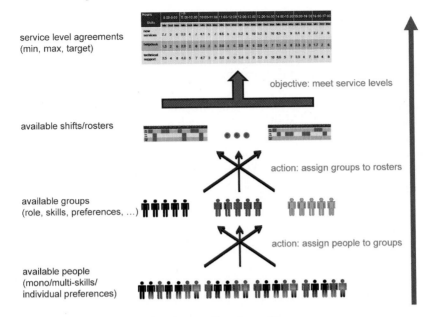

service level agreements
(min, max, target)

objective: meet service levels

available shifts/rosters

action: assign groups to rosters

available groups
(role, skills, preferences, …)

action: assign people to groups

available people
(mono/multi-skills/
individual preferences)

Fig. 9.6 A typical multi-skill shift and roster allocation problem

grades, location, and special status or even driven by the company operations, e. g., for crew pairings for airline industries (Andersson et al. 1997). Each employee holds a number of characteristics and therefore has a certain number of potential groups he can be associated with at each rostering phase. The main objective is, typically, to select a set of shifts/rosters such that the minimum service level in each period is met against minimal costs. To meet this objective, one has the capability to move people from one group to another or allocate a different roster to a group. It is clear that as the number of personnel grows and the planning horizon increases, shift allocation problems become very quickly intractable for a human being to generate valid and optimised shift schedules. To grasp the number of possible solutions, imagine the possible combinations of 100 people to groups and shift allocations that can be made over a period of a few weeks satisfying all the hard constraints, minimising the number of unsatisfied soft constraints and maximising some overall objective such as minimum service level met.

For the following two reasons – planners' time/cost and poor quality of manually generated shifts – there is a strong motivation for automating this process in real-world personnel scheduling. Section 9.3 gives an overview of the different approaches that can be found in the literature to solve the different phases of personnel scheduling problems.

9.3 The Family of Approaches

Shift scheduling and rostering problems have been a subject of interest within both Artificial Intelligence (AI) and Operational Research (OR) communities for a number of decades.

The process of solving personnel scheduling is usually broken down into different phases as described in the previous sections of this chapter. This is due to the complexity of dealing with all these problems – workload prediction, staffing requirements, shift design, and shift allocation – at the same time. This is also motivated by the nature of the enterprise operations where some of these phases may happen at different levels. For example, for many companies changes in shifts (shift design) are relatively rare, happening at a tactical level rather than at an operational level.

But there are always some exceptions where the service demand can be used for building the shifts before allocating people to it (see airline crew scheduling and rostering (Ernst et al. 2004a)). In addition, for each phase, shift scheduling problems exhibit different characteristics across different industries, as we saw with staffing in Sect. 9.2.1 where the workforce requirements could be either fully forecasted, partly forecasted or fully known. Obviously depending on the industry sector and even the company, the nature of these problems change and therefore different approaches need to be developed, e. g., there is no need to use advanced forecasting techniques to estimate the workload if this latter is fully known.

From a theoretical point of view, integrated approaches have generated some interests. Indeed, by integrating staffing and shift assignment[1] phases into one system, one can imagine the optimisation of service levels, shift patterns and shift allocation altogether. But, as explained above, these integrated approaches are mostly not practical and each phase will be solved in sequence with the possibility of going back to a previous phase or even to perform an iterative process between the different phases to improve the overall shift schedules generated.

9.3.1 Solutions to Staffing Problems

Staffing problems are decomposed in two phases: workload estimation and staffing requirements. To estimate the workload when the latter is not known, the main approaches are forecasting techniques and statistical models. Forecasting techniques are usually subject to historical data availability and based upon data analysis techniques to identify relevant patterns within the data that will help estimate the demand (for more details on forecasting techniques, see Chap. 4). Statistical models are appropriate when the demand can be expressed as a probabilistic distribution such as

---

[1] In this chapter, Shift Assignment refers to a single phase potentially including both phases Shift/Roster Design and Shift/Roster allocation

Poisson or Erlang. Incoming calls, customer arrivals or launch of new services can usually be modelled using this technique.

Queuing theory (Gross and Carl 1998), multi-agent systems (Wooldridge 2002), discrete event simulation (Pidd 1998; Brigandi et al. 1994) and heuristic-based modelling (Henderson et al. 1999) are some of the techniques commonly used for generating or estimating staffing requirements from a demand. Finally, in some very complex cases, there is still the possibility to call on consultancy companies that will assess the workforce requirements by simulating the execution of the services by the personnel in a real environment.

It is important to note that most of these techniques work under the assumption that the staffing requirement is independent from the shift assignment phase because of the combinatorial nature of shift assignment problems. However, this is not always true as in many cases staffing requirements will be affected by people being allocated at the shift assignment phase. For example, if greater numbers of nurses are scheduled at the beginning of the day, the waiting lists of patients will be shortened and this may impact the staff requirements for the rest of the day, assuming early and late demands are somehow interrelated.

Thus, the idea of having an integrated approach for staffing and shift assignment has emerged with the basic idea of being able to quickly assess the impact of shift assignment to the required staffing levels using some staffing dynamic models. Such solutions are far from trivial because they imply the same granularity of data at the staffing and shift assignment phases and this is not an easy task to achieve in an organisation. As an example, Bhulai et al. (2005) propose an integrated approach for call centres.

9.3.2 Solutions to Shift Design and Shift Allocation

Integrated approaches, designing shifts at the time of their allocation to people, has been investigated but, for operational reasons, these two phases will remain separated for most of the cases. This is a result of shift building typically being a tactical operation as well as concerning a managerial point of view where changing shifts/rosters too often leads inevitably to confusion and unhappiness of the employees.

As explained in Sect. 9.2.2, the creation of shifts and rosters is usually an organisation-specific task and, generally, is manually executed or in the best case computer-assisted, where the system will ensure shifts and patterns do not break regulation or contract agreements.

As was shown in Fig. 9.6, the problem of allocating people to shifts is a very complex problem due to its combinatorial nature. From a mathematical perspective, this problem belongs to the class of NP-Hard combinatorial optimisation problems. In computer science, this class of problems is well-known for being intractable in a general case for a reasonable period of time. To simplify, this means it is a very complex problem to solve where the time required to find the optimal solution will grow exponentially with the size of the problem (usually the number of staff). The

Complexity Theory tells us that if one minute is required using a computer to find the optimal solution for a group of 10 people, in the worst case it will take up to 17 hours (around 2^{10} longer) to guarantee finding an optimal solution for a group of 20 people!

Thus, the scale and the complexity of this problem prohibit the effective manual allocation of people to shifts, except for the smallest shift scheduling problems. Fully automated systems would seem to be the most appropriate solution but, because of the difficulty to model some of the "ill-defined" requirements as well as the lack of trust in automated systems by shift managers, the most adequate system is usually a semi-automated or computer-assisted approach. In such a case, shift managers request the system to automatically generate shift allocations that they can amend and/or validate later when required. This computer-assisted system only guarantees that no strict rule is broken such as regulation or contractual requirements for the individuals under consideration.

To automatically generate shift schedules, traditional operational research optimisation methods such as enumeration or back-tracking techniques, mathematical programming, and expert systems (Anantaram et al. 1993) have been initially used to solve simple shift allocation problems with few constraints, mono-skill people and a small number of resources. Due to the combinatorial nature of shift allocation problems, incurring an exponential computational cost in the number of staff, enumeration and back-tracking quickly become computationally intractable for all but small problems.

Mathematical programming (MP) solutions are generally based on the famous Dantzig set covering formulation (Dantzig 1954). An important issue with MP techniques is their rather limited modelling capability for constraints and objectives, for instance not always allowing modelling using linear equations. Typically this leads to the adaptation of the problem requirements to the MP technique with the need to develop repair-based techniques to compensate this lack of modelling capability. Thus, developing a specific shift allocation solution based on MP is rather a difficult and time consuming task (see Sitompul and Radhawa (1990) for a review of MP techniques for nurse scheduling).

Other optimisation techniques from the AI community have been explored such as Constraint Programming (CP) (Rossi et al. 2006) and Metaheuristics (MH) (Glover and Kochenberger 2003). In contrast to traditional methods, CP techniques allow complex requirements to be modelled. Pure CP techniques tend to work well for feasibility problems, where a feasible solution satisfying all the requirements has to be found but become relatively inefficient for optimisation problems with an objective function to optimise. Typically, CP can be appropriate for nurses' shift scheduling problems having few admissible solutions or even no solution if we try to satisfy all the constraints, both hard and soft (Seitman 1994; Cheng et al. 1997; Weil et al. 1995).

Metaheuristics are known as approximate search techniques and they propose a different approach for finding good quality solutions in a very short period of time. They work their way through a huge search space approximating the optimal solution without the guarantee to find it.

In this case, the problem is often represented in constraint optimisation terms, where the objective is to satisfy all the hard constraints or core requirements that must be satisfied (such as contractual maximum working hours per day) and minimise the number of other requirements that are not satisfied (such as employee preference). However, the constraints imposed on the problem often cannot be satisfied completely, and the aim changes to one where a solution is found which violates as few as possible.

The application of heuristics and iterative improvement techniques has appeared to be far more promising and efficient for large, complex shift scheduling problems and real-world applications (multi-skills personnel, spatial requirement for field force, large workforce, etc.). They tend to be used when problems cannot be solved with traditional techniques and finding the optimal solution appears to be impossible under certain time constraints. They have the benefits of being easier to implement, more robust, offer an extensive modelling capability based on constraint modelling and propose a better modelling of optimisation objectives.

In this family of techniques, we find MH such as Simulated Annealing (Brusco and Jacobs 1993; Burns et al. 1995), and Genetic Algorithms (Al-Tabtabai and Alex 1997; Cai and Li 2000; Tanomaru 1995) applied to the general personnel scheduling problem. Similiar techniques have been applied to nurse rostering (Aickelin and Dowsland 2000) and bus driver scheduling (Wren and Wren 1995).

However these techniques may have issues when finding a solution for highly constrained problems and some hybrid approaches combining both CP/Greedy Algorithms and MH seem to be the most appropriate in such a case (Monfroglio 1996).

For more details on these different techniques and their applications, the reader can refer to the following survey papers or PhD theses: (Beddoe 2004; Burke et al. 2004; Ernst et al. 2004b; Vanden Berghe 2002).

9.4 Summary

In this chapter, we have discussed the different problems encountered in personnel shift scheduling and rostering problems across different sectors. We presented different computer-based approaches that will enhance the operations of a company providing services to customers. However we have to bear in mind that automated systems are not sufficient because of the complex nature of shift scheduling environments. Firstly, with many conflicting and ill-defined constraints, it is rather difficult to rely solely on a computer-based evaluation. Evaluation by the user is still needed and often necessary. Secondly, the social implications of shift work arrangements are at least as important as the more technical issue of finding an appropriate shift schedule that fits into the constraints model of operation.

However, in recent years, recognition of the importance of flexible employment practices has increased the need for automated rostering tools which can cope with ever more complex problems. The idea of replacing shift work by flexible timetabling through an online system offering the employee the ability to build his working periods sounds very promising. Such a system will handle a large number of parameters such as business policies, operational requirements, employee seniority and performance to propose different working shifts to the employee. This automatically improves staff morale and efficiency. For more details on people and attendance management, the reader can refer to Chap. 11 of this book.

Now that the shifts and rosters of the employees are built and known, the next challenge is to efficiently allocate work to these employees. This vast topic is discussed in the next chapter on work allocation and scheduling that describes different approaches for work allocation and gives some examples across several industries.

Chapter 10
Work Allocation and Scheduling

10.1 Introduction

In the last chapter, we discussed the problem of automating and optimising shift allocations to people in order to meet certain service levels. Now that the number and type of people that need to be rostering in on the day have been determined, there is a need for scheduling work to them. The focus of this chapter is on the challenges in implementing an effective work allocation and scheduling system.

The scheduling of work consists in allocating jobs to a workforce in order to deliver services to customers. More precisely, it is about assigning a job to the right resource in the right place (for the mobile workforce) and at the correct time. The resulting output of a work scheduling phase namely a schedule can be described as the assignments of jobs into time sequences to the resources where one sequence is allocated to each resource. The execution of a schedule processes the assignments of the jobs to the resources over a period of time, ranging from a single day to a few weeks.

In the context of service provisioning, a scheduling system is fed with jobs derived from customer orders or planned work. It then produces work assignments to resources and supervises (mobile) resources in executing the work allocated to them. The main benefits of such a system (ideally) include an increase in customer satisfaction, better efficiency (lower operational costs for service providers) and a certain robustness against disruptions in an operational environment (Gallagher et al. 2006). Having an accurate and efficient scheduling system is, therefore, expected to have a direct impact on the bottom-line business.

In this chapter we first identify the challenges encountered in work allocation motivating the automation of this process. Section 10.3 describes the main concepts in the domain of work scheduling. The different approaches found in the literature for automating work allocation are then described in Sect. 10.4. Finally, we give a summary of this chapter.

C. Voudouris, G. Owusu, R. Dorne, D. Lesaint, *Service Chain Management*
DOI: 10.1007/978-3-540-75504-3, ©Springer 2008

10.2 Challenges in Work Allocation and Scheduling

The challenges with work allocation systems are multiple. Firstly, the availability of input data is critical; the quality, the quantity, and the format of this data need to be carefully investigated. Secondly, the dynamic nature of the environment surrounding work allocation (job cancellation, delays, sickness, regulation change, etc.) forces such a system to be very responsive and flexible. Thirdly, the scale and complexity of work allocation problems can very quickly make the task of efficiently allocating jobs to resources intractable for a human being and therefore motivates the use of automated scheduling systems.

10.2.1 Data Availability

Data availability is a major issue for scheduling systems. The form, source, accuracy and quality of data are always variable, usually depending on whether they are actual, estimated or even unknown (inestimable). The most important sources of information for a scheduling system are obviously those regarding jobs and resources. Without an accurate view of the workload and the resource availability, a scheduling system will not be able to generate any good schedule. Typically in service enterprises, the demand will come from different sources and need to be rationalised before considering moving to an automated scheduling system. In the same manner, there is a critical need for having accurate, real-time information regarding the resources of the company to understand who is doing what, where and when.

Furthermore, some information relevant to scheduling varies in time and space. A good example concerns travel and job durations. The former is usually computed from geographic information systems (GISs) for geographic features or from intelligent transport systems (ITSs) for traffic information (Wang et al. 1999), and the latter is based on historical data from the company allowing some estimation of the job durations. Again, it is essential to understand that with poor estimation and/or low accuracy of input data such as travel times and job durations, a scheduling system will inevitably deliver inefficient schedules leading to poor quality of service and higher cost.

10.2.2 Responsiveness and Flexibility

Work allocation is subject to different laws and regulations regarding different aspects of the work, such as health and safety, working time directives, driving directives and environmental protection. These are challenges for day-to-day high productivity as the scheduling system needs to adjust work allocation to manage disruptions while remaining regulation compliant. In the airline industry, for instance, the application of regulations imposed by the Federal Aviation Administration (FAA)[1] implies taking into account additional restrictions about time slots for landing and leaving (e. g., when bad weather develops around an airport, it reduces visibility for air controllers and pilots, therefore regulations impose to increase the gap of time between each takeoff).

10.2.3 Scale and Complexity

In real-world applications, the number of jobs and the number of resources can be very large leading very quickly to complex work allocation problems. Indeed, there is a combinatorial nature in work allocation as there are many ways of allocating jobs in sequence to resources. In addition, business policies, rules and requirements for allocating jobs are often multiple making the work allocation process even more complex. For example, factors such as regulations (working hours, breaks on routes...), the time windows for a customer's visit, resource features (mobility, capability, capacity...) are some of the requirements that need to be taken into consideration. On top of that, the business usually has some objectives regarding the service level to be met and the cost to be minimised. These business objectives are naturally conflicting as usually achieving a certain service level means increasing operational cost. Consequently, finding a good quality schedule, satisfying all the requirements and optimising some business objectives is a very complex and time consuming task.

By means of an example from the telecommunications industry, BT Plc. (British Telecommunications plc) needs to allocate more than 150,000 tasks to 30,000 field technicians every day. This workforce scheduling is a large-scale problem covering different types of jobs including service provision to business and residential customers, network maintenance, and fault repair. More precisely, it includes the allocation of works and the execution and tracking of jobs. The scheduling problem is defined as follows: given a set of service time-bounded activities and a set of multi-skilled resources, schedule tasks to the right engineer (working periods, skills, breaks, working areas) at the right time (satisfying time windows for appointed visits) while optimising the following business objectives: to maximise the number of tasks allocated, to meet the primary target time for customer visits, and to minimise travel costs.

For all the reasons described above, the automation and optimisation of work allocation has proven to help companies in dealing with the complexity of their scheduling requirements and keeping their operational costs under control (fuel costs, better resource usage, less administration overhead...), while maintaining a certain quality of service. This leads to greater competitiveness and allows a faster response to changing market conditions and customer needs, further increasing customer fidelity as a direct consequence. Automated work allocation may also be

---

[1] The FAA imposes a program of regulations, for more efficient and equitable use of the airspace and airports

beneficial while accommodating customer preferences without compromising the efficiency of the overall scheduling plan.

Conversely, there is a negative effect on the business for not using automated scheduling, particularly on medium and large-sized organisations, where it is virtually impossible for scheduling planners to manually schedule jobs and, at the same time, consider business rules and quality targets. This will lead inevitably to resources being underutilised and work allocation not optimised over the scheduling horizon but rather done in a reactive way without looking beyond the next jobs to be dispatched. This runs the risk of a poor quality of service (QoS) leading to a penalty for the service company since more tasks will be more likely to fail their business targets.

10.3 A General Description of Work Allocation Problems

Typically, work allocation consists in sequencing the jobs to the resources resulting in a set of job sequences where each sequence is assigned to one resource. A sequence is a chronologically ordered list of activities that a resource will execute in sequence. Depending on the service activities of the enterprise, more importance is given to the location of activities (e. g., field force) or to the time when activities are performed (e. g., construction project scheduling, the landing of aircrafts at airport). Scheduling solutions are typically displayed in a Gantt chart (Fig. 10.1) and can be displayed on a map (Fig. 10.2) if there is a location involved.

The underlying computational model is defined as an optimisation problem where the proposed work allocations meet the business requirements so that no inconsistency (e. g., regulation rule broken or task allocated outside its time window) occurs during execution, and where the objectives are usually twofold: to satisfy some service level and minimise the cost. It can be represented by a constrained optimisation problem (COP) with its decision variables representing resource allocations and task start times, a constraint network modelling schedule requirements, and a multi-objective function (evaluating the satisfaction of some soft constraints and the achievement of objectives).

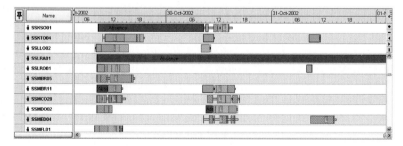

Fig. 10.1 A Gantt chart displaying, for each technician, the sequence of allocated activities (tasks and breaks)

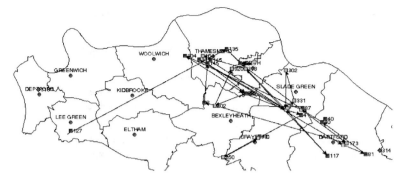

Fig. 10.2 A real world solution for the vehicle routing problem

As shown in Fig. 10.2, when there is a location involved, a scheduling solution can also be displayed as a set of routes corresponding to the journeys currently scheduled by the system to the mobile engineers.

10.3.1 Main Concepts Found in Work Allocation

The main concepts found in scheduling problems are activities, resources, schedules, constraints between activities and/or resources, and objectives.

10.3.1.1 Activities, Resources and Schedules

- *Activity, break and task*: An activity represents any action that a resource can perform. Two types of activities are distinguished which are tasks and resource breaks. A resource break is an activity that must be scheduled usually at a fixed date and with a pre-defined duration (e. g., lunch, home time). A task is an activity that different resources may perform, for instance customer visits. The task's position may vary in the schedule and it is subject to various relations: service time and travel time which may vary for each task-resource pair, time windows, dependencies between tasks, resource compatibility, and splitting over breaks.
- *Resources, crew and fleet*: A resource represents any unit that can undertake activities in sequence. A crew is a team of human resources (a driver, an engineer, a technician) which has complementary skills and can work together to complete particular tasks (e. g., as in air crew scheduling (Qi et al. 2004)). A fleet is the whole set of resources that can be allocated to the problem. Resources may need to pause between activities (resource set-up time), or to spend time travelling in the case of location-based scheduling.
- *Schedule*: A schedule is defined by a set of sequences of activities, the tasks remaining to allocate, together with the consistency and the cost information.

A schedule is defined across a scheduling horizon which is the time interval within which jobs must be allocated and completed. A number of scheduling frameworks provide an explicit representation of the schedule (Ilog 2007; Dorne et al. 2003; Smith et al. 1996).

10.3.1.2 Relations and Constraints

The following typical relations and constraints can be stated in a scheduling problem:

- *Timelines*: Various resource attributes or properties, such as the load capacity of vehicle, affect the allocation of tasks to resources. Resource attributes may also evolve over time due to the allocation of tasks, e. g., the vehicle capacity affected by the delivery or pick-up of goods. On the other hand, a task may require the capacity, the capability or state features from resources and these features may change over the scheduling horizon. Timelines simply capture the evolution of properties over time and are the basis for defining allocation-dependent properties on resources. The most typical timelines are:

  - *Capacity*: Various measurement units are utilised, among them, volume capacity, weight capacity or else maximum working time per day to express regulations for example.
  - *Capability*: A resource capability represents any technician/driver/vehicle technical/technological capability which is required to perform tasks.
  - *State*: A resource state may represent any driver or vehicle state which is required to perform tasks. For instance, in the chemical industry, different chemicals cannot be loaded in the same tank or the tank needs to be washed before loading a different chemical. This means that after a first load, only tasks unloading\loading the same chemical can be allocated to this vehicle or a washing activity has to be included before loading a different chemical. A state timeline allows to represent this type of resource state change during the allocation process.

- *Time window constraints*: These constrain the servicing of tasks to be at a fixed date or within a specified time interval (a so-called time window). Multiple time windows may be defined and the time interval may involve non-contiguous periods of time (service allowed Monday or Friday, or service delivery not possible between 12:00 and 15:00).
- *Precedence constraints*: These are relations that enforce a task to start/end before or after the start/end of another (set of) task(s), eventually with a waiting time between tasks. This type of constraint is particularly useful to represent the order of tasks in project scheduling for example.
- *Parallel constraints*: These enforce several tasks to start at the same time/date simultaneously, for instance a task requiring two technicians working together at the same time can be modelled by two parallel tasks. A delay may be allowed

which, in turn, would mean that there may be a maximum time gap between parallel tasks.

- *Resource compatibility constraints*: These help in capturing compatibility constraints between resources and tasks, and characterise the set of allocations between tasks and resources that are never authorised (e. g., skill requirements between jobs and engineers or a vehicle compatibility with a type of good).
- *Resource constraints*: The choice of the resource assigned to a task may be explicitly constrained by other tasks, as follows:

  - *Same-resource* constrains two tasks to be allocated to the same resource;
  - *Different-resource* constrains two tasks to be on different resources.

10.3.1.3 Scheduling Objectives

Scheduling objectives are a way of qualitatively estimating schedules and solving approaches need them to compare one schedule with another. By means of example, the costing model described below mixes the quality of service evaluation and the operational cost into one overall costing model that, for any schedule under consideration, will return an assessment value of its quality.

- *Task costs*: These are determined by the task service duration, due dates and the type of resource utilised for the allocation. For each task, a cost is incurred for not allocating the task in the schedule (an unallocated cost), for delaying the start of the task (a lateness cost) or for having a resource performing the task (a service time cost).
- *Resource costs*: These are a result of wages, overtime and travelling hours. A cost is defined simply for using each resource and additional costs are incurred for using the resource in overtime, regardless of the task being processed, or for keeping the time the resource needs to set-up (a set-up time cost). There may be a travelling cost too, when the resource has to move to the next job's location.
- *Schedule costs*: This is usually a list of objectives to be met, commonly associated to priority weights to reduce conflicts. Objectives can be related to quality of service (task lateness) or operational costs (set-up time, overtime).

10.3.2 The Dynamic Nature of the Problem

The execution of the schedule corresponds to the effective delivery of services to customers. Scheduled job assignments are forwarded to resources who execute them. Ideally, scheduled start and completion times become release dates at the schedule execution, progressively constituting the actual schedule. The latter involves current time, task and resource variable statuses that are tracked through the execution progress. Due to the inherently dynamic nature of the work allocation environment (task delays, cancellation, sickness, etc.), the scheduling system must continuously update itself with new data and try to minimise the impact of these changes on the current work schedule. Basically we distinguish two distinct cases:

- *Static scheduling*: All inputs are precise and received before the construction of schedules. A backend job allocation process generates optimised schedules based on these precise data and then the schedule is executed accordingly.
- *Dynamic scheduling*: Information is imprecise and updated concurrently with the determination of the schedules. The quality of a scheduling decision can never be guaranteed. Indeed, even if a decision is optimal for what we know at time t, it may be sub-optimal for what we know at time $t + 1$. For instance, choosing the closest technician to perform a task may turn out to be the wrong choice if the technician faces deteriorating traffic conditions on his way.

In addition, events cause deviations in the data as well, to the point that the current schedule is no longer valid, e. g., when a task will now fail according to the plan (in case of overload situations) or a resource is no longer required (underload situations). In daily operations, the environment itself is inherently chaotic (bad weather, mechanical failure); resource availability is subject to last-minute changes and managers may modify provisional schedules and review objectives at any time. In this context, the schedule is likely to be interrupted; for instance, when resources are forcibly allocated to a high priority task that requires immediate work before it fails a business target.

The problem to be addressed by an automated scheduling system is now to keep optimising work allocation over the scheduling horizon (e. g., several days ahead) while re-scheduling activities need to happen very quickly for handling disruptions, exceptions, and events as well as repairing the original schedule when it is no longer executable (Love et al. 2002).

10.3.3 Variants of Work Allocation Problems

Automated scheduling systems have been successfully used in the utility and logistics sectors, where applications are often variants of the general problem, taking into account specific requirements from the domain. In the utility sector, for example, scheduling problems are extensions of standard models such as vehicle routing (Bodin et al. 1983) (routes from central depots to various demand points, each having service requirements), mobile workforce scheduling (Lesaint et al. 2000) (a mix of vehicle routing and skilled work allocation) and stochastic vehicle routing (Bianchi et al. 2004) (when customer demands and travel times follow random distributions instead of being known a priori). Other examples include the water utility, train scheduling, school bus scheduling, flight and aircraft scheduling for landing and takeoff at airports (Qi et al. 2004), field service automation in telecommunications, power/gas distribution and construction. In the logistics sector, a typical system ensures the provision of goods and services from a supply point to a demand point. For example, in transportation (Daskin and Owen 2003), variants of the standard pickup-delivery problem (Parragh et al. 2006) can be applied (tasks have to be assigned per pair, pickup at depot and delivery at destination). In project management services (Braekmans et al. 2005), the building trade, for instance, includes the scheduling of construction plans. The predictive schedule is used as the baseline for executing the project activities while achieving plan stability. In demanding environments, where both the earliness and the tardiness of task allocation with respect to the task's due date are penalised, it is imperative that an item requiring a service must be delivered exactly at the time it is required (Sourd and Kedad-Sidhoum 2005).

10.4 The Family of Approaches

Work allocation approaches aim at generating feasible and high-quality schedules while adapting over time to accommodate the daily dynamic nature of work demand and resource availability (Fig. 10.3).

However, for most of the real-world scheduling problems, it is not possible to find an optimal solution in a reasonable computation time. Indeed, in computer science, such problems are known to be nondeterministic polynomial-time hard (NP-hard) and acceptable algorithms rarely exist to generate optimal schedules in a short period of time, although in some complexity-bounded sub-problems one algorithm may be identified (Lenstra and Rinnooy Kan 1981).

10.4.1 Exact Searches

Exact searches have been known to be one of the most efficient approaches in solving optimisation problems as they can guarantee finding the optimal solution satisfying all constraints and optimising the objective value, if one exists. On the other hand, they can prove as well the non-existence of a feasible solution. The mathematical programming formulation of scheduling problems can be provided

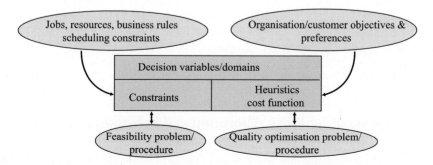

Fig. 10.3 A typical constrained optimisation problem for work scheduling

in some cases, e. g., set partitioning (Domenjoud et al. 1998) or a matrix of linear algebra (Bodin et al. 1983). Generally they follow the usual approach that is to repeatedly solve linear programming problems where constraints are successively relaxed. Other exact searches used in the domain of work scheduling include tree search, branch & bound (Demeulemeester and Herroelen 1992), integer programming (Crevier et al. 2005), dynamic programming (Chang and Pedram 1996) and constraint programming (CP) (Tsang 1993). In recent years, CP has been widely employed to develop real-world scheduling systems (Baptiste et al. 2001). Constraint solvers determine the feasibility of a schedule by checking the constraints that restrict the positioning of tasks in the schedule and by removing the unfeasible set of allocations for each task.

10.4.2 Approximate Searches

When facing NP-hard problems, metaheuristics (MH) (Glover and Kochenberger 2003) and approximate searches are often proposed to quickly obtain near-optimal solutions in lieu of seeking an optimal solution. This is particularly relevant in the context where the schedule is subject to frequent disturbances (the best solution is less important because it will not remain optimal or even valid for a long time). MH methods include techniques such as simulated annealing, tabu search, guided local search, or else genetic algorithms and propose an approach where a heuristic criterion (typically the objective function) is used for guiding the search process through the search space (the set of the possible tasks' allocations). Their search paradigm is based on an iterative process where we start from an initial (feasible) schedule (solution) and makes incremental changes by modifying the current tasks' allocation at each iteration using the objective function to guide this process towards better schedules (a set of solutions).

In the case of population-based MH such as genetic algorithms, the search process maintains a population of solutions throughout the search process instead of a single solution and follows a similar iterative improvement process by applying genetic operators: crossover, mutation and selection. The necessary interface needed by MH to support schedule modifications includes an insertion operation, which inserts a task before a specified activity (tour construction) and a swap operation, which exchanges two tasks (tour improvement). From these operations, more complex moves can be derived (Nanry and Barnes 1999) to help guiding the search more efficiently.

10.5 Implementing Work Allocation and Scheduling

In this section we discuss how companies implement work allocation systems. The main objective is to send appropriate jobs to resources at dispatch time, while maintaining an accurate and optimised work allocation plan over the scheduling horizon. Such a system may follow different business objectives, e. g., limit the number of disruptions from the current work schedule, meet individual and collective requirements (consistency, short-response time, robust and flexible answers, etc.) or ensure that managers are alerted to potential failure by using a task jeopardy management system.

One common approach consists of addressing dynamic scheduling through rescheduling, i. e., through repeated executions of static scheduling operations (Love et al. 2002). There are two possible strategies: either proactive or reactive scheduling (Kizilisik 1999). Proactive scheduling proposes the production of days-ahead schedules for the whole set of resources and tasks which enables optimisation over the scheduling horizon (typically the rest of the day or over a few days) rather than only for the next task (as with rule-based systems). Unfortunately, this is a time-consuming operation which does not fulfil the need for responsiveness in highly dynamic environments. On the other hand, reactive scheduling (Smith 1994) suggests the fast production of short-term schedules for a limited number of tasks and guarantees responsiveness at the expense of global optimality.

However, real-world scheduling problems are generally highly dynamic and they demand careful optimisation. A well-proven successful strategy consists of coupling reactive and proactive scheduling. This can be done by employing a reactive component for online allocation and a background proactive component for global optimisation[2]. The reactive component dispatches scheduled work and is triggered by external events, although it may decide dedicated work assignment, within a scope restricted enough to ensure response within seconds. There is, however, a regular inadequacy between the allocations provided at dispatch time and the actual situation of resources. Three strategies emerge:

- To periodically re-compute a full schedule (in a matter of minutes), and in between, execute a short-term schedule. This can be guided by heuristics such as simulating the evolution of the environment and injecting this knowledge when, or before, scheduling.
- Not to have any predictive schedule and to rely only on business rules to allocate jobs without any view beyond the next jobs (online allocation).
- To rely on teams working together to adjust resources to jobs depending on information which was not known by the scheduler when the schedule was generated.

On the following page, Fig. 10.4 shows an architecture that can be used to manage dynamic work allocation. Architectures usually include: a proactive system computing an estimated optimised schedule, a reactive system allocating work over time, and a schedule controller which evaluates the gap between estimated and actual schedules and decides when to take action through a partial or complete schedule revision process so that the newly computed schedule is optimised based on the latest data. From a functional aspect, the system relies upon an iterative process

---

[2] The reactive component being the ultimate decision-maker may be entitled to override any proactive schedule, yet not without any well-justified reason

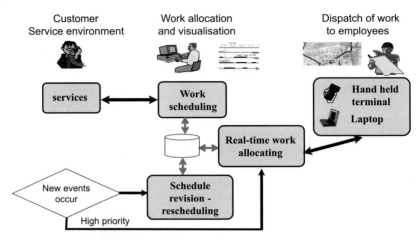

Fig. 10.4 Components involved in dynamic work allocation management

(Gallagher et al. 2006): schedule generation, execution, revision, and constraints relaxation or tightening.

10.5.1 Rescheduling and Disruption Management

When the problem changes over time, objectives such as robustness (to avoid the need for repair) and adaptability (so that the repair time remains affordable) have to be taken into consideration as well as the objectives of feasibility and quality. Built schedules should anticipate and absorb changes quickly and effectively. The update of a schedule in response to changes is called rescheduling. The issue then is to determine the modalities of rescheduling: how often should we reschedule and for how long. The rescheduling process can be triggered every time a change occurs; this assumes that the flow of incoming events may be interpreted as a sequence of elementary changes.

A pragmatic approach consists of rescheduling periodically, the queue of events being all treated in one rescheduling phase. Then the issue becomes to choose a meaningful period of scheduling. On the one hand, short periods should allow the scheduler to account for incoming events as soon as possible. On the other hand, long periods would enable a scheduler to deliver better quality schedules.

Another way of reducing the complexity of rescheduling is to reuse the previous schedule generated during the last run as the starting point of the next schedule. To build new tours, it suffices to identify and remove the invalid portions of past tours.

The rescheduling procedure should also be capable of distinguishing an event that puts in jeopardy all the jobs in a tour from an event that just endangers the last job of the tour. For that reason, a good approach seems to maintain a set of schedules having a similar quality. Firstly, human decisions may be positively influenced by the possibility of choosing among a given set of solutions which are known to be comparable. Secondly, this limits the deviation of cost optimality caused by successive revisions (Aloulou and Portmann 2003). The main benefit is that of avoiding the computation of a new schedule as long as the disruptions can be absorbed by the pre-computed set of solutions (Sevaux and Sorensen 2002).

An alternative way of maintaining robustness consists of inserting idle time into the predictive schedule (Kizilisik 1999) or rescheduling only the part of the schedule which is not about to be executed. Yet, when a global stability is not possible in acceptable time, Gallagher et al. (2006) suggest using incremental scheduling.

10.5.2 Mobility Support

The execution (running) of a schedule by mobile workers regroups the dispatch of pre-scheduled jobs, acceptance by a worker, and feedback transmission between workers and the organisation. An example of information exchange is where there may be task progress, closure, failure, etc. This can be done through a mobility platform, which gives service managers visibility and flexibility with the mobile workers. The goal of a mobility platform is to ensure that an engineering task is properly completed by field engineers by providing them with useful services. These services include delivering task information to corresponding field engineers (e. g., the history of previous jobs), guiding the execution of a customer job, planning a trip to a job location from an engineer's current location, and handling the automatic coordination among workers. When teams are collaborating, workers should be able to control – within limits – their working environment and the order and manner in which they perform tasks. Thus, the location information identification and the tracking functionality as well as the accurate inference of work-related alerts to employees based on the current work context are essential. In addition, knowledge sharing empowers workforces by identifying people who work on similar tasks or in the same locality.

Figure 10.5 shows a solution for supporting mobile workers, where each of the services provided by the mobility platform is separately held.

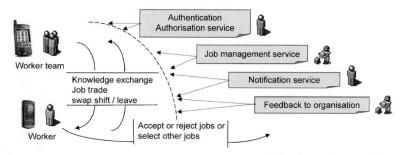

Fig. 10.5 A multi-agent based solution to support mobile workers (Shepherdson et al. 2005)

Mobility platforms introduce new ways of working: service managers know whether an engineer is on-site or has more capacity, or whether a job is running over its scheduled time or has been completed early. Hence they can make the appropriate decisions to dispatch one or more jobs to workers. For more details on engineer empowerment through personalised communications and mobile workforce management, see Chaps. 13 and 19 of this book.

10.6 Summary

In this chapter we discussed the different approaches for scheduling work to resources. We pointed out that the complexity and scale of work allocation forbids the manual generation of schedules and therefore needs to be automated. But, on the other hand, we saw that real-world work allocation problems are very difficult to automate because of their many variants in terms of business requirements and objectives, and a very dynamic surrounding environment. This implies that an efficient work allocation system requires having the ability to generate an optimised schedule over the entire planning horizon, to react almost in real-time for handling emergencies, disruptions and events, and to be very flexible to deal with variants and changes in the business requirements. If these guidelines have to be followed then the impact on the business in terms of quality of service and costs is significant and should not be underestimated in particular for companies having a medium/large workforce or facing strict service level agreements from their customers.

As we explained in this chapter, for any work allocation system, a key issue is the availability and accuracy of the data especially regarding the attendance of the employees. It is critical for a scheduling system to know precisely the number of resources that are available over the scheduling horizon to allocate the jobs efficiently. Following this comment, in the next chapter, we will discuss the challenges and review existing solutions for people attendance management.

Chapter 11
People and Attendance Management

11.1 Introduction

The employees within an enterprise performing tasks in the service chain represent the 'capacity' available and, therefore, directly influence the ability of the chain to process work. This capacity has a number of component parts: the people themselves, their planned attendance and variations – positive through overtime or negative through absence. This 'net availability' must be maintained accurately, and in real time, to enable effective planning, scheduling and reservation of the capacity further along the chain. As well as making this information available to components and functions within the service chain, employees themselves need to view and manipulate it. Enterprises generally do not have a joined up approach to managing this capacity as an entity, rather managing parts of it separately combining manual human resources (HR) processes with limited system support.

Within the service chain there will be employees (the 'capacity') tasked to deliver the service concerned and this capacity is limited. These limits are set not only by the financial constraints of the organisation (it cannot employ an unlimited supply) but by the personal preferences and contractual entitlements of the employee (entitlements to annual holiday, sick leave, rest days, overtime and flexible attendance). The capacity has a number of forces acting upon it, flexing in size up and down on a daily, even hourly basis. In the service chain this represents a challenge as the intake of work is also likely to fluctuate. For any enterprise, insufficient utilisation of employees is a problem and good resource management is about achieving optimal utilisation whilst meeting the various obligations of the employer.

Typically, companies can have up to 30% of the work force on non-effective time at any one time. With employees expected to work flexible shifts, possibly around the clock, imprecise management of attendances and absences can result in too coarse a view of availability which is difficult to manipulate to meet changing demand.

C. Voudouris, G. Owusu, R. Dorne, D. Lesaint, *Service Chain Management*
DOI: 10.1007/978-3-540-75504-3, ©Springer 2008

The challenges for managing attendance are considerable. With increasingly flexible and mobile workforces a static or global attendance template is inadequate. Individual personalisation and direct access is required to the information, over a number of modes – voice, text, web, and handheld amongst others. The process of accepting and authorising absence changes is time intensive and is prone to variations across a company. Furthermore local, legal and company rules to be applied when requesting absence and overtime mean that manual processes become difficult to manage and are unlikely to have sufficient visibility to take into account constraints at the domain or the company level. Finally with information on attendance and absence directly feeding tactical, strategic and operational planning as well as scheduling systems, a clear and comprehensive audit trail of who is changing the information is required. All of the above requires a holistic approach to attendance management and system support to make it work for the enterprise.

Section 11.2 gives a general description of people and attendance management along with its challenges. In the next section current practices for managing people in the industry are reviewed. Section 11.4 argues the case for an automated people and attendance management system. Section 11.5 discusses future trends with regard to people management such as working time flexibility, and shift bidding or plan-driven attendance management that are new approaches emerging from the industry. The final section is a summary of this chapter.

11.2 What is People and Attendance Management?

The capacity within an enterprise is made up of a number of components. Figure 11.1 shows a typical snapshot at any point in time and is similar to an iceberg. The whole iceberg, surrounded with the bold line, is the total resource pool. Above the water line is the available resource scheduled to work for the service chain; below the water line are resources that are unavailable for a number of reasons. Above the iceberg itself is the ability to temporarily inflate the resource pool through overutilising the people within the standard resource pool (e. g., overtime).

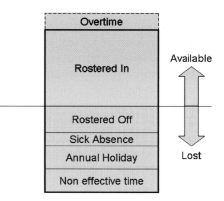

Fig. 11.1 The capacity iceberg

11.2.1 People

Capacity in this chapter's context is all about people. The maximum capacity within the enterprise will be determined by the employees in post, i. e., the resource pool, which will be a mixture of permanent employees and temporary recruits. The latter category will consist of agency, sub-contract or other non-payroll employees. Employees of all kinds will be on a mixture of full and part time contracts. Even without absences and scheduling, this resource pool will flex in size through natural churn and recruitment, or through dynamic engagement and the release of temporary workers.

For larger companies this pool is not equally available to all the demands placed upon it by the service chain. People will have certain capabilities or skills and may have geographical preferences and limitations. This information needs to be held alongside the traditional personnel attributes normally associated with a 'people store.'

11.2.2 Attendance

People need to be scheduled to attend work and the need for a flexibly attending workforce is critical as customers seek to be served outside of the traditional working week's daytime hours. Attendance at its fundamental level is the period within a day when an employee is expected to deliver some work on behalf of the company. Normally, these hours will be part of the contractual agreement entered into by the employee when recruited or engaged. This agreement may include some degree of sophistication, ranging from a basic 'working week' to flexible start times on any day. Attendances may be during the day, over the weekend and increasingly throughout the night. Personal constraints and preferences need to be considered such as health limitations, life-work balance agreements (for example employees signing up to not work particular days or shifts that work within school hours) or part-time working. Companies may choose to offer incentives on particular attendance patterns in return for certain commitments, such as the ability to work Sundays or to be on a night roster. Finally, legislation within the working country may limit attendances to ensure a fair allocation of rest days, and to ensure workers are not scheduled in excess. In Europe, the European Working Time Directive (EWTD) makes such obligations mandatory on companies operating within its remit.

In implementation, this baseline attendance may take the form of a pattern or a shared template of hours. It may be a custom set of shifts, tailored for the individual. Further, it may be selected from a pool of valid shifts, allowing the employee themselves to customise and thus choose a suitable pattern of work. We will return to this later: for more details on shift scheduling and rostering, see Chap. 9 of this book.

On top of this baseline, attendance can be flexed up and down. Flexible working recognises that even with the best planning and optimisation of attendance patterns, at the individual level there will be approximations as demand in a particular area or skill ebbs and flows, or where individual exceptions occur as tasks are undertaken.

For the large variances, and for times when unexpected increases in workload can be foreseen, non-planned attendance is often necessary. This extra capacity requirement can be targeted at the permanent workforce (overtime) or may be implemented with agency or sub-contractor recruitment. In large organisations, resources can also be moved around being redeployed in different areas with possibly different skills for a multi-skilled work force. This allows taking up slack in one area and reducing underutilisation in others (for more detail on resource planning, see Chaps. 3, 4 and 5). However, there will be times when even a deployment plan[1] acknowledges that there is more work coming in than people to do it. In these cases, strategies for temporarily incentivising employees to work more will be required.

For smaller variances, flexible attendance can be adopted. This essentially 'borrows' contractual hours from a later day either positively or negatively, with the balance being restored through paying back the time over- or underworked by a reciprocal arrangement at that time.

It is important to note that attendance management is not time recording, although the two can work together. The latter is an historic exercise about cost recovery and employee allowances whereas the former is about planning employee availability.

11.2.3 Absence

Absences are those periods of attendance where the individual cannot be productive in terms of the service chain. The amount by which the available resource is reduced by absence is termed 'shrinkage'.

Traditionally, when HR systems refer to 'absence management' they generally mean 'sick absence management'. Sick absences are an overhead in most enterprises. Whilst there can be management strategies for dealing with persistent or excessive sick absences, there comes a point at which a degree of shrinkage of the available resource due to sickness must be accepted, a typical figure being around 3–5% of the staff in post at any one time.

The other main absence overhead is holiday entitlement, often referred to as annual leave. This is a contractual entitlement to paid time off, primarily offered to permanent employees. As an entitlement, it has to be expected that while some flexibility can be expected of employees deciding when to take their holidays (and therefore, some demand management can be done), the full year's entitlement should be possible to be taken within the period. This effectively adds further fixed shrinkage to the available resource, typically around 15–20% of the staff in post at any one time.

---

[1] A deployment plan describes for each employee when, where and which skills he will be using over the planning horizon.

Finally, there are other absences over which an enterprise has more control. We split these into two categories. First, non-effective time will be working time, but engaged in tasks that do not directly serve the service chain. For example, time off to get a vehicle serviced, on-the-job training, and team meetings. Second, other absences will be periods of absence, often from work itself, but which are permitted within the terms and conditions of the organisation concerned. Examples might include union duties, compassionate leave, job shadowing.

11.2.4 Maintaining the Mix Between a Fully Automated System and People Involvement

A coherent, consistent view of an organisation's capacity does not exist by itself. The basic unit, the employee, could be deployed manually in very small organisations, but it does not take long (only double figures) before the management overhead of the components of the capacity described above becomes time consuming, onerous and, potentially, non-optimal. Information in the capacity pool needs to be constantly updated and manual management of the same means that this real-time view is not available to other parts of the service chain. When this occurs, either capacity is over-booked (resulting in commitments to customers not being met) or capacity is under-used (resulting in cost and/or lost revenue to the organisation).

Up until now, we have shown a systematic view of what capacity consists of. However, capacity is measured in people and this adds a human resourcing element to the equation. In addition to having visibility and good management of the available pool, the employees themselves need to be directly involved in the process. Ensuring employees are part of the solution has a number of benefits. Most apparent is that the various elements of the capacity within an organisation are effectively stores of information – and this information needs maintenance. Better to engage employees directly in this exercise to increase automation and squeeze efficiency further. A second, but equally important, benefit that follows from this is workforce empowerment – employees that feel they can control and take responsibility for the information flows about them and that drive the service chain are more likely to be satisfied in their job than those who feel centrally controlled.

11.3 Current Practices in People and Attendance Management

People and attendance management solutions are considered under the umbrella term of human resource management systems (HRMS). Automated systems in this space are considered essential for any organisation over around 100 employees due to the cost involved of maintaining the human information within it.

The HRMS space can be categorised into a number of areas covering the user's experience through to the transactional processing of information and strategic planning.

- User experience: Employee and manager interaction, employee communications, and management information and reporting.
- Transactional: Employee records, payroll and benefits, and workforce management.
- Strategic: Training and learning, recruitment, and performance management.

Of the areas relevant to the service chain, workforce management processes, benefits (e. g., annual leave) and a self-service user experience are not well represented in the market leading HRMS solutions.

11.3.1 Analysing the Market Segment for Attendance Management

In September 2006, Forrester Research, Hamerman et al. (2006a), reviewed the market for HRMS solutions, scoring eleven vendors. The research shows the time attendance and absence management areas are consistently the 'poor cousins' in the HRMS space in terms of the weakest support, to the more established strategic and personnel management areas. This does tend to reflect the niche area that Attendance Management has in a Service Management context.

The growth rate of the HRMS market segment is annually around 3%, considerably lower than the leading applications themselves, reflecting the maturity of the market. However, as quoted in Hamerman et al. (2006a), "Workforce optimization, including forecasting and scheduling of hourly workers, is a sub-segment of higher growth potential, as is absence management. This category reflects more and more vertical industry focus to address the workforce needs of specific types of businesses (e. g., retail, healthcare, manufacturing, and transportation). Segment growth: 10%."

Therefore, workforce management and optimisation is not well represented in existing HRMS solutions (due to its narrow field relative to the whole market) but potential for growth is encouraging.

11.3.2 Dealing with Attendance in Organisations

Reviewing current practices in organisations with respect to attendance management shows a similarly low take up of automated support. Whilst many companies running workforces dedicated to service do have work allocation systems, the availability picture tends to be much more static (i. e., effort is put in up front to establish a baseline, but there is little on-going management and adjustment) with locally and manually managed absence management. Opportunities to optimise availability based on individual skills or preferences are also not taken up. This is possibly an artefact of poor system support for these capabilities in the market, but such weaknesses have consequences:

- *Poor or no visibility of capacity.* This is critical – without knowing the extent of the workforce that is able to face and consume incoming work, utilisation cannot be optimised.
- *Inconsistent leave and absence processes.* This has two disadvantages. Firstly, it antagonises employees; secondly, it means an organisation can find it difficult to plan capacity cross-enterprise (due to different approaches to absence approval).
- *Working hours only.* So entrenched are manual processes that some companies are forced to have only an effective view of the workforce when there is manual effort available to maintain it.
- *Granularity of management to one day.* Poor or no system support can mean that intra-day management of availability is too costly. As a result, capacity can be underused within the day.

11.4 Implementing People and Attendance Management

Our approach is to treat the various parts of the anatomy of the capacity available to the service chain in a holistic manner, creating a single attendance management capability. Only by treating the capacity as an entity and managing it as a whole can the best possible utilisation be achieved.

11.4.1 People Management

Traditional HRMS are effective at holding static information about the employees within an organisation and any solution for the service chain should integrate with these capabilities. It makes no sense for an organisation to maintain this information twice. These same systems tend to have a static view of the workforce and are not designed to manage the changes to the person on a daily or hourly basis that an attendance management capability requires. The following list describes the attributes that may need to be exposed by such a system:

1. *Geography*: The employees' and employer's preferences for the working location as well as deployment change during, or prior to, each day should be maintained. This geographic information will be shared with other components in the service chain.
2. *Skills*: People's skill levels and preferences should be held. This may integrate with training databases but from our experience, skills for planning and attendance management tend to be modelled at a higher level than the more low-level specific qualification. Skill preferences can be modelled as well – biasing towards a particular skill (in a multi-skilled workforce) is a method of tuning work scheduling systems where increased demand for a particular skill is forecasted or planned (cf. Chaps. 9 and 10).
3. *Workforce people data*: This capability provides a single source for employee information over and above the traditional HRMS. This will include information

required to support absence and attendance management, as well as employee preferences.

11.4.2 Attendance Management

The baseline position in attendance management is the contractual attendance. The attendance management capability will need to manage this baseline which forms the starting position for the available capacity. All changes (such as absences or overtime) are movements over or under this baseline. The capability should include:

1. *A shift/roster pattern build*: A pattern of attendances is often called a roster. Such rosters can be templates or can be individually built. Either way, a means of designing and assigning expected shifts to an employee is required. Traditionally, patterns of attendance tend to revolve around strict contractual rules and are fixed in advance. As such, they are less flexible when demand changes or flexes. The capability should permit ad hoc customisations and change of shift patterns at the individual level to cope with these inputs (for more details on automated shift scheduling and rostering, see Chap. 9).
2. *Overtime*: Many organisations accept a degree of working over and above contracted hours which may or may not be paid – this responsibility does not belong to the attendance capability – but it should be planned where possible. Additionally, it should be possible for users, or other parts of the service chain, to authorise or limit the use of overtime within areas. Overtime is usually voluntary so the capability should provide self-serving means for capturing volunteers and budgets to permit or restrict their authorisation.
3. *Flexible working*: The ability to dynamically flex attendances for low level peaks and troughs assists the company by providing a cheaper option than paid overtime. It also meets the employee's needs for flexible and short notice small scale attendance changes.
4. *Duty of care*: An automated attendance management capability gives visibility of the planned attendance for individuals and a number of key employer obligations can be supported as a result: firstly, the issue of the safety of the employee at work. In combination with actual sign on/sign off information and knowing planned attendance the capability can monitor and alert violations at the start or the end of the day. Secondly, legislation limiting hours at work or the number of rest days required can also be monitored using the system and actually managed at the integration points (for example, not permitting overtime, even where volunteered and required, when regulation limits have been exceeded).

11.4.3 Absence Management

Many organisations take either a 'command and control' approach to absence management where absence requests need human authorisation or they have too relaxed a view which 'records' absence rather than manages it. The major HRMS offerings treat absence as an attribute to be recorded and reported upon, but not as a dynamic aspect of the overall capacity. In the service chain, enough is known about the demand profile and the available capacity for absence management to be fully automated. Rather than using technology to simply capture requests, the information available within a joined-up view of the service chain can be used to authorise and control absence itself. There are a number of key benefits: firstly, it ensures a consistent process across an organisation with no 'favourites' or local policies; secondly, it can be driven by the individuals themselves, releasing managers from administration; thirdly, by devolving maintenance to the end-user, the quality and freshness of the data can be increased.

When automating absence requests, a number of constraints also need to be modelled to ensure capacity is not depleted in a free-for-all.

1. *Absence management domain*: When evaluating requests for absence, the capability needs to compare like with like. Penalising someone requesting time off in London because capacity is low in Edinburgh is hardly fair. Employees need to be grouped into domains that map the way that work is allocated and reported upon. The domain is likely to be a combination of geography and skill with employees within it sharing a synergy on one or both points. This could of course be exactly the same domain that work is allocated from but, in larger organisations, better results come from having absence management domains that are supersets of the work allocation equivalents. This is because a key element of tactical planning is the ability to move resource between work allocation domains to meet peaks and troughs of demand. Absence managing too low impedes this 'free flow' of resource across boundaries.

2. *Thresholds/budgets*: At the basic level, an acceptable threshold for each absence type should be enforced. This can take the form of a headcount or a percentage of the available work force. For some absence types, such as an annual holiday, this threshold is an overhead the company has to bear. For others, such as training, this may vary as financial demands or work commitments flex. Ideally, these thresholds should be variable, at least by day, to facilitate profiling throughout the year (for example, more employees will want time off in the summer than in the middle of March).

3. *Skill protection*: Absence thresholds work well in a single-skilled absence domain. However, for domains with a multi-skilled workforce, or where the domain has a mix of skills or covers a large geographical area, absence based thresholds can disproportionately deplete the resource pool. For example, work may involve equipment that requires three employees to operate – as a result it is important that the absence domain does not deplete resource below three for that particular skill. As a result it is essential to be able to set and enforce thresholds at skill level either as thresholds/budgets or as fixed minimums designed to 'protect' the scarce resource. This level of protection is also useful in geographically large domains (say in rural areas) to ensure that skills or resources are depleted in one area (which would adversely affect travel time costs for the remainder).

4. *Restricted periods*: Not all days are created equal and it must be possible for ad hoc restrictions to be applied. Examples include major holidays where alternative arrangements may be necessary; reactive restrictions such as those caused by unexpectedly high work volumes; skill level restrictions to permit tighter control on certain skill types, either reactively (in a repair scenario) or proactively if a particular product launch forecast demand for a skill.

5. *Discretion*: In an automated approach to absence management, a purely arithmetical view of the world will not be appropriate in most cases. It is important to bear in mind that such a system deals with people and therefore it is vital to model a degree of 'human discretion into the rules particularly in large multiskilled domains where the chances of violating the rules are high. By means of an example, an employee requesting two weeks of holiday would feel justly aggrieved if his request was rejected simply because on one of the requested days, the resource checks failed.

11.5 Future Trends

This chapter has looked at a first stage in moving attendance management away from written records and approximations and into a unified attendance management capability, lending itself to automated system support. This system creates new opportunities for employee self-service with much of the model accessible and changeable by individuals directly. By exposing the model in this way, a further benefit is that the rest of the service chain itself has direct access to the same operations. This offers a number of new directions in which to take attendance management.

11.5.1 Mobility and Office Solutions

The information maintained within the attendance capability is regularly accessed by all employees. Unlike personnel information in traditional HRMS platforms, which is accessed only occasionally, attendance hours drive the employee's daily schedule with benefits such as annual holiday and overtime availability scrutinised closely. It is effectively the 'diary' of the service chain employee and will be referenced frequently. In enterprises today, there are two other examples of 'regularly touched' platforms. One, particularly in the field workforce, is the mobile device, increasingly used as the work allocation and task management tool of choice. Integration of the attendance capability with these solutions is a natural extension of self-service via the web or voice platforms, bringing the information and the functionality into the hands of end users. Location-based services, available in such products, can supplement and enhance capabilities such as duty of care.

Second is the office productivity suite. Products such as Microsoft Office, Google Tools or StarOffice are now platforms for applications in their own right and are becoming key tools for many employees' daily routine. Integration of the attendance capability with calendar and task management tools can provide the benefits of a richer attendance management focus in the familiar clothing of an enterprise's productivity tool of choice.

11.5.2 Shift Bidding

Much of the current practice in shift allocation centres on a design stage, followed by allocation to the employee. Some degree of employee preference may be taken into account but, generally, shift allocation is company-centred, meeting its needs alone. However, with a unified capacity model that fully understands the skill mix, preferences, geographical and domain assignments, the specific employee performing a particular shift becomes less relevant.

For example, it could be identified that to cover demand in a particular area, a company needs twenty employees per day: ten on early shifts, ten on late shifts, with half the number on Saturday. One solution would be to create a rotating pattern (see Table 11.1), and assign five employees to each week (row) of the pattern.

The problem with this approach is that the pattern becomes complex. To balance Weeks 3 and 4, each employee is required to have a day off during the week. This means that Thursday and Friday will be under-resourced. To resolve this issue requires creating further week patterns (not shown) where the day off moves throughout the working week and the employees assigned to Weeks 3 and 4 re-deployed accordingly across these new patterns. Additionally, while the pattern is a fair allocation of the schedules (insofar as each employee will work identical attendances over the period of the rotation) it does not necessarily meet the preferences of the employees themselves.

An alternative approach is to go back to the original requirement and simply offer some or all of the unassigned shifts (early or late on each day) to the employees. Employees then 'bid' for the shifts they want with preferential terms offered to those who chose to take less popular options (such as weekend or overnight working). A degree of imposition will still be required but it is likely that, in addition to the choices offered to the employee in terms of absence self-service, they will now have a degree of control in terms of designing their own attendance schedule. The

Table 11.1 An example roster pattern (partial)

Week	Mon	Tue	Wed	Thu	Fri	Sat	Sun
1	0700	0700	0700	0700	0700		
	1500	1500	1500	1500	1500		
2	1000	1000	1000	1000	1000		
	1800	1800	1800	1800	1800		
3	0700	0700	0700	0700		0700	
	1500	1500	1500	1500		1500	
4	1000	1000	1000		1000	1000	
	1800	1800	1800		1800	1800	

company also benefits by being able to 'price' shifts that it wants employees to take up. This has the potential for other benefits:

1. *Sick absence reduction.* Much has been written on absence management as a synonym for 'reducing sickness absence.' By increasing choice to employees in the way they design their working attendance, non-genuine sick absence may be reduced.
2. *Employee flexibility.* The employee benefits from the ability to control their own work/life balance. Employees take responsibility for choosing when they want to work shifts the company prefers and when they choose to favour the life's side of the balance. By favouring the former, the chances of being successful in bidding for the latter subsequently increase. Some commercial products already implement a shift bidding component along these lines.
3. *Greater flexibility in attendance delivery.* The more regular review cycles imposed by the bidding process mean that shifts available for bidding can be remodelled each time. This means that by adjusting the mix of shifts available for auction, a company can respond to changes in the demand profile with the potential to reduce costs associated with the failure to deliver enough capacity on the day.

11.5.3 Plan-Driven Attendance Management

With the capacity model of the attendance capability exposed with operations to manipulate and control it, it is now possible to connect these inputs to outputs to the rest of the service chain.

The model depicted in Fig. 11.2 shows that the main output of the attendance management capability is capacity availability. This constitutes the details of the

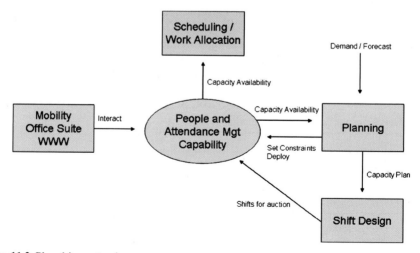

Fig. 11.2 Plan-driven attendance management

workforce and exactly what each employee is doing at a particular moment in time. The inputs to attendance management are the thresholds, budgets and restrictions and the deployment changes suggested by planning. Further, shifts for auction into the bidding process are received from the shift designer.

As this model runs, demand and forecasted demand is understood by the planning component. With a view of existing capacity it can make decisions based on shortages and surpluses. Such decisions can be implemented directly on the attendance management capability and some potential scenarios are described below:

1. *Overtime*: The attendance capability already knows about volunteers and the geography and skill preferences they possess. The planner output can be used to limit overtime budgets or to physically authorise the overtime directly.
2. *Adding agency/sub-contractors*: Extra resources can be injected directly into the capacity pool either as a 'dummy' resource or as particular people.
3. *Tightening or loosening absence constraints*: Where demand is known to fluctuate up or down, particularly in the future, capacity can be managed up or down by adjusting the flow-rate of shrinkage in either direction. For example, in periods of anticipated quiet, more annual leave could be allowed. Conversely, where an anticipated high intake will place demands on particular skills, restrictions can be applied directly by the planner.
4. *Deployment changes*: The work allocation domain, or area where an employee starts their work, may not be optimal for the demand. This can be flexed directly either temporarily or permanently.

11.6 Summary

HRMS applications are usually good at the static model of the person and the complexity of recruitments and contracts. Managing the workforce at the macro level, however, requires a model of capacity that is consistent, maintained in real time, flexible by the minute, accessible and ideally self-service. Shared ownership of this information logically moves it away from a central repository and closer to the main actors, namely the employees. The consistent approach to absence management allows planning to be simplified and employees to be fairly treated.

Offering the attendance capability as service operations to other parts of the enterprise allows for plan-driven attendance management. The very demand hitting the service chain can be used to drive and manage the capacity pool itself, liberating human resources from administration and increasing customer satisfaction through optimal utilisation of the capacity.

Part III
Process, Communications and Information

The manner in which service businesses manage their processes, communications and information around their Service Chain Management solution becomes increasingly important in competitive environments. The degree of maturity in these technologies determines not only the ability of firms to operate but also the degree to which they are gaining a competitive *advantage* by implementing and using IT.

Somebody may argue that commercial off-the-shelf packages in these three areas have really matured and it is only a matter of finding the right vendor to acquire the most suitable middleware, workflow, reporting or communications solution for their service business. We believe this approach is limiting and fails to recognise the opportunities created in several of these areas to improve the way that service firms operate today. In line with this belief, we provide insights on new developments in process, communications and information that can create a difference. More so, we examine how this difference is going to be realised in practice through the implementation of a Service Chain Management solution, along with these technologies, in an agile and incremental way so that, ultimately, user requirements and expectations are met.

This part of the book starts with workflow technologies. In the early days, ERP in factories catered to the process model of production, and that was largely sufficient. As services began to be automated, a requirement to "commoditise" ERP emerged which led to workflow tools which can model any process and not only a production process. ERP process models contain information such as costing, resourcing and other requirements on production associated with each process step; such information is largely missing in workflows. To some extent the semantics need improvement for workflows to be fully integrated into Service Chain Management and used in the same way that ERP uses its process model.

Nonetheless, this has not proved a major limitation. Instead, what has been proved limiting, and a source of frustration, has been the "rigidity" of workflows. In this respect they are better than ERP process models but not flexible enough to model the millions, if not billions, of individual customer service requests that arrive daily at companies.

For example, call a bank, insurance, health, utility or other provider with an issue that is slightly out of the ordinary and immediately you realise the person on the other side will have difficulty processing your request. What you are probably asking is deviating from what is described in the process and this is a major problem for services IT. Chapter 12 looks at the history of the workflow, emerging standards and more importantly new ways to improve workflow flexibility.

The other key area for a service enterprise to search for improvements and benefits is communications. This area has evolved significantly since the days of the telephone and fax, with a proliferation of communication means such as voice, e-mail, SMS, instant message, etc. We believe communications is untapped with regards to empowering employees and customers alike. However for that to happen, developments in personalisation and linking to context, information and, more importantly, business processes would be required. Chapter 13 discusses advances in this technology area and opportunities in unifying and personalising the communications service and experience. This chapter also plays a dual role since the service personalisation methodology discussed could also be suitable for other digital services.

Chapter 14 examines the area of Customer Analytics and Business Intelligence. The chapter goes beyond collecting and storing information to the next level of maturity in information management; to analyse and act on information to improve the operations and customer service of a service firm. Customer Analytics is often the bridge between marketing and operations; Business Intelligence can be seen as closing the feedback loop with regards to Service Chain Management by monitoring performance and supplying key indicators to improve planning and control in an enterprise.

The last chapter in this part (Chap. 15) is devoted to system implementation and the agile delivery of systems. One key principle in this area is that of incremental development and, through the engagement of customers, the validation of systems already developed at the earliest opportunity. Service Chain Management can greatly benefit from such methods. If anything, the lessons from ERP indicate that firms should avoid aiming for the "ultimate system" which increases the risk of failure, but follow instead a step-by-step, incremental approach in automating their processes.

Chapter 12
Flexible Workflows

12.1 Introduction

The concept of effective workflows is deeply ingrained in virtually every industry today. As businesses become more distributed, there is a need for massively networked workflow tools which is reflected in the emergence of the Service-Oriented Architecture paradigm. This large collection of standards brings into workflow the concept of linking together disparate Web Services to form composite applications with some integration of human processes. Most implementations of workflow tools, however, require complete adoption at multiple levels of an organisation as well as agreement in standards to enable inter-service communication in heterogeneous environments. This necessitates significant investment in software management solutions, development time and hardware requirements, all of which can lead to inflexible workflow solutions.

This chapter presents an overview of the development of workflow support systems for the last twenty years from the concept of task granularity to Web Service based workflow design and deployment. The review focuses on flexibility and dynamism in workflows in response to change and exceptions. Key elements are identified in the construction of workflows and different approaches to the design of workflow tools are introduced. The need to abstract workflows and separate design from implementation is then looked at both from a modelling and a language perspective. The chapter concludes with recommendations on potential innovation in the workflow/Web Service product space and suggests a lightweight Representational State Transfer (REST) approach. This loosely coupled approach encourages iterative development, less up front design and hence, more flexible workflows.

The chapter is structured as follows. Section 12.2 reviews the key issues in the construction of workflows and the design and deployment of support tools. Section 12.3 surveys previous work done in the field. Section 12.4 looks at contemporary approaches and introduces methods to handle deviations based on a REST approach. Section 12.5 concludes.

C. Voudouris, G. Owusu, R. Dorne, D. Lesaint, *Service Chain Management*
DOI: 10.1007/978-3-540-75504-3, ©Springer 2008

12.2 What is Workflow and Workflow Support?

A workflow is a formal, or implementation-specific, representation of a business process. Harrington defines a business process as "... any activity or group of activities that takes an input, adds value to it, and provides an output to an internal or external customer. Processes use an organisation's resources to provide definitive results." (Harrington 1991). Organisations typically comprise multiple layers of tasks and services that are co-ordinated to achieve business objectives. Taking an holistic view of organisations is therefore indispensable to understand the notions of workflow and workflow support tools.

12.2.1 Leavitt's Diamond

Leavitt's Diamond provides a good starting point to analyse business processes (Leavitt 1965). As shown in Fig. 12.1, Leavitt's Diamond separates and relates four different aspects of a process, namely, Structure, Technology, People and Task. These aspects are viewed as being integral to a process and of equal importance.

What defines a task, or activity, in a workflow depends upon the granularity at which one chooses to analyse a business process. Once the tasks are identified, an optimal task ordering must be constructed to structure the workflow using algorithms such as the Critical Path Method (DuPont 1950). The tools or technology required to support workflows is another significant component of the analysis. The analysis must also take into account the human factor by considering the people involved in the process and how they will interact with the system. Finally, it must take into account the structure or organisation which represents the set of agents involved in the process.

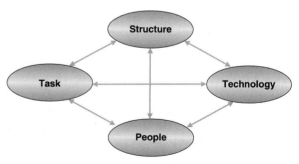

Fig. 12.1 Leavitt's Diamond

12.2.2 A Socio-Cognitive Perspective

Socio-cognitive aspects must be taken into consideration when engineering or deploying workflow technology. A workflow tool will, in some way, replace and interact with employees and customers. The task analysis will be culturally specific (Michelis and Grasso 1994) and, if too restrictive to the individuals interacting with the system, will lead to loss of motivation or abandonment of the system (Hemingway 1998). As quoted from Adams et al. (2003), "Technologies are derived from perceived needs and realised, not in isolation, but through the conventions and norms of their social milieu".

12.2.3 Agents in a Workflow

Today, more so than twenty years ago, a greater number of agents acting in workflows are computer programs or Web Services. Franklin and Glesser define an autonomous agent as a "system situated within and a part of an environment that senses that environment and acts on it" (Franklin and Graesser 1996). This definition does not take into account Web Services as they did not exist at the time of writing. To arrive at a definition of what differentiates a regular computer program from a Web Service is beyond the scope of this chapter.

12.2.4 Control Flow

Another significant aspect in workflow relates to control flow and how computer systems can support collaborative activities and their coordination. Tools that have the ability to monitor and synchronise tasks, enable parallelism and serialism, and handle dependencies and deviation (i. e., exception handling) can generate significant business benefits. For instance, parallelism increases process throughput and reduces latency; handling deviation by providing flexible recovery scenarios minimises business disruptions when tasks end unexpectedly; etc.

12.2.5 Why Are Workflow Support Tools Useful?

As discussed above, workflow support tools have the potential to improve process throughput and reduce overheads in the enterprise, leading towards higher quality of service and lower costs. Workflow tools can also suggest new ways of working to an enterprise by giving the flexibility to model, analyse, and restructure processes. For instance, analysis techniques based on formal models can reveal flaws in workflows such as deadlocks, livelocks, race conditions, unreachable states, and so on. Workflow tools with the ability to handle deviations can make processes more robust and improve the experience of individuals operating within a workflow. Finally, tools providing a suitable level of abstraction can be applied to a variety of business processes, thus allowing enterprises to recoup their investment in workflow technology.

12.3 Previous Approaches

12.3.1 Workflow Management Systems

Workflow tools truly emerged in the eighties and coincided with a move toward a paperless office. The emphasis was on document/data processing and the principle was to capture all the tasks in a process in order to create an optimal workflow. Two examples were the Poise/Polymer system and the Versatile Avionics Shop Test (VAST). Poise and VAST shared a linear view of workflows and imposed a predetermined series of actions on human operators, effectively reducing people to elements in a machine. This was a source of frustration which was compounded by inflexible interfaces and a lack of support for handling deviations.

12.3.2 Running Workflows

The nineties saw the emergence of tools designed to facilitate the running of workflows. A shift from a data-oriented to an agent communication model was deemed necessary from a socio-cognitive and workflow orchestration perspective. The Milan Conversation Model, for instance, advocated the literal capture and transmission of communication between users of a workflow system based on the principle that "any group of persons sharing a social experience, shares a language, a physical space, an agenda, ... without which no interpretation is possible" (Michelis and Grasso 1994). The mapping of face-to-face or e-mail communications was used to track a sequence in a workflow. The problem with this model was that it led to predetermined workflows. Other workflow support tools, such as InConcert (McCarthy and Sarin 1993), focused on data flow and adopted a goal orientation methodology providing the ability to link together diverse activities in order to accomplish a task.

12.3.3 Transactional Model

Up to this point, none of the workflow tools had a robust methodology for recovering from failures. The only available strategy was to express all possible points of failure in the workflow itself. While effective, this strategy can produce overly verbose and complex workflow descriptions. Utilising techniques from the transaction model in database management systems, efforts were geared towards the integration of transactional features into workflow tools (Eder and Liebhart 1996). The principle is to use a transaction run-time model to execute compensatory tasks and roll back a process when a task fails. A transactional model can also help to recover from a failure of the workflow tool itself which is essential when dealing with long-running business processes.

In a transactional model, the act of rolling back via compensatory tasks only applies to the tasks themselves. A workflow tool should not be responsible for an agent's internal roll back since this would break the principle of separation of concerns (Dijkstra 1982). In addition, the transaction model must satisfy the ACID properties, i.e., atomicity, consistency, isolation, and durability. Technically, there are two genres of recovery actions, rolling back (undo) and rolling forward (redo). In a rollback recovery, a significant recovery attempt must be made in the event of a failure when a task has dependencies within a structure. All tasks that are part of a structure and have already committed must have a compensatory action to return the process to a consistent state. In a rollforward recovery, if a task within a hierarchy has no dependencies, the remainder of the process can be executed without leaving the process in an inconsistent state. The Workflow Activity Model takes this into account (Eder and Liebhart 1995).

12.3.4 Workflow Modelling

The next evolution in workflow technology was to develop methods for modelling workflow states. Both graphical models based on bipartite graphs (Petri 1962) and algebraic models based on linear textual descriptions (Milner et al. 1992) were developed. The most significant form of graphical modelling came from an adaptation of Petri nets, known as high-level Petri nets (Riemann 1999) to model data flow, time, and task hierarchies within processes. A significant advantage of graphical models over linear models is that they can be created by non-engineers. Another advantage is that the graphical approach separates the modelling of a workflow from its implementation thus making models portable and free from vendor limitations.

12.3.5 Summary

The progression of work up to this point has been freeing elements of the business process into discrete sections. This process is continuing and set to move the abilities of workflow tools further. "The nineties will be marked by the emergence of workflow software, allowing application developers to push the business procedures out of the applications." (van der Aalst 1998). However, introducing a workflow tool should be more than implementing an electronic version of an already flawed system. If the computerisation of a workflow is merely to recreate an existing system and no time is spent on re-engineering the business process itself, one can be left with "automating a fiction" (Sheil 1983).

12.4 Contemporary Approaches

Advances in computing, network and device technologies have led towards a massively distributed style of working and new forms of interactions and collaborations. We present below the new architectural styles and approaches to workflow tools that have emerged in this context.

12.4.1 Why Enterprises Need Service-Oriented Architectures?

In traditional software development, monolithic applications are constructed to suit enterprise business needs through a slow process of requirements elicitation, system design, development, testing and deployment. This methodology leads to tightly coupled systems which require significant resources to alter when business requirements evolve. A newer approach is that of Service Oriented Architectures (SOA). In this architectural style, smaller software components are created and linked together as networked services, or Web Services. In order to facilitate communication, Web Services have well-defined interfaces known as application programming interfaces (APIs) in this context. This approach makes it possible to connect disparate systems created using different tools and languages, thus loosening the coupling between systems and enabling an agile software delivery process.

12.4.2 Workflow Specification Languages

As has been seen from earlier modelling work (e. g., Petri nets), using abstract workflow specification languages is essential to achieve platform and vendor-independence. We discuss below the design of workflow specification languages in the context of SOA and Web Services and introduce two instances, the Business Process Execution Language (BPEL) and Yet Another Workflow Language (YAWL).

12.4.2.1 Workflow Patterns

Patterns have been originally popularised in the object-oriented community by the Gang of Four book (Gamma et al. 1995). This approach seeks to factorise and express common problems and related solutions in a language-independent way as design patterns that can be reused and applied in different problem domains. Similarly to this research, Russel et al. have formalised and classified workflow patterns into five categories: Control Flow, Structural, State-Based, Advanced Branching and Synchronisation, Cancellation and Multiple Instances (Russell et al. 2003). How best to support these patterns is one of the key challenges in the design of workflow specification languages.

12.4.2.2 BPEL and YAWL

BPEL is the most popular workflow specification language in the enterprise market. It is a notation based on the Extensible Markup Language (XML) for defining business processes via Web Services (IBM et al. 2002). It features a process element that contains other elements, one of which is the concept of a *partnerLink*. This partner-Link allows the definition of other services and roles which allows messages to be passed between services. BPEL also has the concept of exception handling and falls back from exceptions defined in the XML.

One of the key advantages that BPEL offers is interoperability. BPEL is XML-based and therefore agnostic to the platform and execution engine upon which it runs. In relation to BPEL and an Enterprise Service Bus (ESB), there is the concept of *adapter* as a communication mechanism to connect disparate services. Adapters act as an abstraction layer between services. However, many application providers attach significant costs to these types of extensions.

Currently, two versions of BPEL coexist in the market place, BPEL4WS and WSBPEL 2.0. WSBPEL 2.0 is an emerging standard which has not, at time of writing, been finished. Some vendors, however, are already announcing support for WS-BPEL 2.0 in their execution engines. An important point to note about WSBPEL 2.0 is that any processes defined in BPEL4WS will not run on a WSBPEL 2.0 execution engine due to incompatibilities in the schema.

YAWL is an alternative to BPEL which is based on an extension of Petri nets (van der Aalst and ter Hofstede 2005). YAWL has been designed to support a large number of workflow patterns as well as human tasks, via a worklist mechanism. Despite these advantages, YAWL lacks industry support. As BPEL and YAWL are incompatible, the cost and complexity of migrating to YAWL would be non-trivial for enterprises that have invested in BPEL technologies.

12.4.2.3 Problems with Humans as a Component in the Infrastructure

BPEL was primarily designed for system-to-system communications, not for human-to-system communications. To overcome this limitation, current solutions use a task management service that is external to the BPEL core (Clugage et al. 2006). This service, when instantiated, hands back to the BPEL engine once the assigned task has been completed. An issue with this workaround is that human tasks do not have parity with other tasks. The other issue is that current implementations of external task lists are proprietary which kills service integration and significantly reduces their value in the SOA context.

If a BPEL process is dependant on a human component, it is possible for that process to become stuck, i. e., a process will not resume until a human agent has executed their subset of the process. Under the current BPEL specification, the only way to "unstick" a process would be to undo significant parts of the process which could result in poor performance characteristics, especially if the process is long-running. IBM and SAP BPEL have put forward an extension to WSBPEL 2.0 to address this issue called BPEL4People. BPEL4People has the concepts of activities and tasks and adds a new type of activity to BPEL called *People Activities*. Again, this presents a significant problem for adoption as other BPEL tools will have to extend their process execution engine to support People Activities.

12.4.2.4 Open Communication Pathway

A Lingua Franca is necessary for any open communication between Web Services in a SOA. Messages must pass between services and be understood by products to enable a composite application workflow framework. It is significant that Web Services communicate via an open mechanism. This levels the playing field for service developers, meaning that an individual developer is on equal terms with a major vendor. This also paves the way for a greater number of services and encourage a communication-oriented development process. As stated by Metcalfe's law, the value of a telecommunications network is proportional to the square of the number of users of the system.

The main communication mechanism for Web Services is XML (W3C 2006). XML is for the most part human readable and different dialects can be created for specific application, or service, needs. Technically, a service must parse an XML schema in order to participate in a collaboration or workflow. One issue is that XML data can sometimes be overly verbose which makes parsing slow. This has led to the increasing popularity of the Javascript Object Notation (JSON) as an alternative communication mechanism (Crockford 2006). JSON is a serialised data format that is capable of expressing the same data constructs as XML but in a far more compact manner.

12.4.3 Modern Architectural Styles

There are currently two main architectural styles for SOA, the WS-* style and the Web-Oriented Architecture/REST-Oriented Architecture style (WOA/ROA). To understand the differences between the two, it is valuable to break down the overall communication mechanisms.

12.4.3.1 WS-* Monolithic Approach

The WS-* approach consists of a multi-layer application stack, from the top down, service orchestration based on BPEL,

service definition based on the Web Services Description Language (WSDL), service discovery based on Universal Description Discovery and Integration (UDDI), messaging based on the Simple Object Access Protocol (SOAP), transport based on the Hypertext Transfer Protocol (HTTP/HTTPS), and application servers.

Orchestration of workflows in the WS-*architecture is typically managed by a BPEL execution engine. The engine parses and interprets the BPEL code to trigger events. WSDL is an XML-based format used to describe the interfaces of the services being orchestrated (W3C 2001). WSDL provides the ability to build composite applications from service descriptions without having to know or care about the way services are implemented. A WSDL file specifically contains the location of a service, the access to the service and what the service provides. It includes an abstract which defines the SOAP messages in a language agnostic manner as well as a descriptor which details the specifics of the service such as type.

UDDI is a platform-independent XML-based registry used to publish and discover Web Services (OASIS 2002). UDDI is interrogated by SOAP messages and provides access to the WSDL files describing the published Web Services. The process of selecting a service can be abstracted using an ESB. However, UDDI is not a plug and play solution for Web Services since it only describes available communication mechanisms, i. e., the composite application's logic still needs to be written around the UDDI description.

The messaging layer is implemented via SOAP (W3C 2007). Data is wrapped in an envelope with a header and body. The envelope is the root element of the data. A problem with this method is that it breaks a fundamental concept of the Web, the Uniform Resource Identifier (URI). Rather than having each service be described by a unique URI, only the base level service is addressable via SOAP and the subsequent services are addressable from that root node. The transport layer is normally based on HTTP or secure HTTP but other transport protocols may be used. The most common application servers are J2EE and .NET with J2EE having a larger share of the enterprise market thanks to popular open source products such as JBoss and GlassFish.

12.4.3.2 WS-* Standards Proliferation

Multiple WS-* standards have been rolled out as products. As many of these standards are being written by the vendors themselves, it is not necessarily in their best interest to ensure that all their products "play nicely" together. If a vendor can acquire lock-in, it will capture more of the market space and consolidate its business offerings and dominance in the product area. This fragmentation of standards and attempts at acquiring lock-in are, at their core, the complete antithesis of the promise of SOA, i. e., loosely coupled, lightweight, componentised services.

Table 12.1 lists some of the WS-* standards being used or under development. The implementation of this stack varies from vendor to vendor. To address this issue, OASIS, as of October 2006, have started to work on a reference architecture. However, difficult challenges lie ahead. As quoted from (Weerawarana et al. 2005), "there is no universally agreed standard middleware, which makes it difficult to construct applications from components that are built using different programming models ... They bring with them different assumptions about infrastructure services that are required, such as transactions and security. As a consequence, interoper-

Table 12.1 Some of the WS-* standards

Security:	WS-Federation
	WS-SecurePolicy
	WS-Security
	WS-Trust
Transaction:	WS-Addressing
	WS-AtomicTransaction
	WS-Coordination
	WS-Eventing
	WS-Notification
	WS-Transaction
Directory access:	WS-Attachments
	WS-Discovery
	WS-MetaDataExchange
	WS-Policy
Messaging:	WS-Addressing
	WS-Eventing
Reliable:	WS-Reliability
	WS-ReliableMessaging
Management:	WS-Management
	WS-ManagementCatalog

ability across distributed heterogeneous platforms such as .NET and J2EE presents a difficult problem."

12.4.3.3 WS-* vs. WOA

The other architectural style that has become the de facto standard in the Web 2.0 world and has been drawing significant attention from the enterprise community is WOA (Andrews 2005).[1] WOA is based on lightweight messaging technologies such as XML/JSON, HTTP and URI. With Silicon Valley startups pushing out products utilising SOA concepts like mashups and open APIs, one has to start to re-evaluate the heavyweight structure of current enterprise products.

Shortened development cycles, loosely coupled services and faster adoption are the promised benefits of SOA. The large number of protocols required in the WS-* approach seems, however, to contradict these precepts. From one perspective, the complexity of the WS-*application stack can be seen as giving the enterprise community the level of sophistication that it demands but from the lightweight, agile camp, it can be seen as a deliberate attempt to lock-in: "So that was a strategy tax that was imposed by the big companies on some of this technology, where they made it more complicated than it needed to be so they could sell tools." (Anderson 2006).

---

[1] Nick Gall from Gartner Research coined the term Web-Oriented Architecture

Table 12.2 From Web 1.0 to Web 2.0

Web 1.0	Web 2.0
Businesses	Community
Consuming	Contributing
Client/Server	Distributed
Ontologies	Tags
Storing	Collaborating
Roach motels	Open APIs
Eyeballs	Syndication

The WS-* monolithic SOA is designed from a pessimistic view point – the data will be in the wrong format, the service will go down. WOA is more optimistic. The service says how its data will be represented and it is the responsibility of the client or user of the service to insure that the contract is correct for its needs. WOA also has the property of asynchronous contract checking performed on the client end which provides the ability to degrade gracefully if a failure occurs. In the WS-* approach, WSDL mostly checks contract at run-time which leads to a tight coupling between services. While this would be acceptable for a behind-the-firewall deployment, this tight coupling presents issues when opening services up to the Internet.

Sun has recently proposed a new XML-based service description language as a lightweight alternative to WSDL called the Web Application Description Language (WADL) (Hadley 2006). WADL is URI-based rather than node-based. It has specific support for Create, Read, Update, Delete (CRUD) verbs in the schema which is part of the normal transaction process in the Web 2.0/Enterprise 2.0 realm.

From an architectural viewpoint, a significant difference between the WS-* and WOA styles is middleware. WS-* is centred around creating products that act as intermediaries between applications. WOA, on the other hand, is network-oriented and based on the way the Internet has been designed and is being used today in large applications for web sites that serve a significant number of users. One is reminded of the Obasanjo quote: "My website is bigger than your enterprise." (Obasanjo 2006). Although the WOA approach is early in its enterprise usage and is still lacking orchestration capabilities, it represents a significant green field development area for further research.

12.4.3.4 Not Either/Or

When evaluating the WS-*and WOA approaches to SOA and workflow, it should not be considered as an either/or choice as there is a significant difference between green field and legacy development. If an enterprise has legacy systems from a specific application vendor and this vendor has a ESB adaptor to integrate these systems into their SOA platform, this will represent a much easier migration path, whilst preserving the existing investments. However, product interoperability and agility in delivery remain primary concerns. Although the WS-*camp has more vendor support and products in the market place, WOA arguably proposes a more pragmatic roadmap to achieve the vision of SOA.

12.4.4 Recovery Mechanisms and Techniques

Recovery from deviation in a workflow is still very much at the front of support tools. The more facility a workflow tool has to recover from deviation, the more value it will bring to the enterprise and the greater satisfaction to the users of the tool. "Users are forced to work outside of the system, and/or constantly revise the static process model, in order to successfully support their activities, thereby negating the efficiency gains sought by implementing a workflow solution in the first place." (Adams et al. 1998). While building alternatives in workflow models and utilising transactional recovery models remain popular mechanisms for handling deviation, new approaches based on expert systems, data mining and genetic algorithms, appear promising.

12.4.4.1 Expert Systems

Expert systems, or knowledge-based systems, come from the realm of artificial intelligence (Buchanan and Feigenbaum 1978). In the context of a workflow tool, expert systems extend the concept of building in alternative options at specific points in the execution of a workflow. However, in this instance, the tool itself would have control, rather than embedding it within the specification. If an exception occurs, each node may have a handler which forms a list of possible choices at that point in the current execution of the workflow, i. e., a list of anticipated exceptions. In the event of an exception for which no handler exists, either a new handler may be defined or an existing one may be adapted and stored in the knowledge base for future use. Each handler then acts as a self-contained workflow for dealing with deviation at that point in the superset.

Patterns can also be established by looking at the characteristics of exceptions from different perspectives, e. g., status, activity, event, time. From this basis, a tool could attempt to define the nature of the similarity of the deviation from a conceptual hierarchy to provide weighting. The expert system could then form a decision tree to model the exception path, potentially taking into account algorithms for weighting the decision tree in relation to calculation time, in order to provide more effective exception handling.

The problem with these models is when using such a system at scale, the replication of the knowledge base will be non-trivial. Besides, the construction of such decision trees would optimally occur during run-time. If the data were constructed at compile time, the knowledge contained within such knowledge bases would become stale at run-time, particularly if such a workflow has a large number of instances. The difficulties in implementation of a complex process, with potential for a large number of knowledge base lookups to form decision trees on multiple nodes in the workflow, could prove inefficient, leading to undesirable performance characteristics.

12.4.4.2 Worklets

One implementation of the exception decision tree concept is worklets (Adams et al. 1998). Worklets are self-contained sub-processes with associated selection and exception handling rules. Worklets also have the concept of exception Ripple Down Rules for any active step in a workflow. This, in effect, is similar to the redo/undo transactional model but provides more flexibility at a finer level of granularity. In this implementation, worklets refer to three types of recoverable deviations: generic, case-dependent with a-priori knowledge, and case-dependent with no a priori knowledge.

12.4.4.3 Ripple Down Rules

In the Ripple Down Rule model (Compton and Jansen 1990), deviations are conceptually arranged in a binary tree format as shown in Fig. 12.2. This forms the basis of the expert system. Each node in the tree has a true or false option which terminates at a successful deviation solution. The refinement or revision of a deviation path can provide new solutions the next time the tree is formed. If no successful terminal node is in the tree, a new ad hoc step could be created as a new leaf in the tree to be added to the catalogue of recovery steps.

One issue with this approach is that it is dependant upon domain experts to provide ad hoc solutions in a timely manner. This might be acceptable if all the

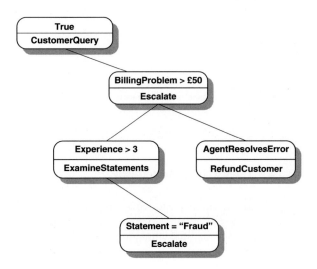

Fig. 12.2 Ripple down rules: a customer billing example

agents of the workflow are human and the workflow is non-critical. However, if some or most of the agents are Web Services, the delay would most likely cause the workflow to abort. Another issue is that, depending on the domain, a large number of deviations may have to be covered in a process. Besides, multiple recovery steps for a similar deviation may be present in the system which could lead to inefficiencies.

12.4.4.4 Data Mining

Data mining (Hartigan 1975), or knowledge discovery, is the process by which patterns are discovered in large volumes of data in an automated manner. By analysing the run-time logs of a workflow, one can derive deviations and performance characteristics. There are two perspectives from which such an analysis may be performed: structure-oriented and performance-oriented. A structure-oriented analysis will reveal modelling problems in the workflow itself, whereas a performance-oriented analysis will show deviations which may lead to bottlenecking behaviour. One can also determine through statistical analysis the frequency of similarly grouped deviations. The noise in the analysis resulting from incorrectly logged events and exceptions may however prove challenging. For example, events may occur multiple times in a process execution so deriving the point at which it occurred may lead to duplicate activities. Hidden activities, events which are not logged but form a fundamental part of the routing process, may also cause issues.

12.4.4.5 Genetic Algorithms

A more experimental approach to deviation recovery is that of genetic algorithms. Genetic algorithms can be used to generate automatically a good, or true, solution to a deviation. Experiments using local and global strategies are reported in (Alves de Medeiros et al. 2005). Local strategies were used to build optimal process models via binary relationships between events, whereas global strategies were based on a one strike search for optimal models. Local strategy cause problems as one stray event can result in damage to the results. Applying genetic algorithms in a global sense, via a Petri net, may present a more effective solution. Whilst an intriguing concept for the automation of recovery from a deviation, this work is still in early phases for adoption into an enterprise-ready solution.

12.4.4.6 Lightweight Mechanisms

Lightweight mechanisms to solve simple deviation problems remain elusive. Rather than attempting to create a highly adaptive global solution, there needs to be a solution, most likely coupled with a lightweight execution engine, that can recover from simple deviations. For instance, in a Web Services context, a tool should be capable of re-routing to an alternative service when a service goes down rather than aborting the process. It should also have the ability to monitor the response times of different Web Services and load balance accordingly.

12.5 Summary

Looking at workflow support tools, a clear progression is evident. The early tools attempted to run as much of the workflow as they could, in as controlled a manner as possible. This, as was discovered, led to overly complex and brittle processes. Tools based on WS-*or WOA/REST principles now focus on enabling workflows and connecting systems together. Although WS-*technologies have received considerable attention, the proliferation of standards and the lack of interoperability between products remain major obstacles to their adoption. The REST approach which proposes a lightweight messaging infrastructure offers a viable alternative that leading companies are already embracing. For instance, Amazon has large-scale products running on open REST APIs, the Mechanical Turk and Simple Storage Service (S3). The Google Maps API is another example of a Web Service that is used in many third-party applications and product offerings. With the trend towards decentralised, communication-enabled business processes and agile service delivery models, the ability to handle changes and exceptions will become increasingly critical. We believe the REST approach can provide a fertile ground for innovation by drawing upon technologies from the fields of Artificial Intelligence, open interoperable APIs and Data Mining.

Chapter 13
Personalised Communications

13.1 Introduction

For decades, circuit-switched telephony has been the dominant form of telecommunications at home and in the office. More recently, services such as voice over IP, instant messaging and short message services have taken centre stage with the widespread adoption of Internet, mobile and broadband technologies. To a large extent, however, these services have evolved in isolation due to the heterogeneity of legacy networks and computing infrastructures. The industry is now embracing next-generation networks (NGNs) and service delivery platforms (SDPs) as a means to unify and integrate communications with IT applications, web services and business processes.

SDPs are a style of service-oriented architecture (SOA) designed for the rapid creation and delivery of multimedia IP communications services. The underlying principle is to turn communications services into software applications that can accommodate a variety of endpoints, perform advanced signalling and media control, be context-sensitive and seamlessly integrate into IT infrastructures. SDPs encompass a range of solutions, products, technologies and standards, notably, the session initiation protocol (SIP) which is used for IP telephony, conferencing, presence, IPTV, video gaming and home appliance control.

Unified communications (UC) services promise enhanced user experience, more flexibility, and gains in personal productivity, workgroup performances and enterprise effectiveness. Still, a disciplined engineering approach is required to mitigate the risks associated to their pervasiveness and complexity. If left uncontrolled, communications services may quickly become counterproductive and lead to repeated disruptions, privacy intrusions and other undesirable side-effects in personal and professional environments. Personalisation solutions are therefore critical to let endusers as well as subscribers (i. e., customers), designers and providers co-configure and control the behaviour and presentation of "their" service.

Personalisation has received a lot of attention in the telecommunications domain over the years. In particular, significant efforts have been devoted to call control in plain old telephony service (POTS) and intelligent network (IN) en-

C. Voudouris, G. Owusu, R. Dorne, D. Lesaint, *Service Chain Management*
DOI: 10.1007/978-3-540-75504-3, ©Springer 2008

vironments. The main outcome of this work has been the conceptualisation and standardisation of call control features (ITU 1993, 1997) and a deeper understanding of the complex challenges inherent to feature engineering such as the management of feature interactions. Although technologies like SIP provide the foundations for modular, compositional and user-centric SDPs, methods and tools for developing feature-oriented SIP-based SDPs and robust personalisation capabilities are lacking while current solutions remain fragmented and limited in scope.

This chapter revisits feature-based personalisation in the context of SIP-based communications services. Section 13.2 first provides an overview of SDPs. Section 13.3 introduces SIP and reviews the main technologies available for creating and orchestrating SIP-based services. Section 13.4 then discusses the issues relating to feature-based personalisation and the principles and elements underpinning feature-oriented SIP-based architectures. Section 13.5 concludes.

13.2 Service Delivery Architectures and Platforms

SDPs are a new style of architecture and platform enabling wireline and wireless carriers, Internet and application service providers, independent software vendors and systems integrators to offer enhanced real-time IP voice, video and data services to their customers. This section reviews the underlying design principles and the range of services supported by SDPs.

13.2.1 UC Services

Beyond basic telephony, SDPs aim to facilitate the creation of UC services, i. e., network- and device-agnostic services blending voice, video and data and integrating into web- and service-oriented architectures. This new breed of services spans over various technology and market segments (Elliot and Lock 2007; Herrell 2006):

- *Live communications* unifying voice over IP (VoIP), video IP telephony, instant messaging (IM) and push-to-talk,
- *Multimodal conferencing* bridging audio, video and web-based conference sessions,
- *Unified messaging* unifying e-mail, voice-mail, fax and short message service (SMS),
- *Enhanced consumer communications services* such as location-based services, IPTV, gaming and home appliance control, and
- *Enhanced business communications services* integrating communications with enterprise applications and processes (e. g., automatic call distribution, contextual presence lists, flexible media and conferencing switching) or enriching in-

formation and collaboration tools (e. g., workspaces, discussion forums, blogs and wikis) with communications capabilities.

UC services are meant to accommodate a variety of endpoints and access network technologies, to perform advanced signalling and media control, to be personalisable and context-sensitive, and to seamlessly interoperate with web services and capabilities, as well as business and operational support systems (BSS/OSS). We discuss each of these concerns below.

13.2.1.1 Access Convergence

The shift towards NGNs and SDPs is primarily motivated by the need to support personal and device mobility. The ambition is to deliver UC services across fixed and mobile access networks (e. g., Tier 1 carrier networks, DSL, cable, Wi-Fi, 2.5G, 3G) and make them accessible through a variety of devices (e. g., corded/cordless handsets, mobile phones, smart phones, personal digital assistants, ultra mobile PCs, laptops, PCs, set-top boxes) and clients (e. g., softphones, UC desktop applications). Popular examples of converged services include find-me/follow-me and mid-call-move.

13.2.1.2 Advanced Signalling and Media Control

Beyond convergence, UC services add value to the basic connection services by performing advanced signalling and media control ranging from the simplest (e. g., do-not-disturb) to the most elaborate (e. g., mobile video sharing with audio conference). To fulfil their role, service applications need to access and control media resources during sessions. For instance, third-party call control applications rely on media servers to bridge participants; interactive voice response applications control media servers to enable voice prompts and auto-attendant capabilities and credit-card calling services are based on dual-tone multi-frequency (DTMF) detection and request media servers to listen for DTMF key inputs and act accordingly.

13.2.1.3 Personalisation and Context-Awareness

Support for personalisation and context-awareness are key attributes of UC services too. The way humans handle interactions typically depend on the type and context of the interaction and the identity and profile of participants. To this effect, UC services need real-time access to static or contextual information. Static data relate to the profile of session participants (e. g., addresses, age, skills, hobbies) and include service-specific operational parameters (e. g., a list of addresses barred by a call-screening service, or a media file played by a music-on-hold service). Static data are provisioned off-line and fetched from dedicated IT applications and systems such as directories and calendars. Context data relate to the type of session (e. g., text chat, or long-distance call) and the situation of participants (e. g., presence status, location, or activity). Context data are acquired through context servers such as home location registers and presence servers.

13.2.1.4 Integration and Service-Orientation

Beyond signalling and media control, UC services may involve web-based user interaction. For instance, multimodal conference services provide a range of web features including participant dial-out, instant chat, selective muting, on-line document sharing and edition, record and replay functions, and so on. More generally, UC services must interwork with IT applications or web services to extend the reach of business processes but also to integrate with BSS/OSS such as customer relationship management and billing systems.

For instance, a field force management system may invoke an intelligent notification and routing service to contact the right employee (e. g., a field engineer, a back-up engineer or a supervisor) based on business rules (e. g., skill-, role- and distance-based routing, with or without escalation and follow-up) and using the most appropriate channel (e. g., VoIP, SMS) and method (e. g., broadcast, personalised) when exception conditions (e. g., the delayed arrival of an engineer on customer premises), alerts (e. g., a power outage) or special events (e. g., an assistance request from a team member) occur.

13.2.2 The Principles and Elements of SDPs

The SDP paradigm is broad and encompasses a range of standards, technologies, products and solutions (Elliot et al. 2006b). This section discusses the design principles and implementation elements common to SDPs as summarised in Fig. 13.1.

13.2.2.1 Protocol and Architecture Layering

SDPs are based on IP networks embracing the IP reference model and protocol stack. The IP model clearly separates the service application, transport and network layers. This separation allows to insulate the service communication logic implemented within applications from transport and network technicalities. It also allows to use different transport protocols such as the transmission control protocol (TCP/IP) or the user datagram protocol (UDP) in combination with application-level protocols such as SIP, the hypertext transfer protocol (HTTP) and the simple object access protocol (SOAP).

Operators and providers also implement horizontal control layers to delineate the access network from their core network and service application layer. Control layers organise elements such as session border controllers and media gateways to manage the interconnection and interoperability of applications and endpoints

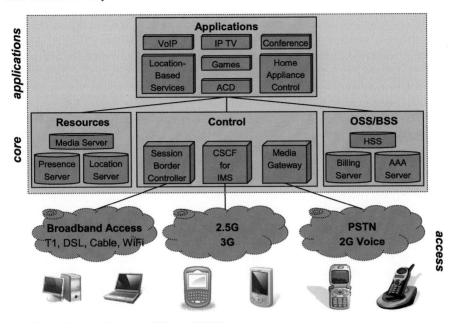

Fig. 13.1 A high-level view on SDPs and NGNs

across administrative domains and heterogeneous access network technologies. The IP multimedia subsystem framework (IMS) designed by the 3rd Generation Partnership Project (3GPP) proposes an architectural blueprint for NGN control layers (Poikselka 2006). The IMS is based on SIP and has been endorsed by many vendors, providers and operators including BT for its 21st Century Network (Crane 2005).

13.2.2.2 Capabilities and Application-Level Protocols

As discussed above, support for advanced signalling and media control, personalisation, contextualisation and seamless IT integration are the main challenges when designing UC SDPs. All design choices must also be balanced against stringent requirements concerning the quality and security of communications (e. g., minimising delays and jitter, preventing denial-of-service attacks), the flexibility, scalability, resilience and manageability of platforms and the overall impact on capital and operational expenditure.

The approach that prevails draws on a separation of concerns and service-orientation principles. SDPs embrace a modular architecture style which decouples service applications from the basic capabilities (media servers, registrars, presence servers, etc.) and support systems (BSS/OSS). This decoupling relies on the adoption of standard interfaces and application layer protocols to manage their interactions. Some proposals such as the 3GPP IMS also include dedicated capabilities to control the access to service applications and their orchestration within administrative domains.

SIP is the predominant application layer protocol used in SDPs to initiate, modify and terminate multimedia sessions (see Sect. 13.3.1). SIMPLE (SIP for IM and presence leveraging extensions) is another popular protocol based on SIP which supports instant messaging and lets applications register for presence information and receive notifications. SDPs leverage many other formats and protocols used by applications to access and control specific resources including VoiceXML to specify interactive voice dialogues and DIAMETER to support authentication, authorisation and accounting operations.

13.2.2.3 Service Creation and Integration

SDPs make extensive use of application programming interfaces (APIs) and domain-specific languages (DSLs) to facilitate the creation of UC services. The objective is to bridge network and information technologies and reach out to a broad developer base by letting independent software vendors and open source communities contribute innovative, standards-based communications services. APIs and DSLs effectively turn communications services into software applications and insulate developers from low-level protocol technicalities. Developers can then concentrate on the logic of their service and rely on familiar programming languages and software development kits to design, program, test and deploy them.

Many APIs and DSLs are for instance available for creating pure and hybrid SIP applications (see Sect. 13.3.3). SIP application server vendors are particularly active in this space and strive to provide converged products integrating SIP into the realm of IT platforms (e. g., J2EE, .NET), protocols (e. g., HTTP, SOAP, Remote Method Invocation or RMI), APIs (HTTP servlets, Enterprise Java Beans or EJBs, web services) and languages (e. g., Java, C#, Business Process Execution Language or BPEL). Consortia like the Parlay group with the Parlay X initiative are also pushing for standardisation through the specification of APIs and web services exposing core communications services and capabilities such as call control, SMS and location. System integrators, service providers and operators also embrace the trend by popularising the concept of network mashups such as BT with its Web21C mashup platform.

13.2.2.4 Service Orchestration and Personalisation

The ability to modularise and compose web services on-demand using business process orchestration technologies such as BPEL is one of the benefits of SOAs (see Chap. 12). Likewise, SDPs aim to facilitate the componentisation and composition of communications services. Beyond application reuse, the main objective is to enable personalisation, i. e., to let users and subscribers pre-configure the run-time behaviour and presentation of their service by specifying the logic governing the selection and orchestration of primitive UC applications.

This approach assumes run-time capabilities to orchestrate the invocation of applications consistently with stakeholders requirements. SIP itself has built-in request routing mechanisms to compose distributed applications at session setup and modify compositions as sessions progress. Various routing APIs and scripting languages leverage these mechanisms and enable programming and executing the orchestration logic of SIP applications deployed to the same application server (see Sect. 13.3.4). Other approaches address orchestration at the architectural level. The IMS control layer, for instance, is built around a SIP routing capability that orchestrates applications deployed within a domain of control.

13.3 SIP Technologies

This section provides an overview of SIP and reviews the main technologies available for creating, deploying and orchestrating SIP-based UC services.

13.3.1 An Overview of SIP

SIP is an application layer signalling control protocol used to establish, modify and terminate multimedia sessions (Rosenberg et al. 2002; Johnston 2003; Sparks 2007). It is text-based, transactional and can be transported unreliably with UDP or reliably with TCP. SIP itself carries the session description protocol (SDP), the protocol which endpoints use to describe their receive capabilities (e. g., codecs, ports) and negotiate media based on an offer/answer model. SIP also relies on the real-time transport protocol (RTP) to carry text, voice, video and data during sessions.

The SIP specification defines the protocol itself together with an abstract communications architecture (Rosenberg et al. 2002). A SIP architecture comprises user agents, back-to-back user agents, registrars, redirect servers and proxy servers. User agents are the endpoints initiating and terminating dialogs. Back-to-back user agents have the ability to take part in different dialogs and to act as endpoints in multi-party sessions. Registrars and redirect servers provide location and redirection services to support mobility. Proxies are responsible for routing messages between, and on behalf of, user agents. All these elements communicate point-to-point by exchanging SIP messages during sessions.

13.3.1.1 Dialogs and Transactions

SIP defines dialogs in terms of request-response transactions between user agents. To initiate a dialog, a user agent sends an *INVITE* request encapsulating a target address in its *Request-URI*[1] field. Once located and reached, the recipient sends back zero or more provisional responses before issuing a final response indicating

---

[1] SIP Uniform Resource Indicator

its acceptance or rejection of the invitation. The client acknowledges the response, which establishes or terminates the dialog. If the dialog is established, user agents directly communicate using RTP. They may renegotiate media through additional *INVITE* transactions, e. g., to add a video channel. Eventually, one of the agents terminates the dialog by sending a *BYE* request.

As shown above, SIP decomposes every dialog into two stages starting with the initial *INVITE* transaction and continuing with zero or more *INVITE* or *BYE* transactions. At each stage, the route connecting user agents is fixed and adjacent entities maintain a client/server relationship on a transaction-by-transaction basis. A proxy acts as a server for its upstream neighbour, that is, the entity from which it receives the request, and as a client for its downstream neighbour, that is, the entity to which it forwards the request.

13.3.1.2 Dynamic Message Routing

SIP allows user agents and proxies to control the construction and evolution of the path followed by messages during dialogs. First of all, an originating user agent can specify a route by encapsulating a sequence of proxy URIs in the initial *INVITE* request starting, for instance, with the URI of an outbound server. The request is then routed to the first proxy in the sequence. Before forwarding it to the second proxy, the latter removes itself from the route. It may also prepend new elements at its discretion by adding, for instance, the URI of an inbound server. The process iterates until the whole route is unfolded at which point the request is routed to the end-point matching the *Request-URI*.

Proxies also influence the paths taken by responses and subsequent requests. A proxy can record itself on the response path by adding its URI to the *Via* header field of the initial *INVITE* request. Such proxies are called transaction-stateful. A proxy can also record itself on the path of subsequent requests by adding its

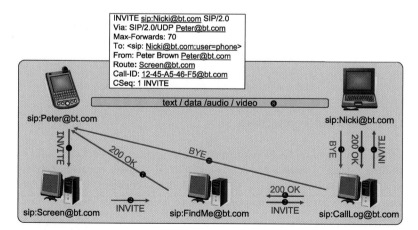

Fig. 13.2 Message routing in a SIP session

URI to a *Record-Route* header field. Such proxies are called dialog-stateful. Figure 13.2 shows the routing of messages in a dialog involving different types of proxies.

13.3.1.3 Back-to-Back User Agents

Back-to-back user agents can bridge multiple dialogs by taking on different user agent roles in each dialog, i. e., the caller or the callee. The way they bridge dialogs is unconstrained. They can therefore be used to emulate dialog-stateful proxies or deliver advanced functionalities such as mid-call-move and conferencing.

13.3.2 SIP Deployments

The SIP specification defines by the means of finite state machines the client and server behaviour of user agents and proxies for handling *INVITE* and non-*INVITE* transactions. It also describes how these elements should manage the lower layers of the protocol stack (see Fig. 13.3). However, it imposes few restrictions on the way they generate and service requests. For instance, servers can choose from a variety of responses to service *INVITE* requests such as *180 Ringing* or *486 Busy Here*. They can apply different routing policies when forwarding requests, e. g., by retargeting messages to multiple addresses through sequential or parallel forking. They can also modify the content of messages, e. g., by adding non-standard header fields to communicate private signals to other entities.

The SIP specification does not impose any restrictions either on the granularity, implementation and organisation of SIP elements or the routing logic applied within a domain of control. This makes SIP a very versatile protocol opened to a variety

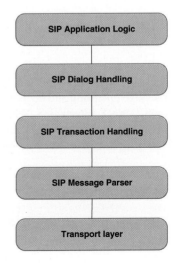

Fig. 13.3 The SIP stack

of implementation technologies and deployment environments. At one end of the spectrum, SIP is suitable for deployments in decentralised environments. SIP may indeed be viewed as an hybrid peer-to-peer protocol since most call signalling (i.e., call initiation, progress and termination) is handled between endpoints. What remains centralised are the location and redirection functions. Recent proposals leverage peer-to-peer technology to alleviate the need for centralised registrars (Bryan and Lowekamp 2007). Such extensions enable SIP to operate in deployments such as small offices, disconnected or ad hoc communications environments, emergency networks, clusters of consumer electronic devices in home networks, and globally decentralised environments such as the Internet.

SIP is equally well-suited for environments where session control and service logic must be centralised. This is required, for instance, by network operators and service providers to manage and monetise their services (Fischl and Tschofenig 2007). As discussed in Sect. 13.2.2, such environments demand open, service-oriented SDPs with embedded orchestration capabilities. In this context, the dynamic routing mechanisms of SIP and the ability to chain proxies between endpoints provide a basic method for composing service applications behaving as proxies – a method known as composition-by-proxying.

A more elaborate method consists of constructing chains that alternate service applications and routing applications. In this way, routing applications are in a position to drive the chaining of service applications. The type (i.e., proxy or back-to-back user agent) and signalling behaviour of all these elements is critical to ensure an orderly routing and the overall quality of communications sessions (Steinmann 2007). In peer-to-peer and proxy-based architectures for instance, the principled separation between signalling and media in SIP ensures that media travels on the most direct route between endpoints while the ability of endpoints to negotiate codecs eliminates the need for transcoding. However, these assumptions are no longer true in architectures based on back-to-back user agents.

13.3.3 SIP Application Creation

SIP implementations for devices and servers expose SIP stacks through high-level APIs or DSLs which abstract away the low-level operations relating to transport, message encoding and decoding, and transaction and dialog management. The style of SIP stack interfacing, API- or DSL-based, and the choice of language implementation technology offer different trade-offs between abstraction, expressiveness, safety, performances and resource control (Burgy et al. 2004).

13.3.3.1 SIP DSLs

SIP scripting languages are the main form of DSLs for SIP services. They allow to program small increments of functionality by the means of scripts combining conditions and actions. Conditions refer to session data such as caller identifier or time of day, whereas actions map to SIP operations such as message proxying or rejection. Scripts are uploaded to network elements and interpreted by embedded scripting engines at run time. Scripting involves filtering, prioritising and firing scripts by evaluating triggering conditions and predefined priorities whenever session events occur. Examples of scripting languages include CPL – an XML-based language for call control services (Lennox et al. 2004), LESS – an extension of CPL targeting endpoint services (Wu and Schulzrinne 2002), and MSPL – Microsoft's SIP processing language.

13.3.3.2 SIP APIs

SIP APIs are the main alternative to scripting languages. Inspired by HTTP servlet and EJB technologies, examples include the SIP servlet API (JCP 2003) and the JAIN SIP API (JCP 2001). The SIP servlet API, for instance, is used for programming and deploying servlet classes to containers. It follows an event-based programming model and exposes methods to handle the reception, proxying, and creation of SIP messages. It also provides classes to process message contents such as header fields or session description data, and to manage dialogs and sessions, e. g., for storing and retrieving state information. A significant benefit of the container approach lies in the ability to program converged applications interacting through SIP and other protocols such as HTTP, SOAP and RMI.

13.3.4 SIP Application Orchestration

SIP APIs and DSLs leave at the discretion of developers to decide how applications influence sessions and, in particular, route messages. If the routing logic is scattered across applications in a given domain, no control can be asserted over their composition without a concerted effort from all the parties involved in service creation. This goes against the precept of SDPs to enable third-party service creation and profile-based routing. To ensure consistency, a holistic approach is required that addresses and separates routing from other concerns. APIs and capabilities dedicated to routing have then been developed to complement SIP APIs and DSLs.

13.3.4.1 SIP Routing APIs

The latest specification of the SIP servlet API introduces a separate router programming interface (JCP 2007). This API provides deployers with a standard, non-proprietary mechanism to invoke SIP servlets written by unrelated parties. Routers programmed with the interface allow real-time or operational control over the invocation of servlets and the ordering of invocations. Servlet selection and composition rules are then automatically enforced with the added benefit that applications can determine on whose behalf, i. e., the caller or the callee, they are being invoked.

13.3.4.2 SIP Routing Capabilities

The IMS proposes a dedicated SIP server, known as serving-call state control function (S-CSCF), to orchestrate the invocation of applications based on user profiles (Poikselka 2006). Profiles are stored in home subscriber servers (HSS) and contain XML-encoded filter criteria. A filter criterion consists amongst other things of an application server address, a trigger point and a priority. The S-CSCF downloads user profiles at registration time and evaluates filter criteria to route SIP requests through applications in the right order. Figure 13.4 gives an example of orchestration in the IMS.

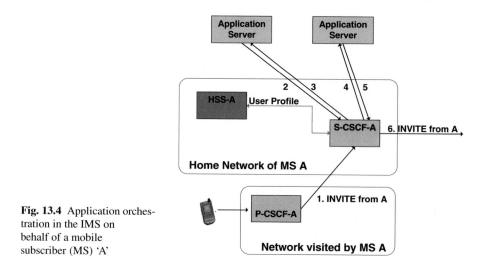

Fig. 13.4 Application orchestration in the IMS on behalf of a mobile subscriber (MS) 'A'

13.4 Communications Personalisation and Feature-Oriented Engineering

Features are fundamental building blocks for engineering personalisable services. While existing SIP technologies and SDP blueprints go some way to support personalisation, none embrace a principled feature-oriented engineering approach. This section revisits feature-based personalisation in the context of SIP services and SDPs and introduces elements of a feature engineering methodology.

13.4.1 Feature-Based Personalisation

Personalisation refers to the process whereby individuals (e. g., subscribers, end-users) configure the behaviour of a service by activating or deactivating primitive functionalities known as *features*. For instance, telephony services are personalised by activating call control features like caller-ID or call-pickup at subscription time. Once activated, features execute automatically (e. g., call-screening) or involve user interaction during sessions (e. g., mid-call-move). Personalisation is not necessarily a one-shot process and may be carried out multiple times during the lifetime of a service subscription. In any case, dedicated interfaces, languages and systems are required to let users configure their service. We list below the main usage requirements on such capabilities:

- *Feature selection*: Users have to select from their providers' catalogue the features that best meet their needs.
- *Feature parameterisation*: Some features need run-time access to operational data, part of which may originate from users, e. g., a call-divert feature assumes a redirection address.
- *Feature composition*: Features, taken individually, cannot suffice to address all the concerns of a user. Therefore, users must have the flexibility to activate multiple features, e. g., log all incoming calls and welcome all callers with voice announcements.
- *Feature sequencing*: Some feature compositions may lead to undesirable service behaviours. In the context of communications sessions, users may wish to specify a chronological ordering in the processing of features, e. g., screen calls, before diverting them.
- *Contextualisation*: Different situations demand different service behaviours. Rather than having to repeatedly activate or deactivate features, users should have the flexibility to program and formulate conditions on the activation of features. Conditions may refer to intrinsic session characteristics such as content (e. g., audio, video), media (e. g., fixed, mobile), type (e. g., local, long-distance), discussion topic, participant identities, devices, status (e. g., busy) and roles (e. g., caller, chairperson) or to extrinsic characteristics relating to the time of a session, participant locations, presence status (e. g., 'be right back'), activity (e. g., seminar), role (e. g., project manager), skills, interests, etc.
- *Preferences*: Allowing users to compose features or request different service behaviours for different contexts can be a source of inconsistencies if features conflict or contexts overlap, e. g., 'call-divert at lunch time' and 'do-not-disturb on Fridays.' If so, user preferences may be leveraged to resolve inconsistencies.
- *Priorities*: Personalisation is not the prerogative of end-users as service subscribers and any third-party in general may have usage requirements too. For instance, the line manager of an employee may impose that he be reachable by customers every morning or a company regulation may bar international calls. Entitlements and priorities may be exploited to manage conflicting viewpoints.

To sum up, a service configuration language should support the selection, parameterisation, composition, sequencing and contextualisation of features. It should also accommodate preferences and priorities to manage inconsistent requirements. Since features are commonly described by trigger-response patterns, one approach consists of designing imperative languages around rule-like constructs allowing users to guard primitive call control actions with context conditions. Examples of this approach for the configuration of SIP services include CPL and LESS (see Sect. 13.3.3).

An alternative is to design declarative logic-based languages supported by automated reasoning tools. In this case, user requirements are specified as goals which inference systems verify and refine into processable service configurations. Examples of this approach for SIP services include the work of Reiff-Marganiec and Turner on policies (Reiff-Marganiec and Turner 2002, 2003, 2004). Whatever the implementation technology, the design of a configuration language is intimately tied to the way features are modularised and compose at run time in the SDP. The management of feature interactions in particular deserves special attention as discussed below.

13.4.2 Feature-Oriented Architectures

Features are ideal component abstractions to modularise application architectures. Conceptually, a feature is an increment of functionality which, once activated, modifies the basic service behaviour in systematic ways (e. g., call-forward-unconditional) or non-systematic ways (e. g., call-divert-on-busy). Because features are meant to be easy to understand and operate by users, they should be fine-grained and orthogonal functionalities. They should also be easily combinable to provide users with the maximum flexibility when configuring their service. The engineering of feature-oriented architectures enabling on-demand feature composition seems therefore a logical approach to the personalisation of communications services.

13.4.2.1 Feature Interaction

One of the challenges in compositional feature-based designs is the management of feature interactions (Calder et al. 2003). Stated informally, a feature interaction is "some way in which a feature modifies or influences the behaviour of another feature in generating the system's overall behaviour" (Bond et al. 2004). The sources of interactions are many and relate to resource sharing (e. g., features sharing an audio channel), signal overloading (i. e., common signals being used for different purposes), the different ways common conditions can be handled (e. g., call-divert and call-waiting on busy), contradictory intentions or expectations from session participants, and other factors.

A systematic methodology is therefore needed to manage feature interactions, that is, to detect them, to discriminate between those that are desirable and those that are not, and to enable the former while preventing the latter, at design time, configuration time or else at run time. We provide below an overview of distributed feature composition (DFC) – a virtual network architecture specifically designed for feature modularity, compositionality and end-to-end feature interaction management (Jackson and Zave 1998, 2003).

13.4.2.2 DFC

DFC comes with its own signalling and media protocols. It applies a composition-by-proxying style and uses routers to invoke the features subscribed by participants. Like the IMS, the DFC routing method sets up dialogs by chaining run-time entities, known as boxes, between endpoints. In addition, it logically partitions every dialog into a source region and a target region, each region comprising one or more contiguous zones. A source (respectively, target) zone is a sequence of feature boxes subscribed by the same address in the source (resp., target) region. DFC routers act as proxies for boxes and reinitialise the route whenever a zone has to be created following a change of region or source/target address. If so, the route is set to the sequence of feature box types (FBTs) to which the address has subscribed. This is the mechanism by which subscribers control the setup of dialogs in DFC networks.

DFC imposes integrity rules on subscriptions to ensure an orderly routing, notably to avoid loops and multiple occurrences of feature boxes. DFC can also accommodate constraints formulated by designers over feature routing orderings. Both rules and constraints are enforced off-line on a subscription-by-subscription basis. The DFC architecture, which is formally specified, serves as a meta-model to represent and reason about rules and constraints and ultimately ensure that every configured subscription is 'interaction-free.' Since feature interactions depend on the type and behaviour of features as well as on the composition method, the DFC architecture introduces and maps various classes of entities including boxes, box types, addresses, features, interaction constraints and subscriptions – see Jackson and Zave (2003) for a formal description.

To uncover feature interactions, designers have to analyse all pairs of FBTs in each region and determine those that are prone to interactions. For each pair, this involves determining which routing order, if any, could lead to an interaction during a session. Any uncovered interaction is then resolved, i. e., avoided or enabled according to its desirability, by formulating a precedence constraint between the two FBT (Zave 2003). Although the scope of the resolution is limited to subscriptions and remains relative to the knowledge encoded by designers, the method is safe and computationally tractable. Overall, this approach enables to reconcile the sequencing preferences expressed by subscribers, the feature interaction constraints formulated by designers and the integrity rules inherent to DFC routing.

13.4.2.3 Towards SIP-based Feature-Oriented Architectures

Virtual architectures with built-in support for feature interaction management such as DFC are attractive in the perspective of personalisation. Yet, no such architecture exists for SIP services and significant discrepancies exist between SIP and DFC. Besides, the specification of the DFC architecture is purely declarative and does not prescribe any particular method to compute 'interaction-free' subscriptions, to reason about interaction constraints, or to handle communication requirements in general.

These problems are reminiscent of knowledge-based configuration tasks arising in product assembly or web service composition domains and for which effective formalisms and techniques have been developed, notably, constraint-based configuration logic systems (Junker and Mailharro 2003; Albert et al. 2005). These systems provide powerful solving methods such as constraint propagation, classification, inheritance, search, and explanations. As significant, they can also be used to incorporate extensions concerning the design of feature catalogues, the integration of context information and the management of subscription preferences and priorities.

13.5 Summary

The shift towards UC is underway with promising applications emerging for business customers (Elliot et al. 2006a; Elliot 2007b). At this stage, return on investment remains difficult to quantify due to limited experience and a lack of success metrics, e. g., how to measure the impact of communications services on human latency in business processes? Still, organisations cannot afford not to invest in UC for risk of losing competitive advantage. Pilots and trials seem therefore the most pragmatic route to assess the benefits of migrating from siloed communications to UC. Above all, developing a vision for how UC can improve the way employees, customers and partners interact is paramount (Elliott 2007a).

From a technology perspective, SIP is predominant. While Internet and application service providers such as Skype and Google have built their success on proprietary protocols in the consumer space, this lock-in approach seems unlikely to attract small and large enterprises. By comparison, there is now a wide variety of SIP applications, devices and platforms available from open source companies (e. g., Asterix, Pingtel), vendors (e. g., Microsoft, IBM), network equipment manufacturers (e. g., Cisco, Alcatel) and device manufacturers (e. g., Nokia, Eriksson) – see (Elliot et al. 2006b) for a comprehensive survey. Likewise, network operators and service providers strive to implement SIP SDPs in their networks consistently with standards such as the 3GPP IMS.

While these actors pursue different strategies to gain market dominance, it is worth recalling that the Internet Engineering Task Force (IETF) is the 'SIP stronghold.' Backed-up by academic and open source communities, the IETF has been driving the evolution of SIP standards with a relentless emphasis on interoperability since the inception of SIP. The situation observed in the SOA/web service space where standards are proliferating, yet non-interoperability between commercial products is the norm (see Chap. 12), seems a remote prospect in the UC/SIP domain. Many technical challenges lie ahead, however, to build SIP-based service-oriented delivery platforms with built-in support for personalisation and contextualisation. Against this background, this chapter has highlighted the need for feature-oriented architectures which are designed for compositionality and the analysis and management of interactions using formal reasoning.

Chapter 14
Predictive Customer Analytics and Real-Time Business Intelligence

14.1 Introduction

Customers should be at the heart of any business. In order to improve processes with customer interaction, businesses have introduced customer relationship management systems. These systems collect large volumes of data about customers which contain valuable information that can allow a business to improve its customer relationships and services. Typically, customer analytics focus on reporting what has happened. However, in order to become pro-active and truly shape the future of a business, it is important to predict what customers want and how they will react. In addition to understanding customers, it is paramount for any enterprise to understand how its business has performed at any given time in the past, now, and in the future. Business Intelligence applications available today focus very much on past performance. However, it is becoming essential that not only is the analysis of business performance done on real-time data, but also actions in response to analysis results can be performed in real time and instantaneously change business process parameters.

Modern businesses gather vast amounts of data about their customers including the use of their products and resources. The computerisation of all aspects of our daily life and the ever-growing use of the Internet make it even easier to collect and store data. Intelligent data analysis (IDA) aims at making use of collected data, turning it into information, and finally into action. Therefore, IDA goes further than simple data mining approaches because it also considers the suitability of the created solutions in terms of usability, comprehension, simplicity, and cost (Berthold and Hand 1999). The "intelligence" in IDA comes from the expert knowledge that can be integrated in the analysis process, the knowledge-based methods used for analysis, and the new knowledge created and communicated by the analysis process.

IDA means combining process knowledge with the collected data. Learning systems based on IDA methods can continuously optimise processes and provide new knowledge about business processes. IDA is therefore an important aspect in modern knowledge management and business intelligence.

C. Voudouris, G. Owusu, R. Dorne, D. Lesaint, *Service Chain Management*
DOI: 10.1007/978-3-540-75504-3, ©Springer 2008

Traditionally, experts are required to run an IDA process. However, the ever-growing need for business automation requires support for non-experts – for instance, in the form of data analysis tools that can run largely unsupervised. IDA capabilities have to be engineered into analytical applications such as business intelligence platforms, customer relationship management (CRM) systems, etc. This requires a certain level of automation in order to make IDA available to domain experts who are not necessarily expert analysts.

An example of such a system is SPIDA (Nauck et al. 2003). SPIDA can automatically build predictive models from data, monitor their performance, rebuild them if required, and provide them as Java code for implementation in applications. However, if we really want to turn such sophisticated technology into a commodity in a business user's tool box, we must take the technology one step further. The technology must be wrapped into user interfaces that focus on the business problem rather than the technology and that are easy to use. Various pointers on such attempts can be found in the remaining sections.

The paper is divided into two parts. The first one deals with techniques for customer analytics – in particular, how to predict customer events like churn and how to find and analyse drivers for customer satisfaction and loyalty. The second part describes the more general area of real-time business intelligence comprising a consolidated semantic data layer, business performance frameworks, how to learn relationships among performance measures and how to make use of these relationships in what-if analysis, business target optimisation and performance prediction.

14.2 Customer Analytics

Customer analytics is essentially concerned with analyzing data and requires standard techniques from areas like statistics (Sheskin 2003), data mining (Fayyad et al. 1996), machine learning (Mitchell 1997) and IDA (Berthold and Hand 1999).

Due to a lack of expertise and tools, data analysis is often done in a too simple or even naive way. Linear models are the most frequently used analysis methods because they are easy to understand and readily available. In many methods from linear statistics, there are implicit assumptions about mutually independent variables and normally distributed values – both are typically not realistic in real-world problems. Linear models cannot take compensatory or reinforcing effects into account. Especially in customer analytics, we observe different types of dependencies among all variables and these dependencies are often non-linear in nature.

Non-linear models are powerful but as mathematical function they are typically unidirectional, i. e., they cannot be inverted. This means that they can only be used to compute the impact on one or more previously selected target variables when some independent variables or drivers change. However, in a typical business scenario we need to understand the effects on all variables. In the next two sub-sections we examine two customer analytics scenarios – predicting customer events and analyzing customer satisfaction. We describe the use of multi-dimensional probabilistic models that are not restricted by linear dependencies, global independence assumptions and unidirectionality. A more detailed description can be found in Nauck et al. (2006).

14.2.1 Predicting Customer Events

Customer service is an important differentiator for service-oriented businesses, such as, for example, telecommunication companies. It is important to understand the contact history between customers and business in order to identify customers who are likely to churn, rescue customers who are under stress due to failed processes, or contact the right customers for cross-selling or up-selling opportunities.

As an example, we see how we can use hidden Markov models (HMM) (Rabiner and Juang 1986) for making time-stamped event predictions. Markov models represent a family of stochastic methods focussed on the analysis of temporal sequences of discrete states. In traditional first-order HMMs, the states are hidden from observation but each of them emits a number of observable variables which could take either discrete or continuous values. As in all Markov models, the current state of an HMM depends only on its previous state which means no prior history of sequence evolution has any effect on the current state. An HMM is fully described by its parameters which are the transition probabilities between hidden states and the probabilities or probability densities of the emission of observables.

Once trained, an HMM can be used for a variety of applications, wherever sequential data and its future evolution are in question. HMMs have started to be appreciated in business analytics. Recent cross-sale models include HMM as one of the most successful approaches for recommending products to those customers who are most likely to buy them given their recent purchases (Li et al. 2005).

HMMs can be used to solve the much more general problem of customer life cycle modelling where the distinctions between hidden states are less sharp and the observables are available mostly in a continuous form that is difficult to process. It assumes that a customer develops a variable behaviour path which starts when he subscribes to a service offered by a business and ends when he decides to cancel the service. The model assumes that customer events or experiences represent observable customer variables generated from unknown (hidden) behavioural states in which the customers find themselves in. The model assumption is that the customers, who behave similarly, i. e., are in the same hidden behavioural state, have the same distribution of the likely events/experiences, i. e., have the same distribution of emission probabilities in the visible states.

In addition to this general analysis of the population of customers, an HMM can be also applied to a single customer, for example, to analyse the churn risk, predict the probability for any other observable customer event or even estimate the time to a particular event.

14.2.2 Customer Satisfaction and Loyalty

Many companies regularly conduct customer satisfaction surveys to understand customer attitudes towards their products, services, and the companies' interaction with the customer. Knowing about customer satisfaction (attitude) and customer loyalty (purchase behaviour) is important for future improvements. It is especially important to understand what drives customer satisfaction and loyalty, and how internal processes play a role.

Customer satisfaction data is typically only analysed with simple linear statistics that assume that drivers of satisfaction are independent of each other. This is not a realistic assumption. Typically drivers of satisfaction are highly non-linearly cross-correlated and that must be taken into account in an analysis. A simple statistic report also does not provide any opportunity to conduct what-if analyses, predictions or target optimisation.

A better alternative is to analyse customer satisfaction data with Bayesian networks (Heckerman and Welman 1995). A Bayesian network is a graphical model that represents variables as nodes with directed connections among them. Connections carry tables with conditional probabilities that specify the dependencies between variables. However, available Bayesian network software is often not suitable because it is aimed at an academic level. These tools do not provide the required levels of automation, intuition, and integration into corporate environments that would make them accessible to business users.

To make a tool for Bayesian networks useful for business users the following functionality should be provided. Firstly, users should be able to simply upload their business data into the tool which then automatically learns the structure of the Bayesian network. Secondly, the tool must automatically identify the main drivers for variables of interest such as customer satisfaction and loyalty, and also the strength of these drivers. And finally, business users are looking for an intuitive user interface that helps them change the value distribution of some variables and see the impact on the remaining ones. An example of such a tool has been presented in Nauck et al. (2006).

14.3 Real-Time Business Intelligence

As with many generic concepts, business intelligence (BI) is not a well-defined term. Some consider BI as data reporting and visualisation while others include business performance management. Database vendors highlight data extraction, transformation, and integration. Analysis tools vendors emphasise statistical analysis and data mining. These different views make it very clear that BI has many facets. To capture them, we globally define BI as the framework for accessing, understanding, and analyzing one of the most valuable assets of an enterprise – raw data – and turning it into actionable information in order to improve business performance.

Current BI systems suffer from a number of obstacles that prevent the realisation of their envisaged potential. The first issue is the transition from data into information is hindered by the shortage of analysts and experts who are required to configure and run analytical software. The second issue is the bottleneck in the transition from information into action. This transition has traditionally been of a manual nature because of the lack of automatic links back into the business process layer facilitating rapid modification of process parameters to improve performance. The third issue is related to the ability to fuse and relate the huge amount of data from the different sources into a timely and meaningful source of information, including the ability to validate the data and deal with quality issues.

The deficiencies of traditional BI mentioned above can be addressed by providing the capabilities for the seamless transition from data into information into action, which we refer to as RTBI (Azvine et al. 2006). This means that RTBI must provide the same functionality as traditional BI, but operates on data that is extracted from operational data sources with adequate speed, and provides a means to propagate actions back into business processes in an adequate time frame. Specifically, RTBI should provide three critical components, namely, real-time information delivery, real-time business performance analysis, and real-time action on the business processes. It must be emphasised here that the concept of real-time does not necessarily equate to zero-latency in the operation of these three components. The concept of real-time indicates the timeliness of the information-decision-action cycle that is relevant to the specific business environment.

In current BI systems, the information flow among operational, tactical, and strategic layers is broken by manual intervention. The challenge is to use intelligent technologies to model the manual intervention present in current systems and

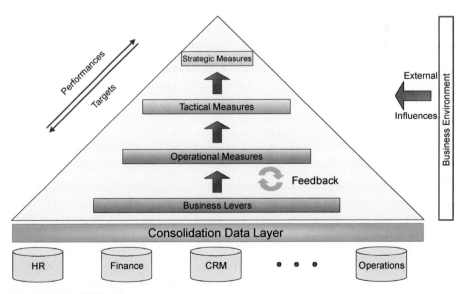

Fig. 14.1 The RTBI vision

to automate both the flow of information from operational to tactical and strategic layers, representing data to the information stage of RTBI, and the actions necessary to translate strategic objectives back to operational drivers to influence strategic decisions in real time, as shown in Fig. 14.1.

14.3.1 A Consolidated Semantic Data Layer

RTBI requires an analytical framework sitting on top of a consolidated data layer that provides real-time ETL (extract, transformation and load) from operational data sources. Although data management communities have talked about the importance of data semantics for a long time, current vendor solutions have not made data semantics explicitly available to end users. For example, data warehouse solutions focus on target schema definitions and ETL. There is hardly any formal documentation, i.e., documentation that could be processed by machines. Even if some informal documentation exists of target schemas and transformation specifications, it is rarely available to the end user because much of the semantics is hidden in transformation codes. As these are not made explicit, performance measures are often defined by dedicated teams who understand the business and the data. The high cost associated with this means that only a few measures could be defined. However, there are many occasions that performance measures should be defined dynamically by end users who may not know the implicit semantics. This means that data semantics as well as contexts have to be available to these users. Business users must have the ability to choose data and data contexts to compose or define new measures, and to get unified data support from any available data sources.

The key requirement to support business users is to relieve them from knowing the details of low-level data integration. Data should be presented to the measure builders in terms they understand. This would address the usual gap between IT departments and business users, who often blame each other for project failure. IT personnel are often unable to understand business requirements while business users are unable to articulate their requirements exactly. Thus, there is a need to supply the data in context for business users to define new measures which in turn would lead to the broad adoption of BI.

The widespread use of BI requires a data layer that allows dynamic integration of new data sources because enterprises cannot afford to build data warehouses for every BI application. Thus, the technologies must be developed to provide the following:

- A unified data layer: A common meta-data structure unifies data access by creating a virtual warehouse view of enterprise data so that all users, regardless of their departments or analytical process, have access to the same values, field names, and sources.
- A streamlined development cycle: This is a step-by-step guide to creating machine-processable meta-data repositories and a mapping between meta-data and concept-based data access.

- An automated data mismatch reconciliation: This is a way of combining data while removing any mismatches between the different data sets.

This type of data layer empowers business users to select data sources suitable for their applications from a pool of siloed data sources without the risk of misusing them. They can safely and dynamically define any measures based on the latest data including data from external data sources. As the data layer provides a unified view of selected data sources, it shortens application development.

14.3.2 Analytical Performance Frameworks

The analytical part of RTBI is composed of an analytical performance framework that links up all operational, tactical, and strategic measures and identifies the business levers for controlling the enterprise. The main building blocks of a performance framework are Business Entities (BEs), each of which represents exactly one performance quantity of a part of the enterprise. Examples are strategic quantities like customer satisfaction or profit, and tactical or operational quantities such as "average time to clear a fault" or "number of abandoned calls in call centre." Furthermore, we distinguish between:

- Internal performance quantities such as the ones just mentioned;
- Business levers which can be changed in order to improve the performance, e. g., the number of call centre agents;
- External influences stemming from the business environment, i. e., anything related to customers, competitors, or other factors, such as weather, which influence the business.

The first step in building a performance framework is to identify relevant performance quantities. The approach is very similar to the ideas formulated in Kaplan and Norton (1996) for Balanced Scorecards. The search for the right quantities is usually driven by the strategy of the enterprise, since we are only interested in those quantities that influence the performance at the strategic level. Typically, answering questions like the following helps identify a set of relevant quantities:

- How can we express our strategic goals in terms of measurable quantities?
- What are the influences of strategic quantities at tactical levels and which operational quantities influence tactical ones?
- What can we control in our business in order to influence the performance?
- What are the external influences we have to take into account?

Once all the relevant quantities have been identified, the following step consists of producing a framework that shows how each quantity affects the rest. As the above questions suggest, we select quantities such that they influence others in the performance hierarchy. Business levers and external influences are at the bottom of the hierarchy, linking to operational quantities above them. These in turn are linked to tactical ones and finally into strategic quantities at the topmost level. Figure 14.2 shows an example framework describing a call centre scenario.

At this point of defining the performance framework, everything has been done at the qualitative level. The quantities to be measured have been defined but not how to measure them. Therefore, the third step is about defining measures for the quantities. For the quantity customer satisfaction, for example, one could compute the relative number of very satisfied customers according to surveys. An alternative could be to measure the average satisfaction level of customers. The decision depends on which measure definition is more relevant for the strategy. In the case of the first one, the distribution of customers who are not very satisfied can be completely ignored, i. e., one does not measure if most of them are still quite satisfied or if they are utterly dissatisfied. The second one takes this into account but still does not tell us anything about the variation of satisfaction amongst customers.

All measures are based on data and for each performance measure, a data source needs to be specified. For example, survey data will be required to measure customer satisfaction. In that context, the role of the data fusion layer is of great importance since the required data is typically distributed between a number of data sources that can be easily described as "disjoint and heterogeneous." This is particularly the case in large enterprises. In order to obtain the correct measurement of a performance quantity, it is possible that a combination of data sources need to be accessed for assembling the required value. The capabilities of the data fusion layer in terms of understanding the data model and relating the contents of different sources, in addition to the management of data quality, are crucial for ensuring the validity of the collected measurements within the performance framework.

Finally, the relationships between the connected quantities need to be quantified. If the relationship is known, an equation or a set of rules expressing the relation-

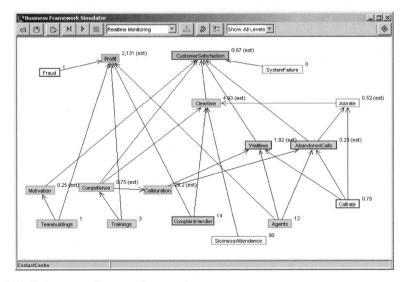

Fig. 14.2 Call centre performance framework

ship can be defined. Many relationships, however, are unknown, ill-defined or of a dynamic nature, i. e., they change over time as the business environment changes. An example of this is the relationship between operational quantities and customer satisfaction. Such relationships can be learnt from historic data as described below.

14.3.3 Monitoring Performance

An important function of a RTBI system is to monitor the performance of an enterprise in real time. Data is collected from operational systems or other internal or external data sources via the data fusion engine and fed into the analytics module. Whenever new data arrives, the performance measures are evaluated. A RTBI platform should provide configurable dashboards to display the resulting performance figures (and optionally a relevant historical view) of each of the quantities within the framework. This approach is considerably different from common reporting where performance is only published on a regular basis like monthly, weekly, or daily. The dashboards can also be set to provide alarms or traffic light type monitors such that warnings can be issued in case of a quantity deviating from its required region of normality.

14.3.4 Learning Relationships

We already pointed out that not all relationships between entities are known, and in most cases, only qualitative knowledge is available about the nature of the relationship. On the other hand, each performance quantity is measured regularly and the values are collected over time. In particular, we can assume that a typical RTBI system will collect the data of related entities. Therefore, we can employ IDA and data mining techniques to learn the relationships from the data. However, learning as such is still not sufficient for RTBI due to the changing nature of some (if not most) of the relationships typically encountered in a business environment. The learning and data analysis must be carried out automatically and repeatedly in a timely manner in order for the results to be relevant for the situation developing at the current time.

Learning relationships from data is not trivial since it consists of a number of steps that each requires data analysis expert knowledge. For each relationship, an appropriate data mining technique has to be chosen and configured and the data has to be pre-processed accordingly amongst other things. Realistically, an expert would set all these steps up based on an initial analysis. Relationships can then be re-learned or adapted at any time using the given setup. Future RTBI systems will be based on technology such as SPIDA (Nauck et al. 2003) which can automate a great deal of the setup and re-learning procedure. Business users will then be able to trigger the learning capabilities of an RTBI platform without the need to understand the learning techniques behind it.

14.3.5 What-If-Scenarios, Target Optimisation and Prediction

Apart from monitoring, two main functions of an RTBI system are running what-if scenarios and target optimisation (i. e., optimise business levers and targets for BEs given strategic targets). What-if analysis answers the question of how business levers and the business environment influence operational, tactical, and strategic performance. We could, for instance, determine how customer satisfaction changes if we increased the number of call centre agents when the number of incoming calls changes.

Another type of analysis is the scenario in which a higher-level target value is set (typically by managers) and it is required to determine how this translates into lower-level targets. Following the example in Fig. 14.2, targets for customer satisfaction and costs have to be translated into targets for clear time, wait time, number of abandoned calls, etc. This target translation is not trivial since the mappings among the business entities we established are unidirectional; generally, they cannot be inverted. The problem of finding targets therefore turns into an optimisation problem. For instance, we might look for targets for all measures such that we achieve a target for customer satisfaction at minimal costs, i. e., maximum profit.

In order to be pro-active, managers have to predict future developments to make the right decisions at the right time. This can be achieved by predicting the development of external influences and propagating predictions through the performance framework similar to what-if analysis. In that way, the future performance of the business can be predicted given the chosen settings of the business levers.

14.4 Summary

Analytics is extremely important for large customer-oriented businesses, especially in areas like customer service and business intelligence. Typical barriers that businesses experience are bad data quality and lack of expertise in analytics. Bad data quality can arise from inconsistent legacy systems and the fact that data gathering is usually done without a subsequent analysis in mind. One way of addressing data quality is to move from outdated legacy systems to a central corporate data model and, for example, a semantic repository as outlined in this chapter. A lack in analytics expertise can be addressed by using highly automated intelligent tools that provide advanced analytics but with an intuitive interface. Business users are domain experts, not data analysis experts. Therefore, we need tools to support them and allow them to focus on their job.

Chapter 15
The Agile Delivery
of Service Chain Management Solutions

15.1 Introduction

For IT leaders, the increasing speed of innovation supported by a strong and flexible enterprise-wide software infrastructure, as well as delivering functionally rich and technically robust services is of primary concern. Increasing responsiveness to business changes and growing requirements ultimately require flexible software systems that can embrace such changes. To realise this, business stakeholders and IT executives are focusing on enhancing their older software delivery models. The goal here is to ensure that the enterprises remain competitive and leading. Agile practices in delivery promises to fulfil such a goal. It addresses the need of building business functionality quickly in circumstances of evolving requirements.

This chapter introduces agile delivery concepts and approaches in the context of global and distributed service chains, and the synergies between the two. The chapter presents a common Application Development Infrastructure for enterprise that influences the agility through service orientation concepts and design, and an adaptive services approach.

15.2 The Need for Agile Delivery

KFC, a subsidiary of Yum! Brands known for its chicken restaurant chain, adapted to the outbreak of the Avian flu in Asia a few years ago by selling fish in Vietnam and other countries. This is a good example of agility – the ability of an organisation to quickly adapt its supply chain, operations, or customer relations in response to unanticipated environmental factors, new business strategies or technology advancements (Mathew 2006). Service chain enterprises with some of the following characteristics would need such an ability to adjust to the changes in surroundings.

- *Global expansion*: Large companies are increasing their service functions to cover many regions and countries and expand their customer base. Advancements in information and communication technologies, free market phenomenon,

C. Voudouris, G. Owusu, R. Dorne, D. Lesaint, *Service Chain Management*
DOI: 10.1007/978-3-540-75504-3, ©Springer 2008

regional trade agreements and outsourcing models have made the service chain global. The trend will continue to stay with ever-changing business policies and consumer trends.

- *Distributed services*: In modern enterprises, business services are distributed across geographies, integrated with disparate technologies, and glued together. This has resulted in an improved, unified and rich interaction platform for consumers. The service chain is comprised of various service links, enterprise and business processes. The integrating units can be located anywhere, either from the same enterprise, external agencies, new acquisitions or shared business models.
- *Heterogeneous services*: Services have become varied for different customer segments. For example, a bank may offer different kinds of loan services for corporates, governmental agencies, or individual consumers.

By leveraging an enterprise wide context aware framework, new revenue generating services can be easily introduced by applying personalised behaviour. Besides customer's experiences can also be greatly enhanced. The characteristics of the service chain mentioned above introduce a conceptual shift in the way enterprises build and deliver services. Enterprises need to serve customers better, faster and cheaper.

IT services delivery processes often focus on addressing the business problems in environments where the business pace is not so fast, and delivery cycles are long. The development flows in downward direction going through multiple stages. Requirements are fixed well in advance, and are fairly stable through the delivery of the solution. The software engineering practices that are being followed, e. g., waterfall model, are sequential development models. This delivery passes through different stages of the Software Development Life Cycle (SDLC) in a sequential way. Firstly, the requirements are gathered and frozen. Secondly, the high and low level design is finalised. Thirdly, the code is finalised. Fourthly, multiple levels of testing such as unit, functional and integration testing are completed. And finally the solution is delivered. As we can see, the decision points are made well in advance to make the delivery successful. More time is spent in creating and maintaining comprehensive documents at each stage, which are not changed often.

These classical methods could pose a challenge in service scenarios as competitors aggressively develop new products to compete which leads to frequent changes in requirements and multiple analysis cycles. These methods need to be enhanced with agile practices to ensure the alignment of IT with service business needs. Agility enables the frequent, incremental delivery of working functionality. It also allows business stakeholders to see parts of the final solution being developed, which also boosts team confidence.

15.2.1 Challenges in Realising Agile Delivery

The notion of having a robust and agile delivery model has been an unfulfilled promise in the enterprises because of missing agile project management techniques to address the challenges involved in the SDLC. We outline the inherent challenges in agile delivery as follows:

- All requirements and design decisions cannot be frozen up front.
- Multiple, and shorter, release cycles need to be planned. To mitigate the risk of not meeting the business requirements, the system integration needs to be validated for a new or varied behaviour of services.
- The constant participation of business and technology stockholders in communicating requirements, validation and feedback is crucial and therefore need to be an integral part of the delivery. Geographical barriers make it more challenging as it is more difficult to seamlessly connect and share ideas.

15.3 Realising Agile Delivery

Having outlined the challenges involved in implementing agile practices in the previous section, this section presents the steps that need to be taken into consideration in SDLC in order to deliver agility. The section also shows that the architecture reengineering should take place to leverage an integrated platform that could act as a key enabler to realise an agile delivery model, with the concept of sharing services and applying variations.

15.3.1 The Development Strategy

An agile development strategy has been defined in many different ways with well-defined sets of values, principles and practices in the designing, programming and delivery of IT solutions (Highsmith 2002). The strategy is very well based upon realities of businesses and not on pre-defined knowledge artifacts. The focus is shifted from older concepts to agility (shown in Fig. 15.1). Here, we point out key practices that have to be followed in order to realise agile delivery.

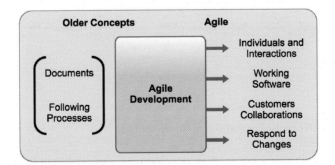

Fig. 15.1 The focus is shifted to agile concepts

15.3.1.1 An Evolutional Approach to Gathering Requirements

The right set of requirements needs to be captured in order to offer the right services to the customer. A systematic requirement analysis is needed for the success of an agile delivery as it could make or break the business. An evolution of the business requirements throughout SDLC is expected. In order to accommodate emerging requirements, a collaboration among users, decision makers, designers and developers has to be seen as an integral part of the development approach.

Requirements can be functional or non-functional. Non-functional requirements focus on the architectural needs and design considerations, whereas functional requirements map to the core business concerns of the solution. A minimal set of requirements should be captured to have a clear understanding of the architectural model and functional requirements at a very high level. It is a difficult and costly affair to repeatedly change architectural requirements of the system. Since the representation and capturing of functional requirements cannot be locked and frozen, the architectural model should be able to provide flexibility and backward compatibility to the solution.

15.3.1.2 Test-Driven Development

Testing of the system as part of the development cycle helps to validate requirements, improve design and ensures conformance. Test-driven development helps to create software in short iterations with a minimal capturing of requirements and up-front design. The test-driven development (TDD) strategy requires iteratively written automated test cases before the functional code. This approach defines iterative cycles of testing and refactoring of code as shown in Fig. 15.2.

In fact, this strategy might have been followed by developers earlier in different forms but it has gained widespread attention in agile delivery practices. Emphasising that the developers first write and fail test cases ensures that a test case works and helps to catch any errors. Test cases that fail are added repeatedly. The process focuses on passing these tests and then refactoring. In the end, it ensures that all the test cases are passed and requirements are met, thus minimising the risks in production.

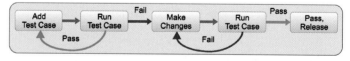

Fig. 15.2 The test-driven development approach: a flow diagram

15.3.1.3 Iterative and Incremental Development

Agile delivery proposes an iterative development paradigm that emphasises progressively improving solutions till the final delivery. The iteration is comprised of

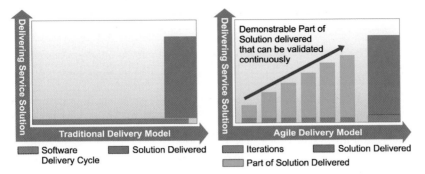

Fig. 15.3 The difference between traditional and agile delivery

requirement gathering, design, development and test phases. This iterative process encourages scaling down the large projects to strategically well-defined functional deployable units that can be delivered in small time frames called iterations. The software unit per iteration is a valuable unit in its own to aid incremental delivery. The iteration includes an individual delivery cycle – planning, designing, construction and testing. Figure 15.3 compares the two different approaches, an older delivery model and an agile model (Ambler 2007).

15.3.1.4 Continuous Integration

Designing and developing a service for an enterprise solution, connecting it to other solutions with the help of well-defined interface boundaries and an architectural model, and testing it frequently is known as continuous integration. As a part of the delivery strategy, integration of functional blocks occurs at each delivery cycle, the effect is to "grow" the system at each "build" phase (Schatz 2006). This practice is a key strategy towards having a reliable build of the software as well as towards getting valuable feedback from service consumers. The system integration is validated regularly for architectural and business requirements, which ensures a clear visibility of the solution as a whole. In each iteration, business stakeholders can see creative ideas being delivered and customers can see improved versions of services. This strategy has proved to be a key ingredient in the agile delivery model. This helps to achieve the following:

- Gaining a competitive advantage.
- Identifying integration problems and fixing them continuously.
- Identifying technology or business complexities, broken and incompatible functionalities, and violations in standards or deviations from requirements.
- Unit testing and integration at each iteration.
- Keeping an eye on Quality of Services (QoS) concerning giving real time business benefits.
- Seeing a return on the investment either partially or wholly.
- Focusing on improvements incrementally by having short feedback cycles.

15.3.2 The Adaptive Service Development Approach

Services can be assembled to design a process that can be integrated as part of an existing or a new service chain. Such services can also be shared among multiple service chains, bringing real-time business benefits. The adaptive nature of service refers to the ability to implement variations in a service at run time by identifying a customer's operating contexts. With the logical division of reusability and variations factor, a service chain can be greatly enhanced, and integration complexities can be reduced.

Different business contexts or technology environments may require changes in the behaviour of the application or service chain. Each change introduces a new version and variation to the service. Applying service variations at run time by using a shared service approach is the key strategy here. The main characteristics of the service that could be varied are:

- *The contract*: New operations have been added into the services or a change has occurred in the message formats.
- *The location*: The service is moved to a different location depending upon its operational advantages.
- *Operational modifications*: The existing operation of a service has been modified.
- *The binding mechanism*: The service end points may also vary for different business needs.

In large enterprises, these varied services need to be handled at a centralised framework level. The traditional strategies for addressing varied services requirements have been to develop multiple applications/systems for different lines of businesess, marketing channels, or geographies etc. The problem with this approach is that it results in the creation of silos of applications/systems with the impact that there is no seamless flow of information across the enterprise. This strategy also results in duplication of the applications and business processes, thus highlighting inconsistencies and bad end user experience. This strategy also results in rigid IT systems resulting in high "time to market" and results in lost business opportunities. The adaptive service approach is a boost to the agility. It provides a well-defined mechanism to apply variations for multiple contexts, without affecting the existing operations. New and personalised services can be added in the service chain easily. A framework that realises this flexibility to the business services or processes is described by Bardram (2004).

A common application platform based upon this approach is a pre-requisite for agile enterprises that could take care of the service lifecycle, service versioning and variations, and enable the addition and enhancement of services for better revenue and performance in an easy plug-n-play manner. It acts as a key strategy to adapt new business models and operational tactics and helps in gaining cost reduction, while not losing focus on customers service.

15.3.2.1 The Common Capability Platform

A capability refers to a business functionality designed and developed in a well-defined way and can be invoked through standard interfaces via well-defined protocols. Each capability has its own set of data, attributes and functional blocks. A common capability platform is a set of transparent and loosely coupled capabilities supported with frameworks, software systems, and data repositories. The capabilities are visible to all, and can communicate with each other through the platform using well-defined message formats.

The platform acts as an enterprise level framework (Deb 2003) that speeds up delivery by leveraging reusable and composed services. It enables the integration of disparate business processes and systems that could span across multiple products and locations in service enterprises with minimal disruption. The platform not only helps to maintain consistency and a standard approach across all the tiers but also helps in responding quickly to new business opportunity. This is possible within reasonable cost only through reuse of existing investments and a service sharing concept. The capabilities are built upon well-defined architectural components as shown in Fig. 15.4. The enterprise level common capability platform as shown here showcases the core service framework and architectural components that promises rich, consistent and uniform user interactions, data integrity, personalisation of services and optimal quality to the software solution. An enterprise application framework design is described by Doddavula and Karamongikar (2005).

Here are some of the key considerations while building a common capability platform for enterprise. The platform must ensure a comprehensive and collaborative strategy to support new products thus bringing the following benefits to the enterprise:

- Improved time to market, flexibility, and lower cost as new business capabilities can be developed and introduced with common architectural guidelines and solution designs.
- Usage of a consistent and shared methodology to develop or design business capabilities with the concept of service orchestration, ensuring low development and maintenance costs.
- Easy configuration and assembly of services and processes.
- Greatly enhancing customer experience since new business innovations can be plugged in as part of a process or capability.

A capability platform should be built based upon the following decision points:

- It should constitute an execution infrastructure with a well-architectured solution. Architecture and design should be based upon industry best practices.
- It should reduce cost by having increased productivity due to the availability of a reusable reference architecture, design models and code components.
- It should provide help in effectively leveraging the organisational knowledge base.
- It should add value through leveraging expertise gained through internal research and application development experience.

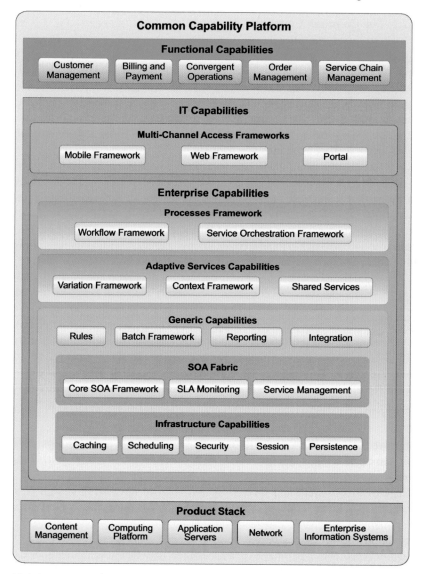

Fig. 15.4 An enterprise application framework showcasing a common capability platform

- It should promise organisation-wide reuse and be able to take care of context specific variations.

Service enterprises need to build or leverage a common capability platform that helps in building organisation-wide common capabilities as business services with the help of tools, frameworks and services – this could ensure the making of right architectural and design decisions and promise a high degree of reuse. The platform must ensure a well-defined, standard-based, proven mechanism in place to create, configure, and host business services. It should help agility, by handling business and service variations with the changing dynamics and opportunities. The platform should provide a standard way to configure the business services for different contexts as a well-organised set of functional units (capabilities) operating in a virtual environment governed by a set of directives based on standard mechanisms.

15.4 Managing Agile Delivery

The delivery model should not only be agile but also be global. The model should emphasise breaking down the work into logical pieces of components, and distributing them to multiple locations, to engineer them where it creates maximum value. The fundamental concept here is to modularise the business processes, the IT applications and infrastructure, and the on-going management, and should be structured with the following best practices:

- Retrain people to develop a good understanding of the model and its implications. An atmosphere of collective ownership need to be established.
- Retain a constant team size to keep the knowledge intact in an evolving project.
- Establish a governance mechanism that should include the formation of a management group to provide effective communication channels.
- Stand-up meetings to happen on daily basis.
- A story board needs to be maintained to have a common view of new requirements in the service chain.
- Test a pilot project to fine tune the model, especially when the technology that is being tried out is new. Any inconsistency in the model or IT infrastructure support can be rectified in earlier stages.
- Establish an open and honest communication environment among business analysts, users, designers, and IT stakeholders.
- Review and continuous feedback should be an integrated approach.
- Establish a check-and-balance mechanism and enable revaluation. Satisfaction surveys help in gathering valuable feedback.
- Establish a continuous improvement mechanism.
- Engage customers to help aligning with business objectives as well as for future operational and execution models in order to have a competitive advantage.

15.5 Summary

For large service enterprises, innovation strategies, competition differentiation and better and faster response to consumers are keys to success. Enterprises must be able to transform their service chains quickly to support change. As oppose to the traditional delivery practices, newer models of delivery that address this culture of change are better suited for these systems. Leveraging well-defined standard based adaptive enterprise architectures is the most pragmatic approach to quickly and flexibly responding to ever-changing customer demand, market opportunities, and external threats.

This chapter discussed the need for agility in service chain management, and demonstrated the practices that need to be followed while engineering software systems and building an agile enterprise solution. We have shown that through service sharing concepts and an adaptive services approach, a unified common capability platform acts as a great value multiplier. This is a new service engineering paradigm that will ensure that dynamically addressing variations in service chain is a painless activity.

Part IV
The Future Service Chain

In previous decades, we saw services emerging from being the domain of the state to be liberalised, cross borders and trade globally. The future service chain will be one where collaboration and competition will prevail. The digitization of services and increased information flows via the Internet will accelerate this leading to a "zero-touch" and fully connected service future where individuals and organisations, under the watchful eye of government and its regulation, will work synergistically (or antagonistically) depending on their interests and the particular context and situation.

Chapter 16 examines how organisations may collaborate to improve forecasting and planning leading eventually to service chains which operate as single entities while competing with each other at the service chain level. This has already been experienced in manufacturing so the indications are that similar trends are to emerge for services too especially if outsourcing and digitisation takes hold – unbundling further vertically integrated service organisations.

Liberalisation of utilities and other government activities worldwide means that services once part of our tax bill are now offered and priced separately with usage by individuals and their specific requirements also coming into play (e. g., road use charging, water metering, repair response times for utilities). This trend will foster the need for pricing to become more efficient and transparent while, more so, conducted online. This can lead to increased savings for customers and profits for organisations especially those that can operate at lower costs taking advantage of the digital networked economy. The subject is investigated in Chap. 17.

The era of central planning for services is gradually giving way to market economics and service trading (something which has largely happened to goods after the decline of the various central planning economies and models). Marketplace technologies geared for services are required to underpin and facilitate this trend. Chapter 18 examines the subject at the enterprise level and in the context of resource trading. This is only one area of application since market economics can also work to empower staff and replace traditional "command and control" structures. Chapter 19 provides ideas on how such empowerment schemes can be devised and implemented.

Chapter 16
Collaborative Demand Forecasting in Service Chains

16.1 Introduction

In Chap. 4, we have discussed in detail the concepts of Forecasting and Demand Planning where the focus was primarily forecasting within the enterprise. With interdependencies of businesses it is imperative for organizations to engage in collaborative demand forecasting across their service chains. This chapter defines collaborative forecasting and highlights the challenges faced in carrying out this process across multiple organizations. It establishes the objective of such collaborative effort and details a framework which can be used by all organizations. It also briefly discusses the popular CPFR framework and its potential application in the service industry.

16.2 What is Collaborative Forecasting?

Wikipedia defines service as the non-material equivalent of a good and thus, it is a non-tangible product provided to a customer by a supplier. The service chain, in this context, does not refer to high carrying stocks or bulky raw material but entails dealing with the challenging issues surrounding "perishability." For example, an engineer who is 'utilized' for only two hours out of an eight-hour working day cannot, once the time has passed, receive work for those 'unutilized' six hours. Thus, the economic opportunity is lost. In a service chain, where multiple business transactions are involved, this could create a cascading effect and result in business inefficiencies for collaborating partners.

We know of a characteristic case where a particular engineering skill was thought to be in demand for a new technology to be deployed as part of several infrastructure projects. The company requiring the skill contacted a subcontractor which, based on the company's forecast, decided to recruit and train engineers in the new skill, even establishing a costly special training school. The demand anticipated by the subcontractor failed to materialize when the original forecast was indicating resulting in the subcontractor having to release or redeploy the newly trained engineers. When

C. Voudouris, G. Owusu, R. Dorne, D. Lesaint, *Service Chain Management*
DOI: 10.1007/978-3-540-75504-3, ©Springer 2008

the company finally needed the engineers, the subcontractor was highly sceptical to collaborate and was only able to satisfy part of the demand for the new skill, resulting in several of the company's infrastructure projects running late.

Scenarios similar to the above happen all the time across the world. They demonstrate how interconnected service businesses are becoming. From the small to the big, they increasingly depend upon each other, more so when operating in near- or real-time. In this context, collaborative forecasting and planning is becoming increasingly important among service chain participants in a globally networked, and increasingly digital, economy.

Collaboration in a service chain is the act of individuals and organizations collaborating or cooperating with the overall objective of achieving a fully responsive, adaptive and synchronized service chain. Forecasting service demand is critical for the operation of any service company, more so, where service is sold in package with the physical product, as service response plays an important part in the customer's product experience.

16.3 Challenges in Collaborative Forecasting

Collaboration for any activity across two organizations requires interaction between people, processes and systems. This introduces multiple challenges in executing the task of collaborative forecasting. They can be categorized into:

- challenges due to human interactions and biases;
- challenges in communication and defining accountability;
- challenges due to the perishable nature of services.

Collaborative forecasting engages people across organizations in sharing information and data. More often than not, information exchanged through such engagement suffers from personal bias and individual interests. Due to the involvement of human interaction, the service chain obtains dynamic properties, like a stock market, where external signals on supply and demand influences human interaction and governs its overall behavior. This makes service chains vulnerable to the phenomenon known as the *bullwhip effect*, i. e., subtle forecasting inefficiencies at customer levels in the service chain rapidly propagate upwards through the chain, distorting and amplifying at each level, resulting in wild swings in forecasting error towards the apex.

Collaborative forecasting also, at times, suffers from repetitive and unproductive communication efforts. Sharing information manually can be very tedious and obstructive. Swings in forecasting accuracy can generate a "blame game" and it requires significant commitment from individuals, and support from senior management, to see through troublesome periods. Common objectives and stage-wise goal setting for the collaborating companies, with clear accountabilities, is often found wanting. The forecasting and demand planning horizon are often different for the various organizations. They may forecast at different aggregate levels and, hence, have different collaboration needs. Quite often, increased effort on collaboration improves forecasting accuracy, but does not result in operational efficiency due to problems with internal integration (Smaros 2007).

Another peculiar challenge faced by service chains is due to "perishability," which means any unutilized time or service cannot be stored, saved or reused. For example, the time lost by a doctor, consultant or engineer cannot be reused or re-billed. Loss of time is loss of revenue. The only hedging strategy against forecasting inaccuracy here, barring customer dissatisfaction and long waiting times, is to have more resources at your disposal to cover up for uncertainty and avoid business losses. This, however, increases costs and reduces resource utilization. To makes things more challenging, changing skill capacity (i. e., the supply side) often requires the training, recruitment or release of personnel, all of which can prove extremely time-consuming and challenging. This further emphasizes the importance of accurate forecasting in the first place.

16.4 The Objectives of Collaborative Forecasting

The overall objective of collaborative forecasting in the service chain is to synchronize service demand forecasts between all customers and suppliers involved in a supply and demand network, such that individual forecasts of self-interested parties acquire synergy and they are based on the fundamental philosophy that a service chain should be operating as a single entity. By achieving demand forecast synergy throughout the service chain, collaborative forecasting will solidly underpin subsequent collective planning processes and lead to efficiencies that will benefit the whole of the service chain.

In supply chain management, a common objective is to achieve optimal inventory quantities such that an inventory is neither under nor over stocked in relation to resource hedging or unanticipated customer demand. In a service chain, the objectives of planning are similar to those of a supply chain, however, forecasting and planning may involve intangible and difficult to quantify services and skills. Forecasting here deals with estimated demand for the consumption of the skills and services. However, in both cases of Supply Chain and Service Chain, collaborative forecasting process aims at reducing "inventory" through the use of information. Thus, it addresses two major challenges:

1. It avoids non-fulfilment of critical service commitments;
2. It reduces the idle capacity.

Collaborative forecasting, in this manner, aims to increase productivity and profitability of the interlinked organizations.

Another advantage of collaborative forecasting arises from its requirement of coordinating and reaching consensus inside and across organisations. Due to its core function of understanding the demand, a forecasting team constitutes a key information centre in the organization. The forecasting team interacts with various stakeholders, internally and externally, obtains market intelligence from sales teams and various industry analysts, monitors macro economic variables and analyzes historical data patterns. The collaborative forecasting process is established between forecasting teams to exchange valuable information to enable uniform decision making across organizations. This allows the service chain to be more flexible and responsive to dynamic market conditions since all information sources are incorporated and collaborators may execute optimal planning of resources based on synchronized forecasts.

16.5 The Collaborative Forecasting Framework

From the discussion above, it is not difficult to deduce that it is very important to have a clear framework within which two or more organizations can collaborate effectively. The stepwise approach, called the Collaborative Forecasting Framework (CFF), described in this section could help in designing such framework. A summary of the CFF is shown in Fig. 16.1.

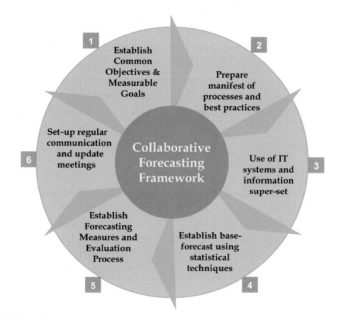

Fig. 16.1 Collaborative Forecasting Framework

Step 1: Establishing Common Objectives and Measurable Goals

Within a single organization, and also across multiple organizations, it is important that a forecasting team has a common set of goals. They should be looking at common measures of forecasting accuracy and these measures should be shared with all the players involved. Any metrics used should aim at pinpointing reasons for not achieving desired targets and become a tool to create an offensive, blame-focussed, environment for the players. Deployment of any forecasting system should be only after open discussion among all the team members and careful analysis of historical data. If forecasting accuracy does not meet expectations, there has to be a way to identify the cause in the process. This requires the process to be completely transparent and each stage of the process to be owned by an accountable person. The team should have a shared vision and a formal statement of objectives, guidelines and approaches to be followed (Jain and Malehorn 2005).

Step 2: Preparing a Manifest of Processes and Best Practices

Across the service chain, each of the organizations will have its own set of processes. After establishing common objective and measure of forecasting accuracy, a team needs to formulate a concise list of processes to manage the internal work and external interactions. Outside entities like suppliers, customers, vendors and other partners would need to agree on a common collaborative process and assume responsibility of inputs and outputs at every stage. This process should be benchmarked with the best in the business, which will help in establishing the goals for process improvement. However, these goals need to be realistic. It is important, therefore, to design maturity stages of the collaborative forecasting process and aim at moving from one stage to another, instead of making short term adjustment to jump through stages.

Step 3: The Use of IT Systems and an Information Super-Set

Although it is likely that the various participants will use different IT systems within each of the respective organizations, it is recommended to use a common system for reporting, accuracy measurements and storing historical forecasts. It is beneficial to combine all distinct and influential data sources from different collaborators into a single data set, and then use this "super" dataset to generate a forecast. This approach would outperform any other strategy and this is the general belief in forecasting research (Granger 1989). However, as all information sources would be pooled into an accessible dataset, it relies heavily upon complete trust between the collaborators. In a tiered service chain comprising of multiple inter- and intra-collaborative relationships, this approach may be unrealistic due to possible business politics, regulatory issues, sensitivity of information and the expense of collecting, aggregating and maintaining potentially inconsistent data (Diebold and Pauly 1990). Creating information supersets requires strong security measures to maintain confidentiality of the sensitive data and information especially so when regulatory issues are at play (e. g., a regulated wholesale division in a telecoms organization would need to protect and separate its forecasts from the retail division which may be competing with some of wholesale's customers).

Step 4: Establishing a Base Forecast Using Statistical Techniques

In comparison to statistical forecasting methods, human judgement produces impaired forecasts. The main problems associated with judgemental forecasting are that humans have a tendency to make predictions about the future which can be affected by a range of decision making and cognitive biases (Tversky and Kahneman 1973) such as the availability heuristic (Kahneman et al. 1982). Within a group, human judgement can deteriorate significantly (Goodwin 2005). Even when presented with a clear view of the situation, a human can make irrational decisions due to group dynamics, peer influence, "group think" (Baron 2005) and a whole range of well studied factors from the field of behavioral psychology.

Hence, one appropriate approach to collaborative forecasting is to generate a base forecast and allow forecast managers to make adjustments according to their understanding of market and experience. Using both statistics and human judgement in the forecasting process can improve the accuracy of a forecasting model, provided any adjustments are justified. The hybrid approach of statistical and judgemental forecast brings benefits from both methods. It brings out subtle patterns from historical data and incorporates them in the base forecast. By allowing collaborators to modify this forecast they can incorporate market intelligence into it.

Step 5: Establishing Forecasting Measures and an Evaluation Process

It is important to periodically monitor the accuracy of collaborative forecasting and performance of the process. Chapter 4 describes some of the popular forecasting measures and pros and cons of using them. It is essential to establish forecasting measures at the start of the process. Key questions such as what to measure, how often to measure, at what level measures will be applied (national, regional, branch, etc.) must be factored in the forecasting process. Statistical measures alone will not serve the purpose for efficient demand planning. Forecasting accuracy must be measured in terms of impact on resource utilization, cost per hour, spare capacity, etc. It is important to assess external situations, such as exceptional events where forecasts were dramatically incorrect. The assessment should also cover internal processes to ensure the collaborative forecast is used in planning and scheduling.

Monitoring these performance measures on regular basis will highlight where improvements can be made in the collaborative process. Deeper understanding of such details also provides an opportunity to improve or modify business processes carried out in particular areas of the organizations.

Step 6: Setting Up Regular Communication and Update Meetings

To maintain an effective process, regular meetings and updates are vital. Members in the collaborative process must attend monthly review meetings; after each meeting, rigorous follow-ups must be done to ensure that the take-away points of the meeting are achieved. Several off-line meetings could be done before and after the review to exchange information. Any process related decisions and/or changes need to be discussed in the review meeting and any issues resolved. Such regular meeting provides an ideal platform for various partners in service chain to meet and it enables faster and more efficient decision making. One of the major outcomes of this meeting is the single forecast on which all the partners will base and initiate their supply planning. The pre-determined nature of the meeting brings in discipline and commitment from participants. Trust, communication and commitment would ensure success of the collaborative forecasting process. A similar framework should be applied within the organization to facilitate cross-functional participation in the demand planning process.

A critical utility of collaborative forecasting is the ability to resolve collaborative forecast exceptions, or disagreements between stakeholders. As mentioned before, such events (which are expected to occur frequently) can be resolved offline or by conventional means. However, in the event that collaborators fail to resolve exceptions, weighted forecast combinations may be used as a tool to combine the conflicting forecasts.

16.6 Learning from Product Supply Chains

The Collaborative Planning, Forecasting and Replenishment (CPFR) framework, developed by Voluntary Inter-industry Commerce Standards Association (VICS) offers significant opportunity for improving forecasting process by collaborating with key trade partners. Information shared between suppliers and retailers aids in planning and satisfying customer demands through a supportive system of shared information. This allows for continuous updating of inventory and upcoming requirements, making the end-to-end supply chain process more efficient. Efficiency is created through decreased expenditures for merchandizing, inventory, logistics, and transportation across all trading partners. Although specific to collaboration in retail industry, the model provides a very useful overall approach for forecasting in service chain.

CPFR formally combines and capitalizes on the intelligence of multiple trading partners in the planning and fulfillment of customer demand (VICS 2002). At the heart of CPFR is the development of a single, shared forecast that supports joint plans of trading partners in the supply chain and drives their mutual replenishment activities. It also provides a framework within which exceptions could be systematically identified and addressed (Lee and Denend 2004). Defining clear performance measures and documenting operational performance expectations allows collaborating participants to assess risk involved with forecasting inaccuracies. All four phases of Strategy & Planning, Demand & Supply Management, Execution and Analysis of CPFR (see Fig. 16.2) are essentials of collaboration also in service chains.

The effectiveness of such collaboration relies upon two factors: the level to which it integrates internal and external operations, and the level to which the efforts are aligned to the service chain settings in terms of the geographical dispersion, the demand pattern and the product characteristics (Holweg et al. 2005).

Although the specifics of this model are geared to synchronizing retailers with manufacturers, we may, in the future, see similar innovative approaches and models develop to benefit service industry verticals by synchronizing demand with supply even in some unexpected areas. For example:

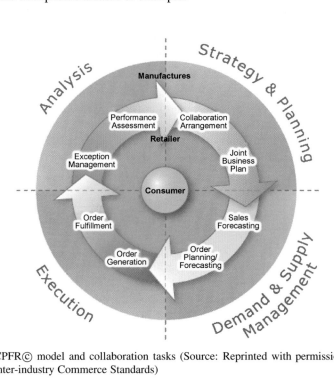

Fig. 16.2 CPFR© model and collaboration tasks (Source: Reprinted with permission from the Voluntary Inter-industry Commerce Standards)

- digital content viewing over the Internet provides instant feedback to content creators (similar to today's Point-Of-Sale systems in retail) leading to near-time or real-time adjustments of the content produced by studios/individuals;
- universities automatically receive forecasts of skills from employers which enables them to co-ordinate on the design of courses and the number of places to allocate to each course?

Increased automation and collection of electronic information is likely to lead in such collaborative directions although the examples above maybe still some years away.

16.7 Summary

The challenges of collaborating and synchronizing across the service chain are becoming all the more important in digitally interconnected and service-dominated economies. This chapter examined some of these challenges and provided an overview of a staged approach to develop a collaborative forecasting practice amongst service companies. Linkages to CPFR recommendations for product supply chains were made along with a perspective on future developments in this promising area.

In the next chapter, we look at another emerging aspect in Service Chain Management. This time we are not looking at service enterprise collaboration but rather competition though pricing and in the context of B2B online commerce.

Chapter 17
Business to Business Online Revenue Management

17.1 Introduction

With the emergence of the Internet, electronic commerce (e-commerce), revenue management and especially applications that combine both are becoming increasingly an area of innovation for service industries. E-commerce has introduced efficiencies across the service chain and it has allowed improvements to take place within and across organizations. Revenue management when combined with e-commerce and done online not only improves resource management but it can be used as a strategic tool to gain competitive advantage. This chapter examines the current approaches and future trends in these very exciting and promising areas.

17.2 The Impact of Internet and E-Commerce on Service Industries

E-commerce is "commercial transactions occurring over open networks" (OECD 1997). Commercial transactions include buying, selling or exchanging products, services and information. The open network being described is the Internet. Business to Business Electronic Commerce (B2B-EC) is when products or services are traded from a business to any other business over the Internet: in our case, we are focusing on B2B-EC in service industries. Sales made over the Internet in service industries have increased every year, particularly for travel, stock trading, electronic banking and insurance. Hence, for firms to remain successful they need responsive business models to continuously meet e-commerce needs.

The Internet has the potential to change B2B-EC tremendously. Businesses with the aid of the Internet are now able to reach out to a global market. They are able to link up to many buyers anywhere around the world without having a relationship with the business in person. Small firms especially benefit since their services are promoted to new markets with which they previously could not afford to be in contact. It has increased opportunities for businesses both small and large to gain more customers at lower costs (Timmer 2000).

C. Voudouris, G. Owusu, R. Dorne, D. Lesaint, *Service Chain Management*
DOI: 10.1007/978-3-540-75504-3, ©Springer 2008

Due to e-commerce, transaction costs are lower as the Internet greatly reduces searching costs for buyers and sellers. The Internet allows the buyers to search for the most advantageous supplier and the sellers to gain potential customers without making physical contact. In the past when buyers purchased a service they would have to shop around in person, going to many suppliers and most probably only locally, for convenience reasons. This is not only time consuming and costly but also the buyer is limited to using a supplier around his area and must accept the available price. Another cost which has extensively decreased is the cost of updating or altering information (e. g., price), sending and storing information. The pace of the performance of these activities has greatly accelerated i. e., by the click of a button (Lee and Lau 1999).

Businesses are also able to enhance their efficiency. They can find out about products and services on their own accord, online, and buy directly from the supplier. Trading partners are able to communicate more directly with each other, avoiding inefficient intermediaries (Turban and King 2003). The use of the Internet also allows immediate and economical access to precise, detailed service information to a very large number of people simultaneously (Malaga 2001). It has also reduced the need for paper and administrative costs (Ramaseshan 1997). This cost reduction allows the supplier to price more competitively, and, consequently, the customers to purchase at lower prices (Bowersox et al. 2002).

The Internet makes information available to both customers and suppliers in real time. Customers are better informed about the service and information such as service pricing, options, availability, and delivery time. The supplier can obtain individual information about customers for customized service; this knowledge can then be used to increase customer satisfaction and loyalty, and, as a result, have a competitive advantage over other suppliers. The supplier can capture the wealth of information the Internet provides and use it to analyze customers' behavior and market segmentation. The Internet also provides the supplier guidance in developing new services or additional attributes to the services for both existing and new customers. The importance for a firm to have access to information is emphasized by Gates (2000): "how you gather, manage, and use information will determine whether you win or lose."

Websites are available 24 hours a day. This prevents the customer frustration of waiting in a queue and also lifts the constraint of time for trading. Accessibility of the service has increased and more people are able to purchase the service at any given time. The global time difference of trading is also overcome. Internet technology can improve the quality and speed of *integration* greatly; it allows the easier coordination of activities within the firm and externally. It can be used to make information flow effortlessly from one part of the organization to another, as discussed in the previous chapter on collaborative demand forecasting. Firms are able to depend on such communication to remain efficient and competitive (Angeles 2000).

The Internet offers new prospects and mechanisms to collaborate and compete with millions of people and businesses online. The electronic market has powered firms to achieve these functions with increased effectiveness and reduced transaction costs, resulting in more efficient markets.

17.3 The Logistics Service Chain: An Example Case of B2B E-Commerce Impact

In this section, we illustrate how B2B e-commerce has led to the improvement of the traditional logistics service chain through the ability to rapidly exchange information. To manage a service chain effectively and efficiently, the exchange of information from one channel to another must be recognized as an essential part of the process; this is allowed through e-commerce which allows buyers and suppliers to share large amounts of information in real time.

The Internet has become the tool used by businesses to exchange information, enabling the real-time control of supplies, orders, inventory levels, service updates and shipment information, and offering a standard approach for order entry, order status inquiry and shipment tracking. A logistics firm can provide information regarding space availability, service updates, and price changes and allows the market to react by placing bids and orders on real-time information. The firm is also able to understand the market demand in real time and take action accordingly. Information exchange between firms in a logistics service chain in real time can significantly lower transaction costs.

Logistics management is an essential activity for businesses which trade goods with other businesses. Transportation of goods is a service which can be carried out by air, road, rail or sea. The transportation service can deliver the goods around the country and beyond. International shipping is accompanied by unavoidable important documentation. Through the Internet the import and export firms can send documentation by taking templates and sending them to its customs broker. This eliminates the need for sending faxes and post. The Internet has resulted in an incredible increase in the speed of information exchange, improved accuracy and pre-clearing shipments (Angeles 2000).

An example of when the Internet can be used to improve the management of the logistics service chain for B2B transactions is a business which uses a third party air freight forwarder to import/export goods. An air freight forwarder (AFF) provides pickup and delivery service under its own tariff, consolidates shipments into larger units, prepares shipping documentation, and tenders shipments to airlines. The Internet allows the business to communicate its needs more readily to the AFF and the AFF to the airline. Thus the business can be more flexible in its orders. The air freight also has more information on a larger number of airlines (suppliers) on space availability and price at low cost and easy access. The strategy of using the Internet to increase efficiency, lower cost and increase profits can be taken a step further. Since using the Internet makes accessing and updating information almost an automated process, there may be no real need for a business to use a third party agent, the business can communicate directly with the airline. The cost of the AFF would be saved by both the airline and the business. The airline can then price more competitively due to the cost reduction. Figure 17.1 illustrates this example of how the Internet can lead to the removal of certain intermediaries in a service chain.

As we can see from the example above, e-commerce procedures are altering the marketplace by changing firms' business strategies (Yau 2002). The Internet has

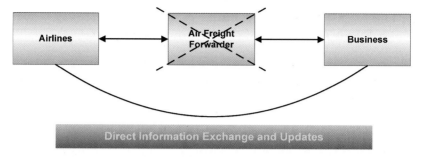

Fig. 17.1 Reduction of the logistics service chain

boosted competition between businesses as buyers are able to make price comparisons and sellers' costs are transparent to the buyers. Companies need to be able to make decisions in real time and must review their business strategies in order to remain competitive.

17.4 Flexible Pricing in E-Commerce

The characteristics of e-commerce have allowed businesses to move away from fixed pricing towards flexible pricing in order to increase effectiveness and efficiency (Bichler et al. 2002). The Internet increases the speed of pricing decisions and firms are now faced with more frequent reviewing and changing of price in order to remain competitively strong. This often manifests itself in differential pricing; a mechanism by which a firm charges different prices across customers (i. e., price discrimination) and on the type of service provided (i. e., product differentiation).

Price discrimination is the practice of a seller charging different prices to different customers for the same or similar service with additional extras. Pigou (1920) described three different forms of price discriminates.

- *First-degree price discrimination*: this is when the supplier sells different units of its service for different prices and these prices may differ from customer to customer.
- *Second-degree price discrimination*: the supplier sells different units of its service for different prices. Customers who buy the same amount of the service pay the same price. Here price is dependent on the amount of service purchased rather than the type of customer. An example of this is volume discounts, i. e., the more you buy the more you save.
- *Third-degree price discrimination*: here, the supplier sells its service to different types of people for different prices. This form of price discrimination usually applies for senior citizens' discounts or student discounts.

Product differentiation is when suppliers personalize their service by adding additional attributes to customize offers to specific customers or market segments. An example can be seen at the Odeon cinemas who offer tea and biscuits as part of their service for the elderly to encourage them to watch films during off-peak times. They also offer parents and toddlers the deal of one toddler to go in for free again during off-peak times. The attraction of additional extras will persuade more customers to visit during times where many seats otherwise go unsold and thus the cinemas are able to generate more revenue.

The airline industry practices differential pricing in a variety of forms. Airlines offer different types of customers' different fares, i. e., senior citizen discounts and frequent flyers. They offer different classes of service, i. e., first class, business class and economy. They also offer different sorts of restricted fares (i. e., advanced purchasing). The telecommunications industry is another example where differential pricing is applied in many different forms. The telecommunications market offers different rates and service to business and residential customers. They offer volume discounts to business customers. They offer calling plans that offer discounted rates based on individual characteristics and usage patterns.

Businesses use differential pricing on the selling of services purposefully to gain revenue on the portion of the market that is willing to pay more than the average price or by offering price sensitive customers deals to convince them to purchase services which would otherwise go unsold. However differential pricing can have the opposite effect if the firm has failed to recognize market segmentation correctly and if differential pricing causes cannibalizations (i. e., customers from the high purchase segmentation start moving to the lower price segmentation) or arbitrage (the service is bought by a third party and at a lower price and sold to customers at a higher price, and the third party makes a profit on the difference). Since the Internet makes information on customer behaviour readily accessible, firms are more able to see the effects of differential pricing and are more knowledgeable on market segmentation. They will also be able to deduce the effects of differential pricing, a negative consequence can be seen in real time and strategies can be altered accordingly.

The Internet market has increased opportunities for B2B to improve their network by using another form of flexible pricing known as *dynamic pricing*. Dynamic pricing is defined as flexible pricing between supplier and buyer in response to supply and demand at any given time. The price changes as the supply and demand in the market change. Dynamic pricing is usually used when there is uncertainty about the price, demand and supply of the service. It can significantly increase revenue. Figure 17.2 illustrates the different types of dynamic pricing models that can be used in B2B-EC over the Internet. We examine these models below.

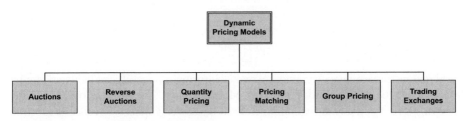

Fig. 17.2 Types of dynamic pricing model

17.4.1 Online Auctions

Many businesses use *online auctions* to sell excess inventories. An online auction is the process where the supplier and buyer offers a service over the Internet for bidding and sells the service to the highest bidder. An auction allows the supplier to determine the value of its service. B2B is usually carried out as a private auction. The Internet allows the process to be carried out electronically with a lower cost, a wide array of support services and with many more buyers and sellers. B2B marketers that use online auctions include marketers of consumer products, electronic parts, artworks, holiday packages and airline tickets. In the service industry B2B, online auctions are increasingly used by electricity transmission capacities, gas and energy options. In the UK, distributors bid for electricity from the suppliers. The distributors have the choice of bidding closer to the time they will need the electricity since they are better informed about the demand or can purchase in advance to ensure they will have enough supply.

17.4.2 Reverse Auctions

The most commonly used mechanism for B2B is *reverse auctions*. Here the buyer sets the price that he is willing to pay and then sellers bid for their service. The buyer has more choice and will be able to receive the best price. The buyer places a bid for the service on a request for a quote (RFQ) system. The suppliers give quotes to the buyer and the supplier that gives the lowest price for the service is the one the buyer will purchase from. Reverse auctions used in B2B are usually set with the condition of entry only through invitation (Anonymous 2001; Spring 1999). The wider range of suppliers increases competitiveness and hence results in the reductions of prices. Many of the B2B electronic trading exchanges offer reverse auctions, for example Ariba (Hix 2001).

17.4.3 Quantity Pricing

A different type of dynamic pricing model is *quantity pricing* (Buscher and Lindner 2004). This is when the supplier offers to sell different units of its service for different prices. Over the Internet the firm is able to put across this information effectively by custom quantity layouts. The firm is able to show that for different units of service, there is a different price. This makes it easier for customers to buy in quantity and understand savings. The Internet makes information readily available and helps to increase the average order, customized to the store. The average order may increase since it is made more attractive and easy to do. This may result in a revenue increase for the firm. An example of this in B2B is PriceHot.com.

17.4.4 Pricing Matching

The Internet makes changing price for services extremely easy, thus making it difficult to continuously know when other competing firms are under priced on homoge-
nous services. *Pricing matching* is a method used by businesses to ensure their customer the security that they are receiving the best price for the service. It is a trade
promise to match or beat all other competitors' prices. The firm promises to re-
fund the difference to the customer if they can buy the same service cheaper. Firms
offer promises to their buyers to match their competitors' price in expectation of
buyers purchasing with them rather than their competitors. The promise is set with
conditions such as a time limit of so many days, and the exclusion of special circumstances like closing down and loss leaders. Proof of pricing of a service prior to
the Internet could have been a bother as a flyer or receipt of the service is required
to provide evidence of the other firms' price. Fortunately over the Internet a website
link showing the other firms' price is sufficient.

17.4.5 Group Pricing

To encourage large group booking a firm can offer *group pricing* (Kauffman and
Wang 2001). The firm offers its service to a group of customers for a rate lower
than the standard rate. The technique of group pricing is common in a range of
services. An example of this is Economytravel.com, which offers group airfares on
15 different airlines.

The individual consolidator rates to different groups negotiated depending on the
circumstances and time. These groups include corporate business groups, musical
groups, band groups, athletic groups, food and wine clubs and weddings/family
reunions.

17.4.6 Trading Exchanges

The final dynamic pricing model mentioned is *trading exchanges*, which are types
of online electronic marketplace where buyers and sellers are brought together to
negotiate for commodities until they reach an equilibrium, thereby setting a price
for the service at a particular point in time or for the future. Using the Internet
a number of specialist trading exchanges have become established for such goods
as oil, chemicals and electricity (Gylnn 2001).

Using dynamic pricing models allows the seller to increase revenue at lowered
costs with improved efficiency to a larger range of buyers. It brings about a mechanism to sell unsold services and to be informed about market demand in real time.
The trade partner has opportunities to purchase at lower prices and has access to
a larger number of diverse suppliers. The supplier can also participate in multiple
auctions at the same time.

The pricing of services over the Internet is gradually underpinned by dedicated revenue management techniques and systems. The subject, already visited in Chap. 8, is examined next not only in an Internet context but also in terms of the models and algorithms that could be used in online applications.

17.5 Foundations of Online Revenue Management

Revenue management is a process of allocating the right type of capacity to the right kind of customer, at the right price, so as to maximize revenue (Smith et al. 1992). The right price and reservation capability is the key mechanism to revenue management. The objective of using revenue management is to ensure the firm makes the highest profits through demand forecasting and optimizing price and inventory accordingly. These techniques involve gaining an in-depth insight into customer buying behaviors, and predicting and reacting by exploiting the knowledge to maximize revenue. The Internet can significantly enhance the revenue management process – revenue optimization and demand management. Kimes (1989) suggested the definition of revenue management is rather restricted in its field of application. The techniques of revenue management are applicable when the conditions in Fig. 17.3 hold true.

Businesses must have a limited or fixed capacity prior to the demand for a service, for example the number of seats in the transportation business, the time slot for advertisements on television and the time of service (8.00 to 17.00) of a hairdresser. To gain the most revenue for a service which has a fluctuating demand, observation, experimentation and thoughtful planning is required in allocating the service

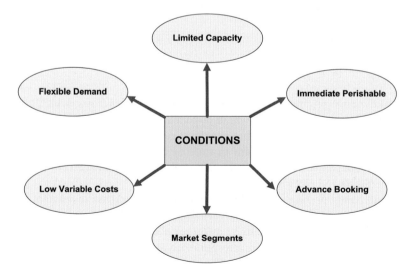

Fig. 17.3 Conditions for revenue management applications

(Phillips 2005). If the capacity is not fixed for the service then there is no need to apply revenue management as capacity can be controlled to suit demand and no loss would be made.

As already discussed elsewhere in the book, a service is *immediately perishable*; in other words, it cannot be stored to accommodate for demand in the future. This is true for the transportation business, for example unused seats on a bus journey cannot be stored for another upcoming journey. Other services include seats in the theatre, cinema and stadium, the time slots of hairdressers, engineer and auto repairers, and rooms in a hotel and apartments. Strategic techniques need to be employed to ensure that revenue is not lost by the service being wasted, i. e., an empty seat. If products can be stored then *inventory management* can be applied instead (Oberwetter 2001).

Advance booking is an important feature as it allows the customer to ensure the service will be available to purchase especially since it is limited. It also allows the business to track future demand and hence it can adjust the price so supply can meet demand (Ryzin and Mcgill 2000). Booking in advance is a feature used to put customers into market segmentation.

Market segmentation allows the firm to charge different customers different prices. Booking ahead of time allows customers to be put into different segments. Price discrimination is not allowed through customer variation. However, customer segmentation can be made through characteristics such as the time of purchase (Weatherford and Bodily 1992) and product differentiation (Kimes 1989). Price-sensitive customers tend to book ahead of time and they are willing to trade flexibly for reduced price. Commonly used is the purchasing of train transport where customers can book on the website in advance for a seat, which allows them to purchase at a cheaper price; they then accept the seat which they are given. Perfect market segmentation would mean the average willingness to pay is different for each segmentation. Market segmentation results in the service being sold at varied prices so as to generate the maximum revenue.

Low variable cost to the supplier is when an additional sale does not cost much but allows the service to be sold at a wide range of prices rather than go unsold. For example, an airline operation has high fixed costs and relatively low variable costs. Once the airline breaks even for a journey of an aircraft with respect to the fixed costs, any revenue gained in surplus of the variable costs (additional seat sold) will go towards profits.

If *demand* for the service is *flexible* then revenue management can be applied to help control the demand. It can be used to help simulate demand when demand for the service is low, for example, by promoting special offers. Alternatively when demand is high they can increase the price and therefore increase revenue. Demand in the airline industry can be flexible due to many factors, some of which include the travel destination, the time of year and particular day, and the holidays, conditions and the political situations of other countries.

As described in Chap. 8, there are five key areas of revenue management research: forecasting, overbooking, capacity allocation, pricing policies and network management. Forecasting is a vital part of planning but it is especially important to revenue management because booking limits, overbooking calculations, cancellations, and no-shows are dependent on its forecasted demand. The practice of overbooking capacity beyond the capacity of the service is carried out to allow for the probability of no-shows and cancellations which is calculated using the forecasts of past data. Capacity allocation is another component of a revenue management system that controls the availability of capacity for different classes. *Network management* is the process of optimising a fixed capacity of services which consists of multiple resources. Network management arises in industries such as airlines with connecting flights or hotel which promote multi-night stays. The price of the inventory is an essential variable which can be used to manipulate demand. It can be used to extract additional revenue when the demand is high or can be used to encourage demand when it is low. Pricing policies which interact with demand behaviur and resource are proposed to extract additional value from perishable resources. Network management is complex since there is a need to consider the interaction between the multi-resources and the effect it has on the ability to sell other services.

17.6 Models and Algorithms for Online Revenue Management

Models are used to represent the different problems addressed in revenue management, capacity allocation, network management, overbooking limits, and pricing decisions, for example. A model is a conceptual and mathematical tool used to describe the problem; it contains a set of variables and their relationships. The model chosen is then used to solve the optimization problem. The effectiveness and success of a model is measured by how well it represents the problem at hand and of course more importantly the amount of revenue generated when using it.

Modelling a problem with numerous interacting variables is a complex task. Research in revenue management was initiated with simple models consisting of only a few variables of the real world problem, holding strong simplified assumptions. For example the revenue management models in the airline industry began with single leg flights with only two booking classes having independent demands. This advanced to multi-booking classes with demand dependences between classes, progressing with models incorporating group bookings, cancellation, no shows, overbooking limits and the inclusion of a penalty cost when failing to honour a reservation. More complex multi-leg flights models were also developed. The development of revenue management models is an active area of research and models are improving with time. When a researcher is modelling a problem the assumptions that he makes will determine the strength of the model, for instance modelling how customers arrive into a system, i. e., simultaneously or sequentially.

Many researchers begin by observing the environment, viewing patterns or behaviors of customers and variables. These behaviors or patterns are used as assumptions the model holds. For example, Bitran and Gilbert (1996) modelled the hotel reservation problem; they did not assume customers would arrive simultaneously on the target day. Based on observation their model made the assumption that customers did not arrive at overlapping times: they specified three groups (customers with 6:00 pm reservations, "walk-in" customers and customers with guaranteed reservations). Their model assumed that customers with the 6pm reservation arrive first, followed by "walk-in" customers and finally those with guaranteed reservations. The market segmentation of customers is another variable which is dependent upon the features the researcher decides to model (i. e., the number of different types of customer segments and the attributes that separate them).

Some of the common decisions made by researchers when modelling an optimization problem is the choice of the selling horizon (the year, month, or week for example), characterizing the flexibility of the service, since flexible capacity allows the seller to allocate perishable resources efficiently based on observed demand rather than forecasted demand. Is the model a deterministic or stochastic model? Stochastic models are more appropriate to describe real-world problems when demand and inventory are unpredictable. When models use demand forecast to make decisions for variables such as pricing of the service, or capacity limits for different market segments, the researcher must decide upon how often the demand forecast is updated (every week, day, or hour, or every time a new customer arrives).

An effective model would be one that can model the problem at hand in an accurate manner and is robust to change. The Internet is a source of motivation for a survey on models. In real time we are able to collect valuable information about demand, inventory levels, and competitors' strategies and process. It also provides us with a laboratory to experiment with price changes. When a customer arrives at a firms' website information can be obtained about the customer. Customers can be divided into more accurate different market segments, each of which has its own attributes. Customers who enter the website and search for services but do not purchase due to price or quality consideration information on their behaviors can also be obtained by storing the path they follow on the website. Pricing decisions in real time require real-time demand data, the available capacity, competitors' strategies, weather, and any other relevant factors. With this information system, we are able to accomplish collecting the right information and making it available at decision points.

A twin problem of the modelling issue is the choice of the computational procedure, i. e., algorithm, to solve mathematically a given model of reality. The most popular algorithm used to solve revenue management problems is the dynamic programming (DP) algorithm (Rothstein 1975). DP models are able to model overbooking limits, cancellations, multi-leg problems and batch booking. However, the algorithm has difficulty solving stochastic problems of the real world with several interacting variables. Using an approximation to the DP algorithm is more appropriate for the Internet environment. Reinforcement learning is an approximation model of DP, which uses simulation to solve optimisation problems.

Reinforcement learning (RL) is an approach which can be used to understand a situation or an environment in order to maximize revenue or to allocate resources more efficiently. The way in which RL is able to achieve this is by learning what to do and how to map situations to actions, to maximize a numerical reward signal. A RL problem aims to be a simple model which captures the most important aspects of the real problem in the presence of a learning agent interacting with its environment to achieve a goal. In RL, the firm improves its performance step-by-step by interacting with an environment and at the same time choosing actions that enable it to explore an environment and to exploit the environment, increasing its profits, e. g., Sutton and Barto (1998).

Martin (2005) modelled a stochastic multi-knapsack booking process of television advertisement with deadlines. Since a TV break is perishable, revenue management techniques can be used to ensure that it is sold at the best price. The model was an online multi-knapsack with deadlines; at each period the agent/operator receives a sequence of arrivals or cancellations. If there is a cancellation then the agent simply updates space availability. At each request for space for the advertisement, the agent must decide whether to accept or reject the client. The algorithm overbooks and calculates the cost of overbooking. A reinforcement learning algorithm is used to find a strategy to maximise the profit in the long run of the accepted spots at the end of the booking process. The strategy is found by using simulation, learning from previous actions and rewards of these actions. It uses linear regression as a strategy to approximate a dynamic situation. The algorithm will determine whether to accept or reject a client according to the length of advertisement and availability of space using past experience. A limitation to the model is that it assumes the clients have no preference to the time their advertisement is shown.

17.7 Summary

The use of online revenue management in B2B-EC allows a firm to learn its customers' willingness to pay and provides the firm with better information on the value of its services. As a result the firm can improve resource management (by allocating the internal resources taking into consideration market preferences) and increases the options available to the customer (by providing a wider range of options regarding quality, speed and price), and consequently, increasing its revenue.

Businesses using the electronic marketplace to trade services with other businesses need to consider not only the advantages but also the disadvantages it brings to the firm. For example, the firm no longer builds personalized relationships because the Internet can accommodate for all the customers' needs. When there is no shortage of supply this may be fine, but if the service becomes scarce then suppliers are more likely to satisfy their established customers first. Another problem which may arise if clear specifications for the service are not given is that the buyer becomes disappointed when expectations are not met and as a result will not trade with the firm again. Nonetheless, e-commerce is here to stay so techniques that automate and improve electronic transactions between companies are becoming essential. This subject is looked at in the next chapter where we examine technologies for implementing electronic marketplaces and more specifically service-oriented resource exchanges.

Chapter 18
Electronic Marketplaces and Resource Exchanges

18.1 Introduction

In the previous chapter, we examined e-commerce, its impact on service chains and the different strategies that can be adopted in online revenue management. An enabler underlying these emerging areas are several new technologies with the most fundamental one being that of electronic marketplaces.

This chapter reviews the state-of-the-art of electronic marketplaces with a focus on the future e-supply chain for both products and services and emerging agent-based marketplaces. It also presents frameworks for new concepts such as service resource exchanges which can underpin intra-organisational and inter-organisational service chain management. Agent technologies seem to be well suited to this domain by providing a distributed environment, are network centric, semi-autonomous and collaborative and can communicate with each other to achieve better optimisation with little human intervention.

18.2 Electronic Marketplaces

Electronic commerce is increasingly assuming a vital role in many organisations. It offers opportunities to significantly improve the way that businesses interact with both their customers and their suppliers. Due to a rapid increase in the number of transactions conducted through electronic channels, such as the Internet, there has been an ever growing demand to develop advanced computational tools to support business to consumer (B2C) and business to business (B2B) eCommerce. Although most of the initial Internet-based eCommerce was in the form of B2C, B2B now constitutes a much larger portion of the overall eCommerce landscape. It is widely believed that B2B will continue to grow and will be the predominant means of doing business in the near future (Shaw 2000). Hence, there is a pressing need to apply sophisticated tools to enhance B2B eCommerce (Sun et. al. 1999; Kurbel and Loutchko 2001). By increasing the degree and sophistication of the automation, on

C. Voudouris, G. Owusu, R. Dorne, D. Lesaint, *Service Chain Management* 251
DOI: 10.1007/978-3-540-75504-3, ©Springer 2008

both the seller's and the buyer's side, eCommerce becomes much more dynamic, personalised and context sensitive.

The characteristics of an electronic marketplace (e. g., membership, regulation, service offer) depend on the organisation that offers the e-marketplace itself. Such organisation is referred to as e-market maker. E-market makers are B2B intermediaries. They operate in the supply chains in various vertical and horizontal industries, with the aim of introducing new efficiencies and new ways of selling and purchasing products and services (Matwin et al. 1991; Timmers 2000). An e-market maker provides content, value-added services, and often (but not always) commerce capabilities. An e-marketplace is managed either by a third-party vendor or by multiple dominant participants within the community. E-market makers aggregate content, provide value-added services, and offer multiple vendor alternatives. At a very high level, e-marketplaces can be segmented into three types. These three types include vertical marketplaces, horizontal marketplaces and enabling technologies (Gipson et al. 1999).

18.3 Agents and Marketplaces

Compared with B2C eCommerce, B2B deals with transactions among organisations. Generally speaking, relationships between organisations are more complex than those between businesses and consumers since they involve the adoption of similar standards with respect to communications and collaboration, as well as joint information technology investment. In particular, one of the main aims of B2B eCommerce is to facilitate more efficient and agile procurement processes (Dou and Chou 2002). Moreover, the tendency for exchanges in the B2B domain is increasingly becoming private. Such exchanges enable companies to trade with their existing partners in a well-defined environment without having to go through some of the early stages of the B2B lifecycle. For the purpose of the B2B lifecycle, smart technologies such as *intelligent agents* (Foss 1998; Fox et al. 2000) are relevant. Also known as *software agents* or simply *agents*, they can aid users by acting on their behalf and performing non-trivial computer tasks which require a degree of reasoning. Agents are most useful in partnership formation, brokering and negotiation stages because these stages all involve complex issues related to decision making, searching, and matchmaking that agent technologies are well suited to (Kurbel and Loutchko 2001).

18.3.1 Partnership Formation

This step may include the forming of a new virtual organisation as well as finding partners that provide products or services in a chain formation. A virtual enterprise (VE) is composed of a number of cooperating companies that share their resources and skills to support a particular product or service effort. One important aspect for agent-based support is service chain management.

Because of business trend towards outsourcing services and resources, service chain networks have become more and more complex. Therefore the emerging software solutions being developed need to be more sophisticated than the current generation of workflow tools. In particular, the various components of the service chain can be viewed as autonomous stakeholders and these various stakeholders need to interact in flexible ways. In B2B or B2C business, companies have to solve a major service chain management problem – how to efficiently incorporate, integrate, and utilise the rich inflows of information provided by multiple suppliers. Thus an agent-based approach can be well suited to this domain. In particular and drawing on the supply chain management experience, agents can be used to execute the scheduling (Fox et al. 2000), negotiate about prices (Sun et al. 1999) and share data between companies (Zeng 2001).

18.3.2 Brokering

Brokering is the process that matches sellers who supply goods/services to the buyers who need them. Brokering in the B2B context typically involves repeated transactions and large volumes. It is becoming more and more expensive and more difficult to find information on companies and their offerings. Hence in B2B commerce this can be done with the help of some form of information broker or matchmaker (Ha and Park 2001) or brokerage centre that acts as an intermediary between customers and providers. The broker in this context could be an agent or multi-agent system. The functions offered by such a broker could include the following: information retrieval and processing, maintenance of a self-learning information repository about the user, profiling of users, monitoring for items of interest for the user, filtering of information, intelligent prediction of user requirements, commercial negotiation between customer and providers, collaboration with other brokers, and protecting the user from intrusive access.

18.3.3 Negotiation

The research domain of electronic negotiation has become more and more important in recent years. Electronic negotiations are fundamental mechanisms to support automated decision making among two or more involved parties by determining the best fitting counterpart for a mutually beneficial deal. Electronic negotiations and multidimensional matchmaking define important building blocks within the research area of electronic markets.

Within the relationship between intelligent agents and electronic negotiations multi-attribute and multi-dimensional scenarios are of prime interest. Over the past few years, these issues have become central in economics and computer science research. The negotiation phase is where the traders aim to reach an agreement about what actions should be performed under what conditions. By establishing contracts on an as-needed and just-in-time basis, sellers can tailor their offerings both to their individual and the prevailing market situation at any given moment in time. Buyers can reduce their service chain costs, benefit from dynamic pricing mechanisms (as discussed in the previous chapter), broaden their supplier database, and streamline the procurement process. Compared with negotiation in the B2C context, B2B negotiation is more complex. The most popular means of conducting B2B negotiation are through auctions (He et al. 2003).

Several approaches to agent-mediated negotiation on electronic marketplaces have been introduced in the literature. However, there is no universally best approach or technique for automated negotiation. The negotiation strategies and protocols need to be set according to the situation and application domain (Kurbel and Loutchko 2001).

18.3.4 Auctions in B2B eCommerce

Support for auction and competitive bidding has become integral part of most software packages for electronic sourcing and procurement. Throughout the past decade many new auction formats have been developed which support more general negotiation and resource allocation tasks. Information systems supporting these types of auctions promise high economic efficiency even in the case of complex preferences, but require special design considerations.

Common classifications classify these auctions into buyer side auctions (one buyer and multiple sellers), seller side auctions (one seller and multiple buyers) and combinatorial auctions, where bidders bid for a combination of related items). An intelligent electronic agent can be either a buyer who submits bids or a seller who provides some products and services in these auctions.

The Kasbah e-marketplace is one of the early attempts at exploiting agent technology for automated negotiations in eCommerce (Maes et al. 1999). The Michigan AuctionBot is a general purpose Internet-based auction server hosted by the University of Michigan (Wurman et al. 1998). Although these kind of e-markets or auction houses are suitable for B2C eCommerce, they are ineffective in B2B ecommerce where multiple negotiation issues are often explored.

Magnet is a secure multi-agent electronic marketplace which supports a variety of transactions from simple buying and selling to complex multi-agent negotiation of contracts with temporal and precedents constraints (Jaiswal et al. 2004). Magnet agents are self-interested and, therefore, we can argue that it's more suitable for B2C commerce than B2B commerce where cooperative negotiation behaviour is possible. As a whole, Magnet is only an e-Auction mechanism with enhanced security facilities, but with multi-agent negotiation.

As many organisations have begun to realise the efficiency of auctions, interest has emerged to extend basic auction types to support negotiation beyond price, and communicate bids with a more complex set of preferences. Different types of auctions: volume discount auctions facilitate negotiations on large quantities of goods (Hohner et al. 2003); combinatorial auctions allow bids for bundles of goods (Cramton et al. 2006), and multi attribute auctions facilitate negotiation on multiple attributes of an auction. These multidimensional auction formats have performed well in the lab, and also in a number of real-world implementations in the field (Bichler et al. 2002).

Bichler and Kalagnaman (2006) propose a software framework for advanced procurement supporting a wide range of versatile auction formats allowing for more flexibility in specifying demand and supply.

Rubinstein-Montano and Malaga (2002) have reported a Genetic Algorithm based negotiation mechanism for multi-party multi-objective optimisation where the negotiation problem is treated as a multi-optimisation problem. The system proposed by them has a centralised decision making model.

On the other hand Lau (2006) proposes an effective and efficient negotiation mechanism to conduct multi-party multi-issue negotiations for individual organisations which is distributed in nature. Genetic algorithms have also been applied to learn effective rules to support the negotiation process (Matwin et al. 1991).

18.4 Resource Exchanges for Service Chain Management

A service chain is a network of customer/supplier relationships, with the exception that the service chain propagates services, as opposed to tangible products and materials. For service providers offering a variety of services over a range of domains, the service chain can become very complex, exhibiting attributes of a graph, rather than a linear chain.

Service chain management is concerned with the optimal provisioning and management of services to customers in order to satisfy customer service demand, whilst minimising the operational costs of supplying services. Supply chain management alone is not generally applicable within the service chain, due to several key differences between the nature of service and supply. Most notably, services are not tangible objects. Supply chain management is concerned with the flow of materials to and from suppliers eventually to the end customer. In the supply chain, materials may be measured by physical quality and quantity, however in the service chain; the definition of quality of service may become abstract. The key difference in this sense is quality of service. Services are inconsistent and dynamic and the human factor could be a hindrance in assessing quality of service. Furthermore, this problem may become even more apparent when the acquisition of services involves supply from contractor service providers.

Marketplaces and intelligent agents have been demonstrated to be useful structures and technologies in the context of supply chain management (Fox et al. 2000; Walsh and Wellman 1999). Could they be also utilised in Service Chain Management to trade services and associated resources? In the rest of this chapter and the next one, we look at how such emerging uses can be realised for trading both service resources (e. g., buying/selling man-hours on specific skills) and service tasks/projects (e. g., specific items of work that need to be performed). At the moment, such trading is mainly conducted in an informal way inside companies (or even between them) and often through complex human interactions and negotiations. Nonetheless, human resources and work scheduling systems described earlier in the book can increasingly enable such trading and negotiations to be automated through marketplaces and intelligent agents.

One such concept examined in this chapter is that of a resource exchange where the allocation of resources in a service organisation (e. g., engineering or construction firm) is accomplished through communication and exchanges between intelligent agents. In such scenario, requests or offers for service resource are often managed through an exchange. Thus, the complex process of acquiring/releasing skilled resources in service enterprises can be automated.

18.5 Business Scenarios for Resource Exchanges

A resource exchange can be approached from two perspectives: the centralised approach and a distributed approach. Obviously, they represent extreme points of view; many combinations between them are possible. In the centralised approach, the focus is on the company's global interests and priorities which solely dictate the allocation of resources. They are expressed via a set of conflicting global criteria. There is no decision power expressed at local management or employee level to reflect a traditional "command and control" way of operation.

In the distributed approach, the focus is on local management interests and priorities with a more "entrepreneurial" spirit being promoted. The company's overall interests and priorities are not explicitly expressed – there is no central manager to enforce them. Their accomplishment should emerge from the individual accomplishment of the local ones.

Embodiments of possible systems implemented based on a common model may be configured to act in different ways to assist in the redistribution of resources between entities within an organisation or across the service chain (e. g., automating the interactions of a company with its service subcontractors). These configurations can be grouped in various types of models based on a number of criteria. Based on a selected set of criteria a number of business scenarios linked to different types of marketplaces can be identified.

18.5.1 Resource Exchange Using a Central Exchange Agent

Our first business scenario relates to a number of divisions or domains (which can represent geographical service areas or defined otherwise) participating in a marketplace trying to optimise the workforce allocation between them by exchanging resources. This can be in the context of electricity, telecom, water or other utility which wants to move resources between divisions as and when required to improve its customer service. Each participating domain or area could have a number of idle or surplus resources (i. e., service personnel such as field engineers) and a number of jobs that need to be resolved. The idle resource cannot resolve the jobs within their own domains because of conflicting preferences or constraints. For example a field engineer might not have the necessary set of skills required to complete a local job however he/she could be deployed to a neighbouring area with pending jobs requiring his/her skill. Figure 18.1 illustrates a two-phase workforce allocation process where the surpluses and shortages left after local allocations are globally distributed. The optimisation process might expand over a shorter or longer planning period. One important aim of this process would be to maximise the number of jobs resolved throughout a region while minimising the travel and lodging costs associated with moving personnel.

The solution will require a collaborative model of the overall centralised system which will have a common objective to fulfil. Several possible agent-based solutions could be envisaged for this scenario. One solution would be that an intelligent *exchange agent* calculates optimal balancing figure for the region based on the region's objectives/priorities/preferences (e. g., maximise the number of jobs resolved while minimising the accommodation and travel cost) and broadcasts all request to all *service seller* agents who in turn will allocate resources to requests based on domain preferences/constraints and respond with resource offers. An optimisation software toolkit could be employed to program the internals of the agents (Voudouris et al. 2001).

Another example is where a common goal for the system could be established to try to optimise the workforce allocation for the entire region; therefore the agents will have this as their main objective, although the system will take into account conflicting objectives of the entities. Examples of conflicting criteria could be minimise travelling distance and maximise use of skill proficiency for resources. In this solution, the Exchange Agent will act as a central matchmaker that tries to satisfy requests by performing a multi-objective optimisation using hard constraints and soft constraints provided by the region's different areas. The Exchange Agent could use a multi-objective optimisation algorithm (Ehrgott and Gandebleux 2002) to se-

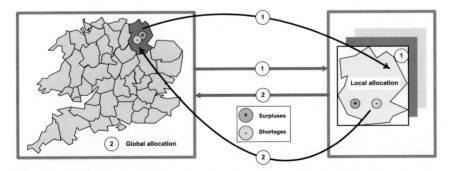

Fig. 18.1 A two-phase workforce allocation model: global allocation of surpluses and shortages left after the local allocation

lect an optimal subset of solutions based on hard constraints. User preferences (soft constraints) will then be used to select the best-preferred solution out of this subset. The intelligent agents representing the areas could then use local constraints to filter out requests or offers for resource that do not satisfy local interests and priorities.

18.5.2 Distributed Agent-Based Resource Exchange

Our second business scenario relates to the number of domains participating in a marketplace and trying to optimise the workforce allocation between them, but in this instance the emphasis is placed on local interests and priorities. In the same way as in the previous scenario, each domain could have a number of idle service resources and the planning period could expand over shorter or longer periods.

The solution will require a competitive model of the overall distributed system where it could also have a common objective to fulfil. The distributed scenario is a promising one where multiple entities have to work together and centralised resource planning looks difficult for a variety of reasons. For example different entities could have potentially conflicting interests or individual entities could have many constraints to consider, and these constraints change dynamically.

Several possible solutions could be envisaged for this scenario from completely distributed models where the region's overall interests are not explicitly expressed and their accomplishment emerges from the individual accomplishment of the local ones to solutions where individual agents have potentially conflicting interests but with an overall goal to maximise completion rates and service quality and minimise travelling distances.

One example would be that the workforce allocation is modelled as an iterative communication process, based for example on a 4-step communication contract net protocol, between *service buyer* agents, on one hand, and *service seller* agents, on the other. Decisions regarding the allocation are made locally, within each agent. A global allocation would emerge from this interaction/communication. The synchronisation of the agents' behaviour, necessary for the realisation of the 4-step communication protocol, is achieved via the Exchange Agent which for example would take the role of a *monitor*. This ensures that a step is initiated only after all the agents have indeed completed the previous step. However, this solution lends itself easily to other methods of timing. An asynchronous model, delegates the decision of when an agent should intervene in the overall environment to the agent itself – this too, then, becomes a matter of a local choice, based on local criteria and/or strategies. A combined solution can be accomplished via a system of deadlines. Agents would be allowed to decide when to initiate a process, but only up to a specific deadline that is enforced by the Monitor. The Exchange Agent may be employed in other types of mediation. Figure 18.2 illustrates a computational model where each domain has a Service Buyer and Service Seller agent associated with them and the region has a *central agency* (i. e., Exchange Agent). Each domain

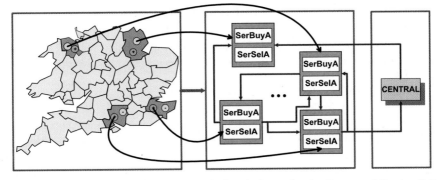

Fig. 18.2 A computational model where each domain has a Service Buyer and Service Seller Agent associated with them with a Central Agency also employed in the allocation process

has associated a Service Seller Agent (SerSelA) and a Service Buyer Agent (SerBuyA). Agents interact (black line arrows in Fig. 18.2) in the process of resource allocation.

However, it is possible to further relax the purely distributed approach, and to enforce certain interaction structures via this Central Agency. Therefore a second example is where individual Service Buyer and Service Seller agents have potentially conflicting interests but there is also a central objective. The business objective in this case is to allow for a distributed market to operate where multiple service providers have to serve multiple service buyers while the central objective is a multi-objective optimisation problem: the central manager has to strike a balance between job completion rates, service quality, travelling distances and other objectives.

18.5.3 A Central Auctioneer-Based Marketplace

Our third business scenario relates to a number of domains and external partners (e. g., contractors) participating in an auction based marketplace aiming at trading resources between them. Each participating domain could have a number of idle or surplus resources and a number of jobs that need to be resolved. External partners would have a number of contractors with the necessary skill sets for the required jobs. The suitable type of auction would be a buyer side auction (one buyer multiple sellers) where service resources would compete over skill requests.

Two scenarios could be considered in this case. In the first scenario the currency based (or single objective) model may be used when buyers and sellers in the marketplace are using comparable currencies (e. g., money). An extra entity would be incorporated in the marketplace model which would be a *contractor agency*. This agency would have *contractor agents* (with similar specification to Service Sellers) that manage a set of contractors, who can be assigned to jobs. In this model the Exchange Agent would act as a central auctioneer assisting in trying to satisfy requests provided by Service Seller, Service Buyer and Contractor Agents on behalf of domains. This central auctioneer would co-ordinate the market. Various auction protocols may be used such as English auction, Dutch auction, or Reverse auction. In this competitive model the individual agents will have as their main objective the optimisation of their own workforce allocation; therefore they would compete in the marketplace to attempt to achieve this objective.

A multi-objective model may be used if it would be impossible to establish a common currency in the marketplace. In this model buyers and sellers use objectives which cannot be directly compared. For this purpose multi attribute auctions facilitating negotiation on multiple attributes of an auction need to be investigated.

18.6 Technologies for Implementation

Initial implementations of some of the business scenarios described above can be engineered as enterprise applications using the three-tier software architecture model (Virginas et al. 2007). As an example, the business logic which contains the intelligent agent components and data layers can be implemented as Enterprise Java Beans (EJB) using the J2EE architecture and eXtensible Markup Language (XML) used as the agent interaction language. Nevertheless, when considering the development of such an agent-based resource exchange as the one described above, one has to consider state of the art agent-based technologies in order to place the framework on a sound platform. The main things to consider are the choice of interaction languages and protocols as well as development tools, technologies and platforms.

Firstly, the agents need to be able to communicate with other agents, with the environment and with humans. Many of the applications use XML. However, most B2B transactions exchange information via the Electronic Data Interchange (EDI) protocol. Nevertheless, there is a common belief that the XML/EDI format will replace the traditional EDI messages. Apart from the Web based applications, the agent field has its own communication and knowledge representation languages like FIPA ACL and Knowledge Query Manipulation language. While these languages are concerned with the format of the message, the content of the message has to be represented in some form, using languages like FIPA SL. Moreover, there are a number of services that aim to facilitate the cooperation among trading partners like the Global Commerce Initiative (Foss 1998).

Secondly, specific development tools can be used which have been specifically developed for the eCommerce domain. For example, AuctionBot is an agent-based auction server that can be used to create automated auctions (Wurman et al. 1998). Furthermore, there are some agent development platforms and tools like the Agent Development Kit (ADK), a Java based eCommerce and workflow management applications environment. While a few interaction languages might become dominant for high level communication, development platforms, once they mature, are likely to increase in use targeting various application areas. The requirements are so varied though that there will continue to be many offerings that are targeted at particular markets. A brief review of interaction languages, protocols, development tools and security issues is given by He et al. (2003).

Finally, as systems are developed that utilise software agents as component building blocks, they will have to interoperate with systems developed using a multi-tier, Web-centric framework. Agent systems may need to interface with other systems (e. g., forecasting, planning and scheduling applications described earlier in the book) to capture their input data. Web services are emerging to provide a systematic and extensible framework for application-to-application interaction, built on the top of existing Web protocols and on open XML standards. A possible solution to this problem is enabling a multi-agent system to offer web services to browser clients of the J2EE Web-centric system. One possible approach to sharing information products developed within the agent system with such other systems and the larger Enterprise is the Web service enabled multi-agent systems (Cavedon et al. 2004). That is, information in an agent-based system would be exposed via Web services. Software clients could be browser clients as well as software agents.

18.7 Summary

There are now many B2B marketplaces on the Web that provide auction services and allow organisations to trade with one another on a global basis (e. g., FreeMarkets and Ariba). Industry analysts estimate that 25% of eCommerce consists of exchanges through such mechanisms (Sachi and O'Leary 2002). However, the several key differences between the nature of service and supply make the service chain management area unique as far as marketplaces are concerned. Little has been reported so far as marketplaces and the service chain are concerned.

Effective service chain management is vital in today's economy and organisations can start investigating the agility and automation offered by agent-based approaches. Agent-based solutions have been extensively reported on partnership formation, brokering and negotiation, primarily in the context of traditional supply chain management, but they hold promise for service chain management too.

In this chapter, we also examined how agent-based systems and market-places can be used to implement resource exchanges in the context of the service chain. Competitive versus collaborative scenarios, multi-objective versus common-currency-based scenarios and internal versus external contractor based scenarios can be considered.

It is our strong belief that marketplace approach is the way forward in this particular problem space and some of these scenarios described here will lead to future successful systems as far resource exchanges are concerned.

Chapter 19
Multi-Agent Systems for Staff Empowerment

19.1 Introduction

In the previous chapter, we examined the concept of resource exchanges based on intelligent agents and marketplaces. In this chapter, we are focusing on how the same distributed decision making models can be used for empowering staff. Human resources are the main resources in a service industry. Success or failure of a service operation is often determined by its personnel management policy. A successful management policy would provide job satisfaction to employees, which will lead to higher morale, productivity and service quality.

Staff empowerment is a management concept. The idea is to give employees autonomy in doing their jobs. The aim is to improve job satisfaction by allowing employees to have control over their operations.

For staff empowerment to work, appropriate management arrangements are required. The philosophy behind staff empowerment recognizes personal needs by individuals. To ensure that the collective behavior of the staff achieves the company's goals, the management must define the authority and responsibilities for each individual or department/division. The assumption behind staff empowerment is that by defining negotiation protocol and assessment criteria properly, the "market" mechanism will ensure that the staff gains autonomy while the company achieves its goals. In other words, everybody wins.

This chapter presents a technological framework for designing a mechanism to implement empowerment in the context of workforce scheduling (examined as a subject in Chap. 10) by using some of the concepts described in the previous chapter. A scenario inspired from BT's field engineering operations is used for illustration. However, the framework and techniques are general and therefore could be used for other job-staff allocation activities, where staff empowerment is to be employed.

C. Voudouris, G. Owusu, R. Dorne, D. Lesaint, *Service Chain Management*   263
DOI: 10.1007/978-3-540-75504-3, ©Springer 2008

19.2 A Workforce Scheduling Problem

The importance of problem formulation is often underestimated (Borrett and Tsang 2001; Freuder 1999). Modelling formalizes the company's considerations; i. e., what are considered important by the company. It also defines the company' objectives, i. e., what the company wants to achieve. In this section, we shall briefly describe a version of the workforce scheduling problem inspired by BT's field service operations (see Chap. 10 for more information on the general problem).

BT has to serve a large number of customers every day. Their needs vary from telephone repairs to network design and installation. Engineers also have to be sent for repair, maintenance and installation of BT's networks. These jobs are geographically distributed. Each job demands engineers of certain skills. Some jobs will take longer time to complete than others – the duration of a job can be estimated through past experience on similar jobs. Some jobs can only be done at certain times. Logically, each job can be assigned a value (how important it is to the company).

To serve the jobs, BT has a large number of engineers. The engineers are also geographically distributed (some of them may start their working days from home). Each engineer may be more skilful on certain types of jobs, but less skilful in others. Therefore, for each engineer, one can logically assign a "preference" to each skill, indicating how efficient they are in serving jobs which require such skill. It is in the company and the customers' interest that the engineers are sent to jobs

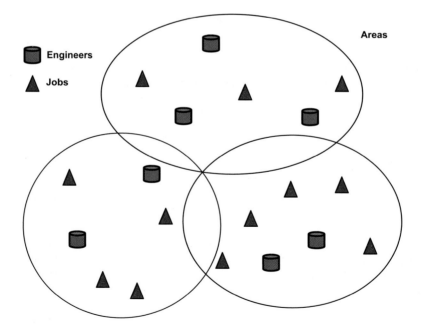

Fig. 19.1 A generic workforce scheduling problem, where the task is to assign engineers to jobs

which they specialize in; i. e., maximizing the "preference" values in job assignments.

The task is to assign these engineers to the jobs, subject to their availability (e. g., some engineers may be willing to work overtime, but others may not). Whenever possible, we would like to minimize the distance travelled by the engineers. Figure 19.1 provides a visual description of the workforce scheduling problem.

19.3 How to Achieve the Goals?

The generic workforce scheduling problem as outlined above is a complex problem. The manager's job is to look after the company's interest, which is a multi-objective optimization problem (Deb 2001). Each area controller/dispatcher has its own scheduling problem, which is also technically a constraint satisfaction problem (Tsang 1993). In particular, this problem can be seen as a constrained multi-vehicle routing problem (Rossi et al. 2006).

The workforce scheduling problem described above can be tackled through central scheduling and optimisation using the approaches outlined in Chap. 10. However, field engineers can introduce delays if they decide to do so. To protect their own interest, controllers may not help other areas freely and so forth. One of the best ways to reduce game playing is through improvement of morale. Staff empowerment is an effective management strategy to maintain morale in the workforce.

One way to implement staff empowerment at the dispatcher/controller level is giving the area controllers permission to look after their own interests (similar scenarios can be developed for empowering team leaders or individual engineers). This means the problem will be formulated as a distributed scheduling problem in which the individual agents have their individual goals as opposed to having shared goals, as stated in (Prosser 1990).

To tackle this distributed scheduling problem, our approach is to model the area controller's activities with intelligent agents. We define a buyer agent and a seller agent for each controller. The buyer agent handles the jobs that the controller has. Its task is to "buy" services to complete the jobs. The seller agent handles the group of engineers under the controller's command and its task is to "sell" services to complete the jobs. Further delegation and empowerment could be achieved if the seller agents operate at even lower levels of granularity such as representing team leaders or individual engineers.

We define a management agent that looks after the company's interest. Ultimately, the management agent will be a program that interacts with the human manager who is in charge of the overall operation. We give the management agent the duty of handling the multi-objective optimization problem. Details of this will be described in the next section.

19.4 Handling Multiple Objectives

One approach to multi-objective optimization is to define mathematically the relative importance of the multiple objectives. This turns the problem into a single-objective optimization problem. One major drawback of this approach is that human managers are often reluctant to define the relative importance of the multiple objectives in abstract, mathematical terms (either due to sheer difficulties or due to their unwillingness to commit themselves). It is, however, relatively easier for one to express one's preference when one is given a few schedules. Therefore, we define the goal of the management agent as to generate a Pareto set of schedules for the human manager to choose.

Our approach is to give the management agent the task of finding a Pareto set of schedules, which will be presented to the human agent for selection. The Pareto set is generated by iterations. In each iteration, the management agent provides the buyer and seller agents the weights for each of their objectives. Thus the buyers and seller agents each have a single-objective scheduling problem to solve. They interact with each other (to be explained later) to generate a schedule. The weights-definition and scheduling-generation process repeats until enough number of schedules have been generated. This is shown in Fig. 19.2.

This approach allows us to neatly separate multi-objective optimization from the rest of the problem. It also reflects the management structure.

Fig. 19.2 A multi-agent based architecture for workforce scheduling

19.5 How to Generate a Pareto Set of Schedules?

Given the architecture defined above, the key question is how the management agent should adjust the weights for the buyer and seller agents. Before we can answer this question, we need to decide on the metric for measuring the quality of a Pareto set. We combine two metrics in our approach: *range and evenness of distribution*. Formal definitions of these metrics can be found in the literature, e. g., see Okabe (2004).

For illustration, let us assume that we have two objectives; this can be represented by two functions, f_1 and f_2 to maximize. Figure 19.3 shows two Pareto sets: the circles and the squares. The circle set has a wider range than the square set, because one of its members has an f_1 value higher than any of the members in the square set; the same applies to f_2. Members in the circle set also more evenly distributed than members of the square set. Therefore, the circle set is preferred to the square set, according to the metrics that we adopt. It provides the human manager a set of solutions to suit different preferences of f_1 and f_2. In other words, the human manager has better chance of finding a satisfactory solution in the circle set than in the square set.

Having decided on the metric to adopt, we have some guidance on how the management agent should set the weights for the buyer and seller agents. For example, good solution to add to the set of square solutions in Fig. 19.3 is where the cross indicates. This solution will extend the range of the square Pareto set.

For the management agent, knowing the target position (such as the position marked by the cross in Fig. 19.3) in its objective space is only the first step towards setting the weights for the buyer and seller agents. The only control that the

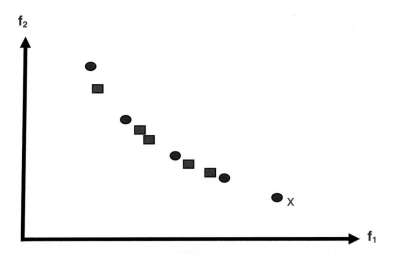

Fig. 19.3 The function space showing the quality of Pareto sets: f_1 and f_2 are two functions to maximize. The *set of circle* solutions is preferred to the *set of square* solutions because they range wider and are more evenly distributed. The mark "x" indicates a desirable member to be added to the set of red solutions

management agent has is in setting the weights. It has no direct control over what schedule the buyers and sellers will generate. In its attempt to generate a schedule in the target position, the management agent must discover the mapping from the weights space to the management agent's objective space. Given that the workforce scheduling problem does not change radically over time, learning of this mapping is possible. Many machine learning tools can be used for this purpose (Mitchell 1997). This is the subject of on-going research on this subject (Gosling et al. 2006).

19.6 Self-Interested Multi-Agent Scheduling

So far we have not explained how the buyer and seller agents interact to generate a schedule. The buyer and seller agents are given their objective functions by the management – the function against which their performance will be assessed. Each agent is free to adopt any methods to generate a schedule to suit their own preference, which (as recognized by staff empowerment) may take into consideration their own agenda which is beyond the management's control.

The problem is basically a self-interested distributed scheduling problem. One of the better methods for tackling this class of problems is the Contract Net, which was developed in the early 1980s (Davis and Smith 1988; FIPA 2002; Smith 1980). The basic principle behind Contract Net is that the buyers broadcast their jobs, and the sellers bid for services provision. The bids vary in quality, from the buyers' point of view. For example, one bid might involve a longer travelling distance, but a better fit of skill. Since the buyer agent has been given the weights to balance between travelling distance and fit of skill (as well as other objectives), it will be able to evaluate different bids. A buyer would make an offer to the best bid. Seller agent has the final say whether to take up the offer. As the seller may get multiple offers for the same engineer, it does not necessarily accept an offer.

The contract net provides a protocol for generating schedules. Unfortunately, it does not necessarily generate the most efficient schedule. Basically, it samples one schedule only, by assigning one job to the locally best engineer ("best" as agreed between a buyer and a seller) at a time. Figure 19.4 shows a scenario involving three regions. In this scenario, Area 1 has one spare engineer. Area 3 has one job that is not served by any engineer. If the company's overall objective is to finish as many jobs

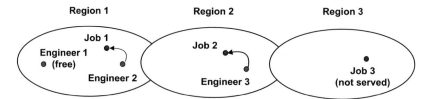

Fig. 19.4 A schedule that could be improved if job-completion is the dominating criteria for solution quality

as possible, while minimizing the travelling distance is of secondary importance, then it would have preferred to assign Engineer 1 to Job 1, Engineer 2 to Job 2, and Engineer 3 to Job 3. This revised schedule would require more travelling, but complete one more job. Unfortunately, this improved schedule will probably not be found by a standard contract net if each area controller were to give priority to its own engineers.

An alternative protocol is presented in the next section which overcomes the shortcomings identified above.

19.7 RECONNET – Local Search over Schedules

An obvious improvement to the contract net protocol is to hill-climb in the space of schedules. A large number of local search methods in the literature could help hill-climbing in the space of schedules, e. g., see Hoos and Tsang (2006). The complication in this problem is that local search requires releasing of contracts and these contracts cannot be released unilaterally; otherwise the situation would be chaotic: an engineer could be sent to a job which has been cancelled by the service buyer, and a job could be waiting to be served by an engineer whose controller has cancelled the contract. This represents a self-interested distributed system. Both buyers and sellers must agree before a contract could be released. To facilitate local search, a contract release mechanism must be designed. The protocol to be described here is called RECONNET (which stands for REtractable CONtract NET).

RECONNET introduces a contract release mechanism to standard Contract Net. When a buyer has a job that needs to be served, it could ask for bids that may involve the release of an existing contract. For example, in Fig. 19.4, the buyer in Area 3 (call it Buyer 3) may ask the seller in Area 2 (call it Seller 2) to make a bid for Job 3. Seller 2 may make a bid to Buyer 3, on condition that the buyer in Area 2 (call it Buyer 2) is willing to release the contract (of buying Engineer 3's service).

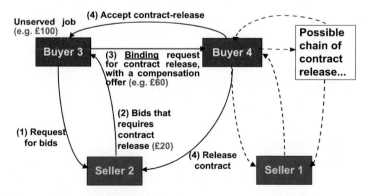

Fig. 19.5 A scenario involving contract release

Buyer 3 may then offer Buyer 2 a compensation for releasing its contract. Buyer 2 may attempt to secure an alternative contract for Job 2 before it decides to take up Buyer 3's offer. The contract release protocol is shown in Fig. 19.5.

Contract release is driven by a market mechanism. To do Job 3, Engineer must travel further than serving Job 2. Therefore, Seller 2 will ask Buyer 3 for a price. Suppose Seller 2 asks for a price of £20, but Job 3 is worth £100 to Buyer 3, then Buyer 3 would be able to offer Buyer 2 anything up to £80 for releasing the original contract. Suppose Buyer 3 offers Buyer 2 £60 to release the contract. Buyer 2 could then use part of it to buy alternative services for Job 2. Since the benefit to a buyer decreases as the chain lengthens, an infinite loop is not a threat to this contract release protocol.

19.8 Dynamic Scheduling

Workforce scheduling is a dynamic problem. New jobs may arrive at any time. Delays may occur, possibly due to complications in service delivery or traffic congestions. This means schedules have to be revised constantly, which adds a new dimension to this complex problem.

To react to new jobs and unexpected delays, rescheduling time is crucial. Like most local search algorithms, the more time the algorithm is given, the more chance it has in finding better solutions. The size of the Pareto set generated by the management agent is also relevant.

The size of the problem varies over areas and time. A problem of realistic size would involve 150 to 300 jobs per area. In a prototype that implements the RE-CONNET protocol mentioned above, a schedule for 7 areas of realistic size took 5 to 15 minutes to generate. (We assumed that each service buyer will buy from 7 sellers – bids from far away sellers are unlikely to be practical, due to travelling cost and travelling time.) There is plenty of room for speed-up in an operational system. It is reasonable to assume a speed-up of at least an order of magnitude over the prototype system. If the management agent needs to generate a Pareto set of 10 schedules, it will take 5 to 15 minutes to reschedule, which is quite acceptable.

When the situation is changed, rescheduling from scratch may not be the best policy. Local search is well suited for schedule-repair. RECONNET is a framework which could support a wide range of local search methods, including Tabu Search (Glover and Laguna 1997; Glover and Kochenberger 2003) and Guided Local Search (Mills 2002; Voudouris and Tsang 2003).

19.9 Research Frontier

In RECONNET, a buyer offers compensation to another buyer for contract release. There is no reason why this compensation cannot be negotiable. Bargaining is a well studies topic in game theory and automated bargaining could play a part in this research (Jin and Tsang 2006).

Each seller agent has to solve a scheduling problem for every objective function defined by the management agent. This is not a standard constraint satisfaction problem (Tsang 1993), hence demands specialized scheduling techniques. For example, assignments have to be agreed by buyer agents and they cannot be undone unilaterally. Exactly how this scheduling problem should be best solved requires a separate study.

The contract release protocol in RECONNET may not be optimal. Research in distributed artificial intelligence may be consulted. In Aknine et al. (2004), Sandholm and Lesser (2002) and Sen and Durfee (1998), agents are allowed to cancel contracts unilaterally. This is viable when all agents are cooperative. Unfortunately, this is not an assumption in our model. We acknowledge the possibility that agents may manipulate the biddings to maximize their own benefit. This, plus the dynamic nature, makes contract de-committing strategies such as those proposed by Raiffa (1982), Sandholm and Lesser (2002) and Sen and Durfee (1998) non-applicable for the problem defined in this chapter. The practical needs in this problem demands new techniques.

We pointed out earlier that the nature of the problem does not change radically over time. Therefore, it is possible to take advantage of information gathered over time in designing the system. Simulation techniques can assist to investigate the various degrees of delays and their impacts. Such a simulation environment is shown in Fig. 19.6. The environment can be used to investigate the impact of delays and

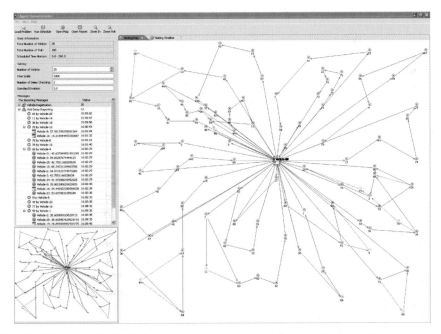

Fig. 19.6 Example of a simulation environment for the workforce scheduling problem

other types of exceptions and also visualize engineer route changes due to them under different scheduling regimes.

19.10 Summary

To summarize, we have used a generic workforce scheduling problem to illustrate how the allocation of work can be combined with staff empowerment. The problem is formalized as a multi-objective, dynamic distributed optimization problem. We have divided this complex problem into sub-problems. This allows us to deal with them separately. It also allows us to bring in established research, such as multi-objective optimization, constraint handling, distributed scheduling, contract net, machine learning and agent-based modelling.

The key to the success of a multi-agent system is in how the authority and negotiation protocol is defined. In the proposed approach, the controllers are given freedom in how they schedule their engineers to serve the jobs – they know how their performance will be assessed. The model can be elaborated to empower at lower levels such as team leaders or individual engineers through the use of intelligent agents modelling their interests and "selling" their services (or buying "services" from others). The approach relies on the market's "invisible hand" to produce schedules that balances the different agents' needs.

Using a multi-agent platform and simulation environment, management can test different designs before they are implemented. This allows the management to identify the overall setup under which desirable results (as defined by the management) could be achieved.

Epilogue

Chapter 20
A Practical Guide to Benefit Realisation

20.1 Introduction

This chapter is a practical guide to help an organisation ensure that it achieves a realistic benefit from introducing new service chain management technologies into its operations. The focus is on Field Force Automation (FFA) and mobile service workers. The viewpoints expressed are based on the work and experience of Paul Cleaver who served in a number of senior management positions at BT over the last 14 years. The examples are mainly drawn from BT's major transformation of the engineering workforce between the years 1993 to 2002 that Paul headed but also from his experience in subsequent roles including his latest highly successful endeavour in delivering ICT solutions for BT's corporate customers.

During the 1990s, BT was under significant pressure and it was essential that the cost per engineering visit was reduced and at the same time customer service was improved. As a result, the company launched a major field force automation and mobility programme to improve the efficiency of its service operations. The key initiatives included the introduction of an advanced work scheduling system to automate the dispatch of jobs to the mobile workforce, the introduction of resource management software to ensure that the workforce started work in the correct location, the introduction of ruggedised laptops and PDAs to eliminate the need for paper and also an important initiative to improve the quality of the engineering work to reduce repeat visits which can seriously affect customer service and costs. The lessons learnt are important when it comes to service chain management for fieldforces but can be just as useful in the context of salesforce, officeforce and other serviceforce situations.

20.2 What Does Automation Mean?

This is a very important question as many managers who are responsible for the mobile workforce have no appreciation of what can and should be achieved through an automation initiative. It is absolutely not about providing the mobile worker with

C. Voudouris, G. Owusu, R. Dorne, D. Lesaint, *Service Chain Management*
DOI: 10.1007/978-3-540-75504-3, ©Springer 2008

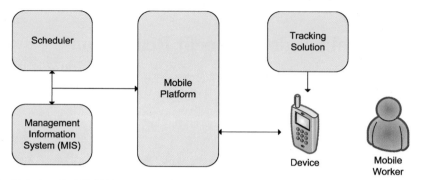

Fig. 20.1 A typical Field Force Automation solution

a device and then saying "you are automated; achieve a 15% productivity gain tomorrow." The device should be decided last; it is not the important ingredient in achieving the necessary gains. The key is the software applications that enable the gains to be made. Figure 20.1 is a very simple pictorial explanation of a typical field force automation solution.

20.2.1 The Scheduler

Scheduling as a technology subject was covered in depth in Chap. 10. For several companies, a simple but flexible work scheduling software application is sufficient to initiate them into field force automation. This will be able to improve work ordering so that work is more efficiently completed. The solution must be able to chase productivity when appropriate, but also be able to be driven by customer service objectives. The scheduler must be able to work in real time and update work schedules throughout the day to reduce manual intervention by dispatching personnel. It also needs an excellent link to the management information system to be described below.

20.2.2 The Mobile Platform

The Mobile Platform is the method of transferring the information from the "backend" software to the mobile worker and back again. Often, the solution represents a relatively simple piece of technology but rather essential to facilitate communications between the company and its field workers.

20.2.3 Tracking

More and more GPS-based tracking linked to a scheduler is the norm. The tracking element lets the organisation know where the mobile worker actually is and linked to the scheduler enables the most efficient work distribution to take place. It would be wrong to name companies but when Company A introduced scheduling linked to tracking and good management information 200 mobile workers were found to do little work if any! Company B introduced a combined work allocation and tracking solution and found that 7% of their workforce was full time couriers for another company and were using their company vans for another organisation! Managers may be blind to reality if they believe that this cannot possibly be happening in their organisation.

20.2.4 Device Selection

Once an organisation understands field force automation and what it is trying to achieve device selection can take place. The service environment plays a major role in the decision. For example, a mobile worker and his van is a much harsher environment than that experienced by sales people and managers and a plastic non-ruggedised device will most likely break. A company that we worked with had their automation programme derailed because the devices kept breaking which ruined the perception of the whole programme.

When considering which device to choose do not base the decision solely on the upfront cost. A ruggedized or semi-ruggedized device will be more expensive but on how much money does the mobile worker cost the company not being able to work due to a broken plastic device? It is often the case that a device that is difficult to break will pay for itself many times during its 3 year life. For some reason, this fact is just ignored as managers cannot resist the cheap option which is in fact extremely expensive in the long run. The scenario below illustrates this point by providing indicative figures on the failure rates of devices and associated costs:

- Failure rate plastic device   50% per annum
- Failure rate semi-ruggedised device   5% per annum
- Failure rate ruggedised device   1% per annum
- Approx. cost per mobile job lost   £60
- 5000 jobs lost through plastic failure   £300,000
- 500 jobs lost through semi-ruggedised   £30,000
- 100 jobs lost through ruggedised failures £6000.

The problem is that very few companies translate the device failure rate into lost jobs; there is generally only a comparison of actual costs of the various devices.

20.2.5 Management Information

Management Information is another key subject often neglected. We often hear a project manager say "we will think about the management information after we have implemented the project." This is the "wrong" approach. The first item to be considered is the key information that will be needed to ensure that the anticipated benefits are being realised. Often a maximum of up to six reports is sufficient to provide with all of the productivity and customer service information that is required. It can ideally be available in real time and definitely no later than the next morning so that corrective actions can be taken. Up to date information is essential to enable an organisation to understand what is happening hour-by-hour, day-by-day.

20.3 What Does Benefit Achievement Mean?

Before embarking on the path to automating the processes for an organisation which is going to be relatively expensive, time consuming and will undoubtedly lead to serious cultural issues needing to be addressed, the organisation must understand what the benefits really are. From our experience, the key benefit areas are often the following:

- Productivity gains;
- Customer service improvements;
- Faster invoicing;
- Standardisation;
- Implementation of service policy and customer priorities;
- Better quality of work leading to a reduction in repeat work;
- Better understanding of the real performance of the organisation.

20.3.1 Productivity Gains

Automating the processes around the mobile workforce is likely to lead to productivity gains; however managers must not fall into the trap of believing that a theoretically calculated gain will happen in practice. Sales and consulting organisations who sometimes advice that a 50% gain in productivity is achievable through an FFA initiative are way off what reality suggests. In our experience, a figure between 10% to 20% is possible depending upon the starting position. Productivity has to be judged on completed work i. e., 7 jobs completed per worker per day becomes 8 jobs completed per worker per day. Do not let people take you down a route of 5 minutes saved per job equates to X% productivity gain. The saving has to be able to materialise hence a hard measure has to be used as mobile or other service workers are often expanding or contracting true working time to complete their "traditional" number of tasks per day. This is a difficult circle to break hence a simple view that productivity will increase by one or more tasks a day is a simple but effective method. The more complicated the calculation becomes; the less likely it will be delivered in reality.

If an organisation has 1000 mobile field workers each costing circa £50K per annum (including all vehicle and equipment costs) a 10% saving equates to £5,000,000 per annum which can translate into new work and revenue that can be brought into the organisation maintaining the same level of resources. This can pay for the automation programme within the first year of implementation.

Productivity can also be split into two different areas, the mobile workforce and secondly the office based scheduling and dispatch teams. If scheduling or dispatch become automated it is obvious that major savings will occur in the latter area too. The nature of the job for dispatchers will also change into a jeopardy management activity which should result in a higher percentage of appointments and other commitments being achieved to be discussed in more detail below.

In general, it is wise to avoid wild claims and ensure that common sense is used at all times. This particular area is important to get right since financial savings are essential to justify technology investments.

20.3.2 Customer Service Improvements

Reducing customer churn is vital to the success of most organisations. Automating the mobile field force, if done properly, will reduce missed appointments. It should also ensure that a correctly qualified person is sent to the job. The general service improvement and impact on customers is quite difficult to quantify correctly as an action taken today may not be reflected in "churn" for up to 6 months. It is best to be careful when measuring churn and a minimum 3 month period should be allowed before the benefit of automation is assessed against any churn figures. If an organisation wants to measure this properly it is also important that no other initiatives are implemented that will affect churn during the measurement period e. g., price increase or reduction, new products, special offers, etc.

Alternatively, a measure for customer service is the number of appointments or other commitments made to customers that are achieved on time. An automated solution can often enable a 15% improvement to be made on successfully completed appointments and commitments at the promised time.

20.3.3 Faster Invoicing

Faster invoicing is a very important side benefit from fully automating a service process. Post-automation, it should be possible to send the relevant information back into an organisation's billing system on the same day that the work is completed. On a number of occasions experienced firsthand, this has saved up to 5 working days from the invoicing cycle which can considerably improve the cash flow of an organisation. This should be seriously considered as an important financial gain and be included in the financial benefits of the business case to be realised in the first stages of solution deployment.

20.3.4 Standardisation

It is very difficult to identify a financial benefit from standardisation across a company's mobile workforce. However, regardless of the financial case, there are undoubted soft benefits from standardisation that is brought about through automation. The same process will be followed throughout the organisation ensuring that quality and brand can be managed and maintained across the full geography. On the more practical side, if there is an urgent need to move field workers from one geography to another then they can immediately receive work through their device and without first having to understand and adjust to potentially unfamiliar local practices. Such worker moves may only happen once or twice a year, but when they take place, it is usually in a crisis and the last thing that anybody wants is to have to spend days training in order that a person can work in a new geography.

20.3.5 The Implementation of a Service Policy and Customer Priorities

This area of benefits is related to customer service improvements mentioned above but more specifically on how the organisation enforces its service policy and manages customer priorities. If an organisation currently has a group of dispatchers (also known as controllers) allocating work manually to the mobile workforce then the service policies and customer priorities of the organisation can easily fall out of control. Management will normally set these policies based on the company's service strategy and customer segmentation. In the simple case, this results in a list like the following that is used for prioritising incoming service requests:

1. Premier repair;
2. Bronze repair;
3. New installation worth over £300;
4. New installation worth £100 to £299;
5. New installation worth under £99.

In more complex cases, a Service Level Agreement (SLA) may be defined for each customer group (or specific customer contract) with specific response times promised and also penalties in case one or more targets/deadlines are missed.

In reality, it is very difficult to ensure that priorities and/or SLAs are followed in a manual allocation environment. This position is further compromised by the relationship between the dispatcher and the mobile workers which can seriously influence who receives what work. Once automation is realised, all of the smoke and mirrors disappear and the allocation rules and priorities are entered into a system which can consistently implement the company's service policy. An online reservation facility can be coupled to the FFA solution to manage the customer interface. Work allocation adheres to priorities and SLAs by design thus avoiding penalties and meeting simple or complex customer requirements and SLAs.

20.3.6 Better Quality Work

Although not directly related to automating the service process, the quality of work is a very important element in terms of potential cost savings and improved customer service. As automation takes place, the perception of mobile workers is that the company has much more information available about them and the work they are doing. This will be true but not necessarily to the extent that may be perceived. Organisations can leverage this perception to drive through an improvement in the quality of the work at the same time as rolling out the automation of processes. Improving the quality of work is highly linked to mindset. It requires considerable management effort to force the benefit home and potentially training for a number of the mobile workers. It is often the case that a minority of mobile workers are causing the majority of "repeat" work and they can be the target of such training programmes. Paradoxically, the people with the highest productivity and completion rates may also be responsible for pure workmanship. It is definitely worth considering complementing an automation initiative with a quality initiative especially if an organisation has a serious repeat work problem.

20.3.7 A Better Understanding of the Real Performance of the Organisation

This is an important but also a highly contentious topic. In a manual environment, do managers really know how accurate key performance indicators are? There may be a serious amount of "sharp pencil" practice taking place which distorts the figures to make them look much better than they actually are? Do not believe that this cannot be possibly happening in your organisation, hopefully it is not but it needs to be checked. Why do we raise this point? If productivity is artificially inflated in a manual environment when an organisation automates the process and eliminates "massaging" of the productivity figures then performance will appear to have gone down when in reality it will be a true reflection of at least what was already happening in the organisation and hopefully an improvement.

This perceived performance drop can kill a successful project in an instant; hence it is important that the manual collection of data is 100% understood before comparisons are made pre and post automation. It is similarly probable that job completion times are manipulated in a manual environment to turn customer satisfaction failures into apparent successes! This again needs to be fully understood as it can cause the same problem as the productivity problem. The ultimate benefit is for the organisation since measures can be taken to improve performance once the real picture emerges.

20.4 Understanding Existing Processes

Before embarking on a field force automation project for the mobile field workforce, it is essential that there is a full understanding of the operational environment "as is." This will not only help in the debates about the potential benefits that can be gained from automation but ensure that the project team understands what really goes on in the depths of their operation.

For example, it is essential that the project team understands what happens at the start of the day. This is not about what the process says. This is about what really happens. Do you have 50 people trying to contact the dispatch office on their mobiles at 8:00 am? This can lead to up to an hour's delay before some mobile workers are on the way to their first job. After receiving the job or jobs, does the mobile worker then queue up for kit to complete the work? On a process diagram these two activities will look very straight forward and no time consuming at all. In reality, some mobile field workers may still be in the depot 90 minutes after starting work. There will be a large and immediate productivity gain at the start of day if the jobs have been automatically downloaded to the person's device and the kit required delivered to them beforehand.

Another key time is the end of the working day, do the workers slowdown to enable them to complete the last job where they want to be rather than where the organisation wants them to finish. These areas need to be looked at in detail in order that the new automated process can eliminate as many of these black spots as possible.

A secondary advantage to completing this basic but detailed process mining is that the organisation will have at least one or more experts who fully understand what is really happening and can then sensibly map the automated process with a large degree of confidence. This person(s) will play a leading role in ensuring that the new software actually fulfils expectations. Time spent properly understanding existing workflows will lead to a much greater probability of the business case benefits being achieved. If this work has not been completed and the wrong solution is implemented then this may result in a failed project. The failure is not due to the fact that it is hard to successfully implement a field force automation solution but rather down to a lack of good solid basic process work at the start of the journey.

Once the current process is understood, the project team can design the new process and associated systems; in effect a blueprint to get the organisation from the "as is" to the "will be" position. At least a year should be anticipated as the implementation and settling down period.

20.5 Selecting Suppliers and Products

Once the project objectives and end goals are clear then the team can proceed with selecting the software first and subsequently the device and other elements of the solution. The following guidelines can help in making such choices especially in terms of identifying suitable suppliers:

1. Do not "go cheap" as in day-to-day life you get what you pay for. The financial and customer service benefits run into millions of pounds per annum so why try to save a couple of thousand by going with the cheapest software supplier possible.
2. Make 100% sure that the software can do what you need it to do! Test the software and any associated claims.
3. Do not listen to wildly exaggerated estimates of up to 50% improvement. The theory will definitely show very high potential benefits, but there is a significant difference between the theory and practice. If you cannot have a rational debate with the software company about reality then it is probably because they do not understand the practicalities of a mobile field workforce.
4. Do not purchase software from a company who in effect want to hand over the software to you and run! This is unfortunately common practice in this particular space. In effect, they are not interested in whether you can achieve the benefit; they just want to make the sale.

At the end of the day, the key is to go with a supplier that you can trust and who will stay with you until the agreed benefit has been achieved. This chapter mentions that between 10 to 20% improvement in productivity is often achievable. If you can identify a supplier to link into this and work with you towards this target then a successful project is likely to ensue.

Moving away from software, if your organisation is not really equipped to manage the project and achieve the benefits then choose a supplier that will provide hardened, experienced, project and benefit achievement management. The benefits are high and it is worth investing to ensure that they are realised to their full.

Choose the device last not first! The software is the key and should take precedence. Nonetheless, the device needs careful consideration and should be based on the "will be" vision that was produced at the design stage. For the majority of mobile field workers, a PDA is sufficient but there are definitely serviceforces where a tablet or laptop are essential, primarily if detailed network records and safety records need to be studied before completing a job. Device selection must not be prejudiced by initial cost outlay as discussed but take into account total costs including device failure rates and associated loss of time.

Once, the suppliers and their products are carefully selected then the project can move into the piloting and implementation phase.

20.6 Piloting and Implementing

The link between benefits and solution implementation is a very important one. The project team would need to ensure that essential management information is available before you commence a pilot and during it as you need to measure and compare performance. An obvious statement, but on many projects the management information is ignored as "too difficult, to be completed later."

Definitely do a meaningful pilot, up to 10% of the workforce. By their very nature, pilots are easy to manipulate (e. g., the pilot area selected may be the most high performing) and the project team may be able to show very good benefits. It is reasonable to expect only part of that benefit level to be realised from a full and company-wide "roll-out!" A 15% productivity gain indicated by a pilot may often result in a 10% productivity gain when the system is used company-wide.

The pilot also has to prove that all of the elements of the solution are working properly and achieving the correct end result. Do not rush the pilot, if it is to run for 3 months, let it run for 3 months even if it is shown to be working successfully after 4 weeks. The pilot period can be used to build the confidence in the organisation which will make a bigger implementation much easier. Complete a factual closure report on the pilot as documented evidence of the results.

A successful pilot will make organisational roll-out easier, nonetheless particular care would need to be taken to plan the roll-out in absolute detail and ensure that the plan is adhered to and updated regularly. A post-implementation review should also be initiated and completed and the information and learning points from the project ideally used in other company initiatives.

Be very wary that the organisation does not slip into the mode of getting the project finished and "forgetting" the benefits. It is not acceptable for everybody to pat each other on the back at the end of the project as technically a successful implementation with the original "return on investment" totally forgotten under the relief of completing the exercise. The benefits do not just appear. They have to be "chased" to be achieved. The management information has to be studied and acted upon. The employees will need to actively use the system.

It is paramount to stress this last point of using the technology not just implementing it. It is often the case that the majority of effort is devoted to implementing a service chain management solution rather than encouraging and training personnel to use the solution to the benefit of the organisation. Given that benefits are linked to IT usage rather than deployment (Marchand and Hykes 2006), the division of effort is misbalanced for the majority of projects with CIOs and other senior managers considering the work complete after the delivery of a system. Ensuring usage is an especially meaningful activity to define as part of the overall project plan and follow it through with execution.

If we were to summarise the steps to a successful project discussed so far then we can think of a six stage overarching plan as depicted in Fig. 20.2.

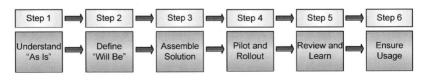

Fig. 20.2 The six steps to a successful project and realisation of benefits

20.7 Summary

In this chapter, we looked at some of the practicalities and hurdles when realising the benefits from technology investments. The experiences and advice shared hopefully provides a realistic guide to those seeking to embark on an automation project for field service or other types of service operations.

Clearly, the proper and productive use of a system is where the "real" work starts and the pay offs lie. Organisations will be much more successful in their IT projects if this mindset takes hold. With this message, we rather draw to a close this book and look forward to expanding on the issue of improving IT adoption and usage in service industries at a future occasion.

References

Adams M, ter Hofstede A, Edmond D, van der Aalst W (1998) Facilitating Flexibility and Dynamic Exception Handling in Workflows Through Worklets. In: Belo O, Eder J, Pastor O, Falcao E, Cunha J (eds) Short Paper Proceedings of the CAiSE'05 Forum FEUP. Porto, Portugal 161:45–50

Adams M, Edmond D, ter Hofstede A (2003) The Application of Activity Theory to Dynamic Workflow Adaptation Issues. In: Proceedings of the 7th Pacific Asia Conference on Information Systems (PACIS-2003), Adelaide, South Australia

Aickelin U, Dowsland K (2000) Exploiting Problem Structure in a Genetic Algorithm Approach to a Nurse Rostering Problem. Journal of Scheduling 3(3):139–153

Akkermans H, Vos B (2003) Amplification in Service Supply Chains: An Exploratory Case Study from the Telecom Industry. Production and Operations Management 12(2):204–223

Aknine S, Pinson S, Shakun M (2004) An Extended Multi-agent Negotiation Protocol. Autonomous Agents and Multi-Agent Systems 8(1):5–45

Al-Tabtabai H, Alex A (1997) Manpower Scheduling Optimization Using Genetic Algorithm. In: 4th Congress on Computing in Civil Engineering, American Society of Civil Engineers. Philadelphia PA, pp 702–709

Albert P, Henocque L, Kleiner M (2005) Configuration-Based Workflow Composition. In: IEEE International Conference on Web Services (ICWS 2005), IEEE Computer Society. Orlando FL, pp 285–292

Aloulou M, Portmann M (2003) An Efficient Proactive Reactive Scheduling Approach to Hedge Against Shop Floor Disturbances. In: Kendall G, Burke E, Petrovic S, Gendreau M (eds) Proceedings of the Mutlidisciplinary International Conference of Scheduling: Theory and Applications (MISTA'03). Springer-Verlag, Nottingham, UK

Alves de Medeiros A, Weijters A, van der Aalst W (2005) Using Genetic Algorithms to Mine Process Models: Representation, Operators and Results. BETA Working Paper Series 124, Eindhoven University of Technology. Eindhoven, Holland

Ambler S (2007) Agile modeling. Tech rep, Ambysoft, http://www.agilemodeling.com/

Anantaram C, Joshi P, Deshpande K, Trivedi P (1993) Crew Rostering System – An Expert System for Scheduling Crew for Indian Airlines. In: Proceedings of the 9th Conference on Artificial Intelligence for Applications IEEE Computer Society. Orlando FA, pp 63–70

Anderson E, Morrice D (2000) A Simulation Game for Service-Oriented Supply Chain Management: Does Information Sharing Help Managers with Service Capacity Decisions? Journal of Production and Operations Management 9(1):40–55

Anderson T (2006) WS-* vs the REST.
http://www.regdeveloper.co.uk /2006/04/29/oreilly_amazon/

Andersson E, Housos E, Kohl N, Wedelin D (1997) Crew Pairing Optimization. In: Yu G (ed) OR in Airline Industry. Kluwer Academic Press, pp 1–31

Andrews W (2005) Whoa! We've got WOA.
    http://blog.gartner.com/blog/index.php?itemid=400
Angeles R (2000) Revisiting the Role of Internet-EDI in the Current Electronic Commerce Scene.
    Logistics Information Management 13(1):45–57
Angus I (2001) An Introduction to Erlang B and Erlang C. Telemanagement (187):6–8
Anonymous (2001) Reverse Auctions Are Creating False Savings for Manufacturers. Manufacturer
    News 8(10), http://www.manufacturingnews.com/news/01/0531/art1.html
Aral S, Brynjolfsson E, van Alstyne M (2006) Information, Technology and Information Worker
    Productivity Task Level Evidence. In: Straub D, Klein S, Haseman WD, Washburn C (eds)
    International Conference on Information Systems (ICIS). Milwaukee, WI
Armistead C, Clark G (1994) The "Coping" Capacity Management Strategy in Services and the
    Influence on Quality Performance. International Journal of Service Industry Management
    5(2):5–22
Armstrong J, Collopy F (1998) Integration of Statistical Methods and Judgement for Time Series
    Forecasting: Principles from Empirical Research. In: Wright G, Goodwin P (eds) Forecasting
    with Judgement. John Wiley & Sons, pp 269–293
Arthur Andersen Consulting (1997) Yield Management in Small and Medium-Sized Enterprises in
    the Tourist Industry. Tech rep, Arthur Andersen, Brussels: Directorate General XXIII
Auh S, Bell S, McLeod C, Shih C (2007) Co-Production and Customer Loyalty in Financial Ser-
    vices. Journal of Retailing 83(3):359–370
Azvine B, Cui Z, Nauck D, Majeed B (2006) Real Time Business Intelligence for the Adaptive En-
    terprise. In: Proceedings of the IEEE Joint Conference on E-Commerce Technology (CEC'06)
    and Enterprise Computing, E-Commerce and E-Services (EEE'06), IEEE Computer Society.
    Palo Alto CA, pp 222–229
Band W, Schuler I (2007) Case Study: Big River Telephone Executives Lead The Charge for CRM
    Adoption. Tech rep, Forrester Research
Baptiste P, Pape CL, Nuijten W (2001) Constraint-based Scheduling – Applying Constraint Pro-
    gramming to Scheduling Problems. Kluwer Academic Publishers
Bardram J (2004) Java Context Aware Framework (JCAF). Tech rep, Centre for Pervasive Comput-
    ing, Department of Computer Science, University of Aarhus, http://www.daimi.au.dk/~cfpc/
    publications/files/bardram_jcaf_2004.pdf
Barnett F (1988) Four Steps to Forecast Total Market Demand. Tech rep, Harvard Business Review
    66(4):28–38
Baron R (2005) So Right It's Wrong: Groupthink and the Ubiquitous Nature of Polarized Group
    Decision Making. In: Zanna M (ed) Advances in Experimental Social Psychology. Elsevier,
    San Diego CA 37:219–253
Barr A, Feigenbaum A (1986) Handbook of Artificial Intelligence. Addison Wesley Longman
    Publishing Co
Beck J, Prosser P, Selensky E (2003) Vehicle Routing and Job Shop Scheduling: What's the Dif-
    ference? In: 13th International Conference on Automated Planning and Scheduling. Trento,
    Italy
Beddoe G (2004) Case-Based Reasoning in Personnel Rostering. PhD thesis. University of Not-
    tingham, Nottingham, UK
Bermudez J, Agutter J, Westenskow D, Foresti S, Zhang Y, Gondeck-Becker D, Syroid N, Lilly B,
    Strayer D, Drews F (2000) Data Representation Architecture. Visualization Design Methods,
    Theory and Technology Applied to Anesthesiology. In: Clayton M, Vasquez de Velasco G
    (eds) Association for Computer Aided Design in Architecture (ACADIA2000). Washing-
    ton DC, pp 91–102
Bhulai S, Koole G, Pot G (2005) Simple Methods for Shift Scheduling in Multi-skill Call Centers.
    Tech Rep WS 2005–10. Free University, Amsterdam, Netherlands
Bianchi L, Birattar M, Chiarandini M, Manfrin M, Mastrolilli M, Paquete L, Rossi-Doria O, Schi-
    avinotto T (2004) Metaheuristics for the Vehicle Routing Problem with Stochastic Demands.
    In: Proceedings of the 8th International Conference on Parallel Problem Solving from Nature
    (PPSN-VIII), Springer, Lecture Notes in Computer Science 3242:450–460

Bichler M, Kalagnanam J (2006) A Non-Parametric Estimator for Reserve Prices in Procurement Auctions. Information Technology Management 7(3):157–169

Bichler M, Kalagnanam J, Katircioglu K, King A, Lawrence R, Lee H, Lin G, Lu Y (2002a) Applications of Flexible Pricing in Business-to-Business Electronic Commerce. IBM Systems Journal 41(2)

Bichler M, Kalagnanam J, Lee H, Lee J (2002b) Winner Determination Algorithms for Electronic Auctions: A Framework Design. In: Bauknecht K, Tjoa AM, Quirchmayr G (eds) 3rd International Conference on E-Commerce and Web Technologies (EC-Web 2002), Springer, Aix-en-Provence, France, Lecture Notes in Computer Science, vol 2455

Bill G (1999) Business @ The Speed of Thought: Using A Digital Nervous System. Warner Books

Bitner MJ (1990) Evaluating Service Encounters: The Effects of Physical Surroundings and Employee Responses. Journal of Marketing 54(2):69–82

Bitran G, Caldentey R (2003) An Overview of Pricing Models for Revenue Management. Manufacturing Service Operation Management 5:203–229

Bitran G, Gilbert S (1996) Managing Hotel Reservations with Uncertainty Arrivals. Operations Research 44(1):35–49

Bitran G, Mondschein S (1995) An Application of Yield Management to the Hotel Industry Considering Multiple Day Stays. Operations Research 43(3):427–443

Bjerring-Olsen K (2006) Productivity Impacts of Offshoring and Outsourcing. STI Working paper 2006/1, OECD

Bodin L, Golden B, Assad A, Ball M (1983) The State of the Art in the Routing and Scheduling of Vehicles and Crews. Computers and Operations Research 10(2):63–211

Bolkestein F (2004) Right of Establishment and Freedom to Provide Services. Directive Proposal COM/2004/2, European Commision

Bond GW, Cheung E, Purdy H, Zave P, Ramming C (2004) An Open Architecture for Next-Generation Telecommunication Services. ACM Transactions on Internet Technology 4(1):83–123

Borrett J, Tsang E (2001) A Context for Constraint Satisfaction Problem Formulation Selection. Constraints 6(4):299–327

Bowersox D, Closs D, Copper M (2002) Supply Chain Logistic Management. McGraw-Hill Higher Education

Box G, Jenkins G (1970) Time Series Analysis: Forecasting and Control. Holden Day

Boyd E, Bilegan I (2003) Revenue Management and e-Commerce. Management Science 49(10): 1363–1386

Braekmans K, Demeulemeester E, Herroelen W, Leus R (2005) Proactive Resource Allocation Heuristics for Robust Project Scheduling. Research Report 0567, DTEW, K.U. Leuven, Belgium

Brigandi A, Dragon D, Sheehan M, Spencer T (1994) AT&T's Call Processing Simulator (CAPS) Operation Design for Inbound Call Centers. Interfaces 24(1):6–28

Brown R (1959) Statistical Forecasting for Inventory Control. McGraw-Hill

Brown R (1960) Smoothing, Forecasting and Prediction of Discrete Time Series. Prentice-Hall

Brusco M, Jacobs L (1993) A Simulated Annealing Approach to the Solution of Flexible Labor Scheduling Problems. Journal of the Operational Research Society 44(12):1191–1200

Bryan DA, Lowekamp BB (2007) Decentralizing SIP. ACM Queue 5(2):34–41

Buchanan B, Feigenbaum E (1978) DENDRAL and Meta-DENDRAL: Their Applications Dimension. Artificial Intelligence 11(1–2):5–24

Burgy L, Caillot L, Consel C, Latry F, Reveillere L (2004) A Comparative Study of SIP Programming Interfaces. In: 9th International Conference on Intelligence in Service Delivery Networks (ICIN 2004), Bordeaux, France

Burke E, Causmaecker PD, Berghe GV, Landeghem HV (2004) The State of the Art of Nurse Rostering. Journal of Scheduling 7(6):441–499

Burnham M, Kern M, Anim-Ansah G, Owusu G (2006) A Model to Improve the Strategic Alignment of Resources to Demand. GCTO Technical Report, British Telecommunications plc

Burns A, Hayes N, Richardson M (1995) Generating Feasible Cyclic Schedules. Control Engineering Practice 3(2):151–162

Buscher U, Lindner G (2004) Ensuring Feasibility in a Generalized Quantity Discount Pricing Model to Increase Supplier's Profits. Journal of the Operational Research Society 55(6):667–670

Cai X, Li K (2000) A Genetic Algorithm for Scheduling Staff of Mixed Skills under Multi-criteria. European Journal of Operational Research 125(2):359–369

Calder M, Kolberg M, Magill EH, Reiff-Marganiec S (2003) Feature Interaction: a Critical Review and Considered Forecast. Computer Networks 41(1):115–141

Cavedon L, Maamar Z, Martin D, Benatallah B (eds) (2004) Extending Web Service Technologies: The Use of Multi-Agent Approaches. Springer

Chang J, Pedram M (1996) Energy Minimization Using Multiple Supply Voltages. In: Horowitz M, Rabaey JM, Barton B, Pedram M (eds) Proceedings of the International Symposium for Low Power Electronic and Design IEEE. Monterey, CA

Chang S (2002) Handbook of Software Engineering and Knowledge Engineering. World Scientific Publishing Co

Cheang B, Li H, Lim A, Rodrigues B (2003) Nurse Rostering Problems – A Bibliographic Survey. European Journal of Operational Research 151(3):447–460

Checkland P (1990) Systems Thinking, Systems Practice. Wiley

Cheng B, Lee J, Wu J (1997) A Nurse Rostering System Using Constraint Programming and Redundant Modeling. IEEE Transactions on Information Technology in Biomedicine 1(1):44–54

Chiang W, Chen I, Xu X (2007) An Overview of Research on Revenue Management: Current Issues and Future Research. International Journal of Revenue Management 1(1):97–128

Ciancimino A, Inzerillo G, Palagi L (1999) A Mathematical Programming Approach for the Solution of the Railway Yield Management Problem. Transportation Science 33(2):168–181

Clement R, Wren A (1995) Greedy Genetic Algorithms, Optimizing Mutations and Bus Driver Scheduling. In: Daduna J, Branco I, Paixao J (eds) Computer-Aided Transit Scheduling Lecture Notes in Economics and Mathematical Systems, vol 430, Springer-Verlag, pp 213–235

Clugage K, Shaffer D, Nainani B (2006) Workflow Services in Oracle BPEL PM 10.1.3. http://www.oracle.com/technology/products/ias/bpel/pdf/bpel-workflowservices-1013.pdf

Collins J (2001) Good to Great. Random House Business Books

European Commission (2007) i2010 – Annual Information Society Report 2007. Tech rep, European Commission, http://ec.europa.eu/information_society/eeurope/i2010/docs/annual_report/2007/comm_final_version_sg/com_2007_0146_en.pdf

Compton P, Jansen R (1990) Knowledge in Context: A Strategy for Expert System Maintenance. In: Proceedings of the 2nd Australian Joint Conference on Artificial Intelligence (AI'88). Springer-Verlag, Adelaide, Australia, pp 292–306

Constable J, New C (1976) Operations Management. John Wiley and Sons

Conway A, Dorne R, Voudouris C (2001) iNetwork – A Framework for Network Optimisation. In: Proceedings of the International Network Optimization Conference (INOC 2003). Evry, France, pp 163–168

Cook TM (1998) Sabre Soars: Keynote Address. Tech rep, ORMS

CPFR (2007) Collaborative Planning, Forecasting & Replenishment. Voluntary Interindustry Commerce Solutions, http://www.vics.org/committees/cpfr/

Cramton P, Shoham Y, Steinberg R (eds) (2006) Combinatorial Auctions. MIT Press

Crane P (2005) A New Service Infrastructure Architecture. BT Technology Journal 23(1):15–27

Crevier B, Cordeau J, Laporte G (2005) The Multi-Depot Vehicle Routing Problem with Inter-Depot Routes. European Journal of Operational Research 176(2):756–773

Crockford D (2006) The application/json Media Type for JavaScript Object Notation (JSON). RFC 4267 (informational), Internet Engineering Task Force http://www.ietf.org/rfc/rfc4627.txt

Cusumano M (2006) Services in Industry Lifecycles and Technological Discontinuities. In: MIT eBusiness Conference and CIO Symposium

Dantzig G (1954) A Comment on Eddie's Traffic Delay at Toll Booths. Operations Research 2(3):339–341

Daskin M, Owen S (2003) Location Models in Transportation. In: Wal R (ed) International Series in Operations Research & Management Science, Handbook of Transportation Science, vol 56, Springer, pp 321–370

Davenport T, Harris J (2007) Competing on Analytics: The New Science of Winning. Harvard Business School Press

Davis R, Smith R (1988) Negotiation as A Metaphor for Distributed Problem Solving. In: Bond A, Gasser L (eds) Readings in Distributed Artificial Intelligence, Morgan Kaufmann, pp 333–356

Deb K (2001) Multi-objective Optimization Using Evolutionary Algorithms. John Wiley & Sons

Deb S (2003) Building IT Architectures for Enterprise Agility. Tech rep, Infosys http://www.infosys.com/technology/cutting_edge_CE-08–03.pdf

Demeulemeester E, Herroelen W (1992) A Branch-and-Bound Procedure for the Multiple Resource-Constrained Project Scheduling Problem. Management Science 38(12):1803–1818

Dickersbach J (2003) Supply Chain Management with APO. Springer-Verlag, Berlin

Diebold F, Pauly P (1990) The Use of Prior Information in Forecast Combination. International Journal of Forecasting 6(4):503–508

Dijkstra E (1982) On the Role of Scientific Thought. Selected Writings on Computing: A Personal Perspective. Springer-Verlag

Disney S, Towill D (2003) Vendor-managed Inventory and Bullwhip Reduction in A Two-level Supply Chain. International Journal of Operations & Production Management 23(6):625–651

Doddavula S, Karamongikar S (2005) Designing an Enterprise Application Framework. Tech rep, JAVA.NET, http://today.java.net/pub/a/today/2005/04/28/soadesign.html

Domenjoud E, Kirchner C, Zhou J (1998) Generating Feasible Schedules for A Pick-up and Delivery Problem. In: Maher M, Puget J (eds) Proceedings of the 4th International Conference on the Principles and Practice of Constraint Programming 1998 (CP'98). Springer-Verlag, Pisa, Italy, Lecture Notes in Computing Science 1520:467

Dorne R, Voudouris C, Liret A, Ladde C, Lesaint D (2003) iSchedule: An Optimisation Toolkit based on Heuristic Search to Solve BT Scheduling Applications. BT Technology Journal 21(4):50–58

Dou W, Chou D (2002) A Structural Analysis of Business-to-Business Digital Markets. Industrial Marketing Management 31(2):165–176

Dube P, Hayel Y, Wynter L (2005) Yield Management for IT Resources on Demand: Analysis and Validation of a new Paradigm for Managing Computing Centres. Journal of Revenue and Pricing Management 4(1):24–38

DuPont Corporation and Remington Rand Corporation (1950) The Critical Path Method

Durman P (2007) BT Steps in as Rivals are Hit by Broadband Cost. Tech rep, The Sunday Times http://business.timesonline.co.uk/tol/business/industry_sectors/telecoms/article1751585.ece

Eder J, Liebhart W (1995) The Workflow Activity Model WAMO. In: Proceedings of the International Conference on Cooperative Information Systems (CoopIS'95), Vienna, Austria, pp 87–98

Eder J, Liebhart W (1996) Workflow Recovery. In: Proceedings of the 1st IFCIS International Conference on Cooperative Information Systems (CoopsIS'96). IEEE, Brussels, Belgium, pp 124–134

Ehrgott M, Gandebleux X (2002) Multiple Criteria Optimisation: State of the Art Annotated Bibliographic Survey. Kluwer Academic Publishers

Elliot B (2007a) Discovering the Value of Unified Communications. Tech Rep G00144673, Gartner Research

Elliot B (2007b) Three Killer Business Communication Applications. Tech Rep G00149038, Gartner Research

Elliot B, Lock C (2007) A Framework for Unified Communications. Tech Rep G00145337, Gartner Research

Elliot B, Blood S, Hafner B (2006a) Achieving Agility through Communication-Enabled Business Processes. Tech Rep G00137838, Gartner Research

Elliot B, Blood S, Kraus D (2006b) Magic Quadrant for Unified Communications. Tech Rep G00139822, Gartner Research

Elmaghraby W, Keskinocak P (2003) Dynamic Pricing in the Presence of Inventory Considerations: Research Overview, Current Practices, and Future Directions. Management Science 49(10):1287–1309

Ernst A, Jiang H, Krishnamoorthy, Owens B, Sier D (2004a) An Annotated Bibliography of Personnel Scheduling and Rostering. Annals of Operations Research 127(1–4):21–144

Ernst A, Jiang H, Krishnamoorthy M, Sier D (2004b) Staff Scheduling and Rostering: A Review of Applications, Methods and Models. European Journal of Operational Research 153(1):3–27

Ertin E, Dean A, Moore M, Priddy K (2001) Dynamic Optimization for Optimal Control of Water Distribution Systems. In: Priddy KL, Keller PE, Angeline PJ (eds) Applications and Science of Computational Intelligence IV, Society of Photo-Optical Instrumentation Engineers (SPIE) Conference, vol 4390:142–149

Fayyad U, Piatetsky-Shapiro G, Smyth P, Uthurusamy R (1996) Advances in Knowledge Discovery and Data Mining. AAAI Press and MIT Press

FIPA (2002) FIPA Contract Net Interaction Protocol Specification. Tech rep, Foundation for Intelligent Physical Agents, http://www.fipa.org/specs/fipa00029/SC00029H.html

Fischl J, Tschofenig H (2007) Making SIP Make Cents. ACM Queue 5(2):42–49

Fitzsimmons JA, Fitzsimmons MJ (2001) Service Management: Operations, Strategy, and Information Technology, 3rd ed. Irwin/McGraw-Hill

Fixler D, Siegel D (1999) Outsourcing and Productivity Growth in Services. Structural Change and Economic Dynamics 10:177–194

Fleischmann M, Hall JM, Pyke DF (2004) Smart Pricing. MIT Sloan Management Review 45(2):9–13

Forecasting Principles (2007) Forecasting Principles. http://www.forecastingprinciples.com

Forum T (2006) Enhanced Telecom Operations Map. Tech rep, TM Forum
    http://www.tmforum.org/

Foss J (1998) Brokering the Info-Underworld. British Telecommunications Eng 17(2):202–206

Fox M, Barbuceanu M, Teigen R (2000) Agent-Oriented Supply Chain Management. International Journal of Flexible Manufacturing Systems 12(2/3):165–188

Franklin S, Graesser A (1996) Is it an Agent, or Just a Program? A Taxonomy for Autonomous Agents. In: Muller J, Wooldridge M, Jennings N (eds) Proceedings of the 3rd International Workshop on Agent Theories, Architectures and Languages (ATAL-96), Springer-Verlag, Budapest, Hungary, LNCS 1193

Freuder E (1999) Modeling: the Final Frontier. In: Proceedings of the 1st International Conference on the Practical Application of Constraint Technologies and Logic Programming (PACLP'99), London UK, pp 15–21

Galbreath J, Rogers T (1999) Customer Relationship Leadership: A Leadership and Motivation Model for The Twenty-first Century Business. The TQM Magazine 11(3):16–17

Gallagher A, Zimmerman T, Smith S F (2006) Incremental Scheduling to Maximize Quality in a Dynamic Environment. In: Proceedings of the International Conference on Automated Planning and Scheduling (ICAPS'06). AAAI Press, Cumbria, UK

Gamma E, Helm R, Johnson R, Vlissides J (1995) Design Patterns: Elements of Reusable Object-oriented Software. Addison-Wesley

Gates W (2000) Business @ the Speed of Thought: Succeeding in the Digital Economy. Warner Books

Gilliland M (2005) Alternative Metrics for Forecasting Performance. In: Jain C, Malehorn J (eds) Practical Guide to Business Forecasting. Graceway Publishing Company, pp 412–418

Gipson M, Runett R, Wood L, Clawson P (1999) The Electronic Marketplace 2003: Strategies For Connecting Buyers and Sellers. Tech rep, Simba Information Inc

Glover F (1989) Tabu Search: Part I. OSRA Journal on Computing 1(3):190–206

Glover F, Kochenberger G (eds) (2003) Handbook of Metaheuristics. Kluwer Academic Publishers

Glover F, Laguna M (1997) Tabu Search. Kluwer Academic Publishers

Goodwin P (2005) How to Integrate Management Judgment with Statistical Forecasts. Foresight: The International Journal of Applied Forecasting 1(1):8–12

Gosling T, Jin N, Tsang E (2006) Games, Supply Chains and Automatic Strategy Discovery Using Evolutionary Computation. In: Rennard J-P (ed) Handbook of Research on Nature Inspired Computing for Economics and Management, vol 2, Idea Group Reference, chap XXXVIII, pp 572–588

Granger C (1989) Invited Review: Combining Forecasts – Twenty Years Later. Journal of Forecasting 8(3):167–173

Green K, Armstrong J (2004) Structured Analogies for Forecasting. Forecasting Principles, http://www.forecastingprinciples.com/paperpdf/Structured_Analogies.pdf

Gross D, Carl M (1998) Fundamentals of Queueing Theory. John Wiley & Sons

Gylnn D (2001) Clicking once... Clicking twice. Sunday Business Magazine

Ha S, Park S (2001) Matching Buyers and Suppliers: An Intelligent Dynamic Exchange Model. IEEE Intelligent Systems 16(4):28–40

Hadley M (2006) Web Application Description Language (WADL). https://wadl.dev.java.net/

Hamerman P, Leaver S, Gaynor E (2006) The Forrester Wave: Human Resource Management Systems. Tech rep, Forrester, http://www.forrester.com

Hamerman P, Ragsdale J, Schooley C, Schuler I, Gaynor E (2007) HR/HCM Applications: Strategic Processes Move To The Forefront. Tech rep, Forrester, http://www.forrester.com

Hansen B (2000) Sample Splitting and Threshold Estimation. Econometrica 68(3):575–603

Harper P, Shahani A (2002) Modelling for the Planning and Management of Bed Capacities in Hospitals. Journal of the Operational Research Society 53(1):19–24

Harrington H (1991) Business Process Improvement: The Breakthrough Strategy for Total Quality, Productivity, and Competitiveness. McGraw-Hill

Harteyeldte H, Epps SR (2007) Self-service Check-in Clicks with Travellers. Tech rep, Forrester Research

Hartigan J (1975) Clustering Algorithms. John Wiley & Sons

He M, Jennings N, Leung H (2003) On Agent-mediated Electronic Commerce. IEEE Transactions on Knowledge and Data Engineering 15(4):985–1003

Heckerman D, Wellman MP (1995) Bayesian Networks. Communications of the ACM 38(3):27–30

Hemingway C (1998) Toward a Socio-cognitive Theory of Information Systems: An Analysis of Key Philosophical and Conceptual Issues. In: Proceedings of the IFIP Working Groups 8.2 and 8.6 Joint Working Conference on Information Systems: Current Issues and Future Changes, Kluwer Academic Publishers, Helsinki, Finland, pp 275–286

Henderson S, Mason A, Ziedins I, Thomson R (1999) A Heuristic for Determining Efficient Staffing Requirements for Call Centres. Tech rep, Department of Engineering Science, University of Auckland, Auckland, New Zealand

Heracleous L (1998) Strategic Thinking or Strategic Planning? Long Range Planning 31(3):481–487

Herrell E (2006) Unified Communications: What You Need To Know. Tech Rep G00141343, Forrester Research

Herrell E (2007) Contact Centre Workforce Management Tools: Network and Communications Essentials. Tech rep, Forrester

Heskett J, Sasser W, Schlesinger L (1997) The Service Profit Chain: How Leading Companies Link Profit and Growth to Loyalty, Satisfaction, and Value. Free Press

Highsmith J (2002) What is Agile Software Development? Tech rep, CrossTalk Magazine, http://www.adaptivesd.com/articles/cross_oct02.pdf

Hix N (2001) The Business Guide to Selling Through Internet Auctions: A Proven Seven-step Plan for Selling to Consumers and Other Businesses. Maximum Press

Hogarth R, Makridakis S (1981) Forecasting and Planning: An Evaluation. Management Science 27(2):115–138

Hohner G, Rich J, Ng E, Reid G, Davenport A, Kalagnanam J, Lee S, An C (2003) Combinatorial and Quantity Discount Procurement Auctions Provide Benefits to Mars, Incorporated and its Suppliers. Interfaces 33(1):23–35

Holland J (1975) Adaptation in Natural and Artificial Systems. University of Michigan Press

Holt C (2004) Forecasting Seasonals and Trends by Exponentially Weighted Averages. International Journal of Forecasting 20(1):5–10

Holweg M, Disney S, Holmstrom J, Smaros J (2005) Supply Chain Collaboration: Making Sense of the Strategy Continuum. European Management Journal 23(2):170–181

Hoos H, Tsang E (2006) Local Search for Constraint Satisfaction. In: Rossi F, van Beek P, Walsh T (eds) Handbook of Constraint Programming, Elsevier, chap 5, pp 245–277

Hormer P (2000) The SABRE Story: The Making of OR Magic at AMR. Tech rep, *OR/MS Today*

Humby C, Hunt T (2003) Scoring Points: How Tesco is Winning Customer Loyalty. Kogan Page

IBM (2006) IBM Corporate Responsibility Report. Tech rep, IBM
    http://www.ibm.com/ibm/responsibility/pdfs/IBM_CompanyCollab.pdf

IBM, BEA Systems, Microsoft SAP AG, Siebel Systems (2002) Business Process Execution Language for Web Services – Version 1.1.
    http://www.ibm.com/developerworks/library/specification/ws-bpel/

Ilog (2007) Logistics: Planning and Scheduling. Tech rep, Ilog, http://www.ilog.com/

Infosys (2007) Radien: J2EE Application Framework. Tech rep, Infosys
    http://www.infosys.com/services/application-development-maintenance/platform-services/
    Radien.pdf

Ingold A, Yeoman I, McMahon U (2000) Yield Management: Strategies for the Service Industries, 2nd edn., Thomson Business Press

International Telecommunication Union (1993) Introduction to Intelligent Network Capability Set 1. Recommendation Q.1211, Telecommunication Standardization Sector of ITU (ITU-T), Geneva, Switzerland, http://www.itu.int/rec/T-REC-Q.1211

International Telecommunication Union (1997) Introduction to Intelligent Network Capability Set 2. Recommendation Q.1221, Telecommunication Standardization Sector of ITU (ITU-T), Geneva, Switzerland, http://www.itu.int/rec/T-REC-Q.1221

Jackson M, Zave P (1998) Distributed Feature Composition: A Virtual Architecture for Telecommunications Services. IEEE Transactions on Software Engineering 24(10):831–847

Jackson M, Zave P (2003) The DFC Manual. AT&T
    http://www.research.att.com/~pamela/dfc.html

Jain C, Malehorn J (2005) Practical Guide to Business Forecasting, 2nd edn. Graceway Publishing Company

Jaiswal A, Kim Y, Gini M (2004) Design and Implementation of a Secure Multi-agent Marketplace. Electronic Commerce Research and Applications 3(4):355–368

Java Community Process (2001) JAIN SIP API Specification. Java Specification Request 32, http://www.jcp.org/en/jsr/detail?id=032

Java Community Process (2003) SIP Servlet API Version 1.0. Java Specification Request 116, http://jcp.org/en/jsr/detail?id=116

Java Community Process (2007) SIP Servlet Version 1.1. Java Specification Request 289, http://jcp.org/en/jsr/detail?id=289

Jensen K, Barnsley P, Tortolero J, Baxter N (2006) Dynamic Modelling of Service Delivery. BT Technology Journal 24(1):48–59

Jin N, Tsang E (2006) Co-adaptive Strategies for Sequential Bargaining Problems with Discount Factors and Outside Options. In: Yen GG, Lucas SM, Fogel G, Kendall G, Salomon R, Zhang BT, Coello CAC, Runarsson TP (eds) IEEE Congress on Evolutionary Computation (CEC), IEEE Press, Vancouver, Canada, pp 7913–7920

Johnson D, Gilfedder T (2002) Evolution of Optical Core Networks. BT Technology Journal 20(4):11–18

Johnston AB (2003) SIP: Understanding the Session Initiation Protocol, 2nd edn. Artech House

Johnston R, Clark G (2001) Service Operations Management. London: Financial Times/Prentice Hall

Jones P (2000) Defining Yield Management and Measuring Its Impact on Hotel Performance. In: Ingold A, McMahon-Beattie U, Yeoman I (eds) Yield Management, 2nd edn., Thomson Business Press, pp 85–97

Jones TO, Sasser WE (1995) Why Satisfied Customers Defect. Tech rep, Harvard Business Review 73(6):88–91

Jopling E (2006) New Entrants Will Shake Up the Telecom Industry. Tech rep, Gartner

Junker U, Mailharro D (2003) The logic of ILOG (J)Configurator: Combining Constraint Programming with a Description Logic. In: Workshop on Configuration of the 18th International Joint Conference on Artificial Intelligence (IJCAI-03), Acapulco, Mexico

Kahneman D, Slovic P, Tversky A (eds) (1982) Judgment Under Uncertainty: Heuristics and Biases. Cambridge University Press

Kaplan R, Norton D (1996) Balanced Scorecard: Translating Strategy into Action. Harvard Business School Press

Kar J (2006) Adopting Agile Methodologies in Software Development. Tech rep, Infosys, http://www.infosys.com/technology/toc-platforms-enterprise-agility.asp

Kauffman R, Wang B (2001) New Buyers' Arrival Under Dynamic Pricing Market Microstructure: The Case of Group-Buying Discounts on the Internet. Journal of Management Information Systems 18(2):157–188

Kern M, Anim-Ansah G, Owusu G, Voudouris C (2006) FieldPlan: Tactical Field Force Planning in BT. In: Bramer M (ed) Artificial Intelligence in Theory and Practice, Springer, Santiago, Chile IFIP International Federation of Information Processing, vol 217

Kimes S (1989) The Basics of Yield Management. Cornell Hotel and Restaurant Administration Quarterly 30(3):15–19

Kimes S (2000) A Strategic Approach to Yield Management. In: Ingold A, McMahon-Beattie U, Yeoman I (eds) Yield Management, 2nd edn., Thomson Business Press, pp 3–14

Kimes S (2003) Revenue Management: A Retrospective. Cornell Hotel and Restaurant Administration Quarterly 44(5/6):131–138

Kimes S, Chase R (1998) The Strategic Levels of Yield Management. Journal of Service Research 1(11):156–166

King W (1988) How Effective is Your Information Systems Planning? Long Range Planning 21(5):103–112

Kirkpatrick S, Gelatt C, Vecchi M (1983) Optimization by Simulated Annealing. Science 220 (4598):671–680

Kirovski D, Jain K (2006) Off-line Economies for Digital Media. Business & Technology. Tech rep, Microsoft Research
http://research.microsoft.com/users/darkok/papers/nossdav.pdf

Kizilisik O (1999) Predictive and Reactive Scheduling. In: IE 672 Theory of Machine Scheduling, Springer

Kurbel K, Loutchko I (2001) A Framework for Multi-agent Electronic Marketplaces: Analysis and Classification of Existing Systems. In: International ICSC Congress on Information Science Innovations (ISI'2001), American University in Dubai, U.A.E

Laithwaite R (1995) Work Allocation Challenges and Solutions in a Large-scale Work Management Environment. BT Technology Journal 13(1):46–54

Lau R (2006) Towards a Web Services and Intelligent Agents Based Negotiation System for B2B eCommerce. Electronic Commerce Research and Applications 6(3):260–273

Leavitt H (1965) Applied Organisational Change in Industry: Structural, Technological, and Humanistic Approaches. In: March J (ed) Handbook of Organization, Rand McNally, pp 1144–1179

Lederer A, Salmela H (1996) Toward a Theory of Strategic Information Systems Planning. Journal of Strategic Information Systems 5:237–253

Lee HL, Denend L (2004) West Marine: Driving Growth Through Shipshape Supply Chain Management. Academic Papers GS-34, Stanford Graduate School of Business

Lee HL, Whang S, Peleg B (2005) Toyota: Service Chain Management. Tech Rep Case GS41, Stanford University

Lee W, Lau H (1999) Factory on Demand: The Shaping of an Agile Production Network. International Journal of Agile Management Systems 1(2):82–87

Lennox J, Wu X, Schulzrinne H (2004) Call Processing Language (CPL): A Language for User Control of Internet Telephony Services. RFC 3880 (standard), Internet Engineering Task Force, http://www.ietf.org/rfc/rfc3880.txt

Lenstra J, Kan AR (1981) Complexity of Vehicle Routing and Scheduling Problems. Networks 11(2):221–227

Lesaint D (2006) A Modular and Combinatorial Formulation for Strategic Manpower Planning. Tech rep, British Telecommunications plc

Lesaint D, Voudouris C, Azarmi N (2000) Dynamic Workforce Scheduling for British Telecommunications plc. Interfaces 30(1):45–56

Li S, Sun B, Wilcox RT (2005) Cross-Selling Sequentially Ordered Products: An Application to Consumer Banking Services. Journal of Marketing Research 42(2):233–239

Li Y (2006) Verb-Noun Directory for Telecommunications Services Look-up. In: Proceedings of the IEEE/WIC/ACM International Conference on Web Intelligence and Intelligent Agent Technology, Hong Kong, China, pp 307–311

Li Y, Voudouris C, Thompson S, Owusu G, Anim-Ansah G, Liret A, Lee H, Kern M (2006) Self-service Reservation in the Fieldforce. BT Technology Journal 24(1):40–47

Littlewood K (1972) Forecasting and Control of Passenger Bookings. In: Proceedings of the 12th AGIFORS symposium, Israel, vol 12, pp 95–117

Longley PA, Goodchild MF, Maguire DJ, Rhind DW (2005) Geographical Information Systems: Principles, Techniques, Management and Applications, 2nd edn., John Wiley and Sons

Lopez MD, Brown EG, Metre EV (2007) Telcos Should Look to Location-Based Services for Growth: X Internet Services Will Make Location-Based Services Relevant To Firms. Tech rep, Forrester Research

Love M, Sorensen K, Larsen J, Clausen J (2002) Disruption Management for An Airline – Rescheduling of Aircraft. In: Applications of Evolutionary Computing (EvoWorkshops 2002), Springer, Kinsale, Ireland, Lecture Notes in Computer Science, vol 2279, pp 315–324

Ludwig B (1997) Predicting the Future: Have You Considered Using the Delphi Methodology? Journal of Extension 35(5):1–4, http://www.joe.org/joe/1997october/tt2.html

Luenberger D (2003) Linear and Non-Linear Programming, 2nd edn. Springer

Maes P, Guttman R, Moukas A (1999) Agents that Buy and Sell. Communications of the ACM 42(3):81–91

Makridakis S, Wheelwright S, McGee V (1983) Forecasting: Methods and Applications, 2nd edn., Wiley

Makridakis S, Wheelwright S, Hyndman R (1998) Forecasting: Methods and Applications, 3rd edn., Wiley

Malaga R (2001) Consumer Costs in Electronic Commerce: An Empirical Examination of Electronic versus Traditional Markets. Journal of Organizational Computing and Electronic Commerce 11(1):47–58

Maoz M, Clark W (2007) Magic Quadrant for Field Service Management. Tech. Rep. G00148407, Gartner

Marchand D, Hykes A (2006) Designed to Fail: Why IT-enabled Business Projects Underachieve. Perspectives for Managers (138):1–4
http://www.ecis2007.ch/mod_docs/IMD_PFM138_Marchand-Hykes_Oct_2006.pdf

Martin B (2005) Combinatorial Aspects of Yield Management: A Reinforcement Learning Approach. Tech rep, Bouygues SA, Guyancourt, France

Mathew G (2006) Infosys Thought Leadership for Enterprise Agility. Tech rep, Infosys
http://www.infosys.com/technology/platforms-enterprise-agility.pdf

Matwin S, Sapiro T, Haigh K (1991) Genetic Algorithm Approach to a Negotiation System. IEEE Transactions on Systems Man and Cybernetics 31(1):102–114

McCarthy D, Sarin S (1993) Workflow and Transactions in InConcert. IEEE Data Engineering Bulletin 16(2):53–56

McDonald M, Dunbar I (1998) Market Segmentation, 2nd edn., Macmillan

McGill J, van Ryzin G (1999) Revenue Management: Research Overview and Prospects. Transport Science 33(2):233–256

Michelis G, Grasso M (1994) Situating Conversations within the Language/Action Perspective: The Milan Conversation Model. In: Proceedings of the 1994 ACM Conference on Computer-Supported Cooperative Work (CSCW'94), ACM Press, Chapel Hill NC, pp 89–100

Miller K, Waller H (2003) Scenarios, Real Options and Integrated Risk Management. Long Range Planning 36(1):93–107

Mills P (2002) Extended Guided Local Search. PhD thesis, Department of Computer Science, University of Essex, Colchester, UK

Milner R, Parrow J, Walker D (1992) A Calculus of Mobile Processes – Part I. Information and Computation 100(1):1–40

Mitchell T (1997) Machine Learning. McGraw-Hill

Mithulananthan N, Oo T, Phu L (2004) Distributed Generator Placement in Power Distribution System Using Genetic Algorithm to Reduce Losses. International Journal of Science and Technology 9(3):55–62

Monfroglio A (1996) Hybrid Genetic Algorithms for a Rostering Problem. Software – Practice & Experience 26(7):851–862

Nair S, Bapna R (2001) An Application of Yield Management for Internet Service Providers. Naval Research of Logistics 48(5):348–362

Nanry W, Barnes J (1999) Solving the Pickup and Delivery Problem with Time Windows Using Reactive Tabu Search. Transportation Research Part B 34(2):107–121

Nauck D, Spott M, Azvine B (2003) SPIDA – A Novel Data Analysis Tool. BT Technology Journal 21(4):104–112

Nauck D, Ruta D, Spott M, Azvine B (2006) Being Proactive – Analytics for Predicting Customer Actions. BT Technology Journal 24(1):17–26

Nuijten W, Pape CL (1998) Constraint-Based Scheduling with ILOG Scheduler. Journal of Heuristics 3:271–286

OASIS (2002) UDDI Version 2 Specifications. http://www.oasis-open.org/committees/uddi-spec/doc/tcspecs.htm

OASIS, UN/CEFACT (2007) Electronic Business using eXtensible Markup Language. http://www.ebxml.org

Oberwetter R (2001) Can Revenue Management Land a Starring Role in the Movie Theater Industry? OR/MS Today, 28, 40–44

OECD (1997) Measuring Electronic Commerce. http://www.oecd.org/dataoecd/13/23/2093249.pdf

Okabe T (2004) Evolutionary Multi-Objective Optimization: On the Distribution of Offspring in Parameter and Fitness Space. Informationstechnik, Shaker Verlag

O'Reilly T (2005) What Is Web 2.0: Design Patterns and Business Models for the Next Generation of Software. Tech rep, O'Reilly
http://www.oreillynet.com/pub/a/oreilly/tim/news/2005/09/30/what-is-web-20.html

Owusu G, Voudouris C, Dorne R, Lesaint D (2002) Developing a Profiler in the ARMS Platform. In: Proceedings of the 6th IASTED International Conference on Artificial Intelligence and Soft Computing, Banff, Canada, pp 541–546

Owusu G, Voudouris C, Kern M, Garyfalos A, Anim-Ansah G, Virginas B (2006) On Optimising Resource Planning in BT with FOS. In: IEEE International Conference on Services Systems and Services Management, IEEE/SSSM06

Paatero J, Sevón T, Lehtolainen A, Lund P (2002) Distributed Power System Topology and Control Studies by Numerical Simulation. In: Proceedings of the 2nd International Symposium on Distributed Generation: Power System and Market Aspects, Stockholm, Sweden

Pak K, Piersma N (2002) Airline Revenue Management: An Overview of OR Techniques 1982–2001. Tech Rep EI 2002–2003, Econometric Institute

Parragh S, Doerner K, Hartl R (2006) A Survey on Pickup and Delivery Models. Working paper, Chair of Production and Operations Management, University of Vienna, Vienna, Austria

Pentland A (2004) Social Dynamics: Signals and Behaviour. In: International Conference on Developmental Learning (ICDL), IEEE Press, San Diego, CA

Petri C (1962) Kommunikation mit Automaten. PhD thesis, Institut für instrumentelle Mathematik, Bonn, Germany

Phillips R (2005) Pricing and Revenue Optimization. Stanford University Press

Picard R (1997) Affective Computing. MIT Press

Pidd M (1998) Computer Simulation in Management Science, 4th edn., John Wiley & Sons

Pigou A (1920) The Economics of Welfare. Macmillan London

Poikselka M, Mayer G, Khartabil H, Niemi A (2006) The IMS: IP Multimedia Concepts and Services, 2nd edn., John Wiley and Sons

Prahalad C, Ramaswamy V (2004) Co-Creation Experiences: The Next Practice in Value Creation. Journal of Interactive Marketing 18(3):5–14

Prosser P (1990) Distributed Asynchronous Scheduling. PhD thesis, Department of Computer Science, University of Strathclyde, Glasgow, UK

Qi X, Yang J, Yu G (2004) Scheduling Problems in the Airline Industry. In: Leung J (ed) Handbook of Scheduling: Algorithms, Models, and Performance Analysis, Chapman & Hall/CRC Press, Chap 50

Rabiner L, Juang B (1986) An Introduction to Hidden Markov Models. IEEE Signal Processing Magazine 3(1):4–16

Raiffa H (1982) The Art and Science of Negotiation. Harvard University Press

Ramaseshan B (1997) Attitudes Towards the Use of Electronic Data Interchange in Industrial Buying: Some Australian Evidence. Supply Chain Management 2(4):149–157

Reichheld F (2003) Loyalty Rules: How Leaders Build Lasting Relationships. Harvard Business School Press

Reiff-Marganiec S, Turner KJ (2002) Use of Logic to Describe Enhanced Communications Services. In: Peled D, Vardi MY (eds) 22nd IFIP WG 6.1 International Conference on Formal Techniques for Networked and Distributed Systems (FORTE 2002), Springer, Houston TX, Lecture Notes in Computer Science, vol 2529, pp 130–145

Reiff-Marganiec S, Turner KJ (2003) A Policy Architecture for Enhancing and Controlling Features. In: Amyot D, Logrippo L (eds) Feature Interactions in Telecommunications and Software Systems VII, IOS Press, Ottawa, Canada, pp 239–246

Reiff-Marganiec S, Turner KJ (2004) Feature Interaction in Policies. Computer Networks 45(5):569–584

Riemann R (1999) Modelling of Concurrent Systems: Structural and Semantical Methods in the High-Level Petri Net Calculus. PhD thesis, Universite de Paris XI, Orsay, France

Roland Berger Strategy Consultants (2003) Yield Management and Mobile Communications – Lessons from the Airline Industry. Briefing 2, InfoCom Executive

Rosenberg J, Schulzrinne H, Camarillo G, Johnston AB, Peterson J, Sparks R, Handley M, Schooler EM (2002) SIP: Session Initiation Protocol. RFC 3261 (standards), Internet Engineering Task Force, http://www.ietf.org/rfc/rfc3261.txt, updated by RFCs 3265, 3853, 4320

Rossi F, van Beek P, Walsh T (eds) (2006) Handbook of Constraint Programming (Foundations of Artificial Intelligence). Elsevier Science

Rothstein M (1975) Airline Overbooking: Fresh Approaches are Needed. Transport Science 9:169–173

Rubinstein-Montano B, Malaga R (2002) A Weighted Sum Genetic Algorithm to Support Multiple-party Multi-objective Negotiations. IEEE Transactions on Evolutionary Computation 6(4):366–377

Russell N, van der Aalst W, ter Hofstede A, Edmond D (2003) Workflow Patterns. Distributed and Parallel Databases 14(3):5–51

Russell S, Norvig P (2003) Artificial Intelligence: a Modern Approach. Series in Artificial Intelligence, Prentice Hall

Sachi C, O'Leary B (2002) The Role of Internet Auctions in the Expansion of B2B Markets. Industrial Marketing Management 31:103–110

Sandholm T, Lesser V (2002) Leveled-commitment Contracting: A Backtracking Instrument for Multiagent Systems. AI Magazine 23(3):89–100

Sasser W (1976) Match Supply and Demand in Service Industries. Harvard Business Review 54(6):133–140

Schatz B (2006) SOA and Agile Development. Tech rep, AgileJournal http://www.agilejournal.com/index2.php?option=com_content&do_pdf=1&id=67

Schmenner R (1995) Service Operations Management. New Jersey: Prentice Hall

Scott D (2007) Survey Shows the RTI Journey Continues. Tech rep, Gartner Research

Seddon J (1992) I Want You to Cheat: The Unreasonable Guide to Service and Quality in Organisations. Tech rep, Vanguard Consulting Ltd

Seifert R (2003) adidas-Salomon AG: The 'mi adidas' Mass Customization Initiative. Teaching Note IMD 6–0249-T, IMD, Lausanne, Switzerland

Seitman D (1994) In-house Medical Personnel Scheduler – A Computerized On-Call Scheduling Program. Journal of Clinical Monitoring and Computing 11(1):1387–1407

Sen S, Durfee E (1998) A Formal Study of Distributed Meeting Scheduling. Group Decision and Negotiation 7(3):265–289

Sevaux M, Sorensen K (2002) A Genetic Algorithm for Robust Schedules. In: Proceedings of the 8th International Workshop on Project Management and Scheduling (PMS'02), Valencia, Spain, pp 330–333

Shapiro C, Varian HR (2000) Versioning: The Smart Way to Sell Information, HBR OnPoint Enhanced Edition edn., Harvard Business Review On Point

Shaw C, Evans J (2002) Building Great Customer Experiences. Palgrave Macmillan

Shaw G, Brown R, Bromiley P (1998) Strategic Stories: How 3M is Rewriting Business Planning. Harvard Business Review 76(3):41–50

Shaw M (2000) Electronic Commerce: State of the Art. In: Shaw M, Blanning R, Strader T, Whinston A (eds) Handbook of Electronic Commerce, Springer, Chap 1, pp 3–24

Sheil B (1983) Coping with Complexity. Office: Technology and People 1:295–320

Shepherdson J, Lee H, Mihailescu P (2005) Multi-agent Systems as a Middleware to Automate Mobile Business Processes: State of the Art. In: Proceedings of the 5th International Conference on Information Science and Communications, Malta

Sheskin D (2003) Handbook of Parametric and Nonparametric Statistical Procedures, 3rd edn., Chapman & Hall

Shostack G (1977) Breaking Free from Product Marketing. Journal of Marketing 41(2):73–80

Silver E (2004) An Overview of Heuristic Solution Methods. Journal of the Operational Research Society 55(9):936–956

Simchi-Levi D, Kaminsky P, Simchi-Levi E (2000) Designing and Managing the Supply Chain: Concepts, Strategies, and Case Studies. Irwin McGraw-Hill

Simpson J, Noble A, Egan B, Morton D, Richards T, Burstin M (1995) Experience in Applying OR Techniques to the Solution of Practical Resource Management Problems. BT Technology Journal 13(1):16–28

Sitompul D, Radhawa S (1990) Nurse Scheduling: A State-of-the-art Review. Journal of the Society for Health Systems 2(1):62–72

Smaros J (2007) Forecasting collaboration in the European grocery sector: Observations from a case study. Journal of Operations Management 25(3):702–716

Smith B, Leimkuhler J, Darrow R (1992) Yield Management at American Airlines. Interfaces 22(1):8–31

Smith R (1980) The Contract Net Protocol: High-level Communication and Control in a Distributed Problem Solver. IEEE Transactions on Computers 29(12):1104–1113

Smith S (1994) Reactive Scheduling Systems. In: Brown D (ed) Intelligent Scheduling Systems, Kluwer Academic Publishers, pp 155–192

Smith S, Lassila O, Becker M (1996) Configurable, Mixed-Initiative Systems for Planning and Scheduling. In: Tate A (ed) Advanced Planning Technology, AAAI Press

Sourd F, Kedad-Sidhoum S (2005) An Efficient Algorithm for the Earliness-Tardiness Scheduling Problem. http://www.optimization-online.org

Sparks R (2007) SIP – Basics and Beyond. ACM Queue 5(2):22–33

Spirit D, O'Mahoney M (1996) High Capacity Optical Transmission Explained. John Wiley & Sons

Spring T (1999) Reverse Auctions: A New Spin on E-Commerce. Tech rep, PC World, http://www.pcworld.com/

Stadtler H, Kilger C (2000) Supply Chain Management and Advanced Planning. Springer, Berlin

Steindl C (2005) Agility Defined. Tech rep
http://www.ocg.at/ak/software-prozesse/files/051205_steindl.pdf

Steinmann MJ (2007) Unified Communications with SIP. ACM Queue 5(2):50–55

Sun R, Chu B, Wilhelm R, Yao J (1999) A CSP-Based Model for Integrated Supply Chain. In: Proceedings of the AAAI-99 Workshop on AI for Electronic Commerce, Orlando, FL

Sutton R, Barto A (1998) Reinforcement Learning: An Introduction. MIT Press, Cambridge, MA

Talluri K, van Ryzin G (2004) The Theory and Practice of Revenue Management. Springer

Tanomaru J (1995) Staff Scheduling by a Genetic Algorithm with Heuristic Operators. In: Proceedings of the 1st IEEE International Conference on Evolutionary Computation IEEE Press, pp 456–461

Tateson R, Bonsma E (2003) ShoppingGarden – Improving the Customer Experience with On-line Catalogues. BT Technology Journal 21(4):1358–3948

Tersine RJ (1988) Principles of Inventory and Materials Management, 3rd edn., New York: North-Holland

Thompson S, Cioffi M, Gharib H, Giles N, Li Y, Nguyen T (2006) From Trips to Telcos, Next Generation Service Portals. BT Technology Journal 24(1):27–39

Timmers P (2000) Electronic Commerce, Strategies and Models for Business-to-Business Trading. John Wiley & Sons

Tsang E (1993) Foundations of Constraint Satisfaction. Academic Press

Turban E, King D (2003) Electronic Commerce. Prentice-Hall

Tversky A, Kahneman D (1973) Availability: A Heuristic for Judging Frequency and Probability. Cognitive Psychology 5:207–232

Urban G (2006) Don't Just Relate – Advocate: A Blueprint for Profit in the Era of Customer Power. Wharton School Publishing

Urban G (2007) Introduction to Customer Advocacy and Morphing. In: MIT Center for Digital Business, Annual Conference and CIO Symposium

van der Aalst W (1998) The Application of Petri Nets to Workflow Management. Journal of Circuits, Systems and Computers 8(1):21–66

van der Aalst W, ter Hofstede A (2005) YAWL: Yet Another Workflow Language. Information Systems 30(4):245–275

Vancil P, Lorange R (1976) Strategic Planning in Diversified Companies. Harvard Business Review 53(1):81–90

van Ryzin G (2005) Models of Demand. Journal of Revenue Pricing Management 4(2):204–210

van Ryzin G, McGill J (2000) Revenue Management without Forecasting or Optimization: An Adaptive Algorithm for Determining Airline Seat Protection Levels. Management Science 46(6):760–775

VICS (2002) CPFR Voluntary Guidelines: Nine Step Process Model. Tech rep, Voluntary Interindustry Commerce Standards Association, http://www.vics.org/committees/cpfr/

Vigoroso M (2004) The Field Service Optimization Benchmark Report: Tapping the Service Supply Chain for Profit and Competitive Advantage. Tech rep, Aberdeen Group Report

Virginas B, Ursu M, Tsang E, Owusu G, Voudouris C (2007) Intelligent Resource Allocation – Solutions and Pathways in A Workforce Planning Problem. In: 1st KES Symposium on Agent and Multi-Agent Systems – Technologies and Applications, Wroclaw, Poland

Vitasek K (2006) Glossary of Supply Chain Terms. Tech rep, Supply Chain Visions, Bellevue, Washington, http://www.scvisions.com

Vollmann T, Jacobs WBR, Whybark D (2004) Manufacturing Planning and Control Systems for Supply Chain Management. McGraw-Hill, New York

Voudouris C, Dorne R (2002) Integrating Heuristic Search and One-Way Constraints in the iOpt Toolkit. In: Voss S, Woodruff D (eds) Optimization Software Class Libraries. Kluwer Academic Publishers, Chap 6, pp 177–192

Voudouris C, Tsang E (1999) Guided Local Search and Its Application to the Travelling Salesman Problem. European Journal of Operational Research 113(2):469–499

Voudouris C, Tsang E (2003) Guided Local Search. In: Glover F (ed) Handbook of Metaheuristics, Kluwer Academic Publishers, Chap 7, pp 185–218

Voudouris C, Dorne R, Lesaint D, Liret A (2001) iOpt: A Software Toolkit for Heuristic Search Methods. In: Walsh T (ed) Proceedings of the 7th International Conference on the Principles and Practice of Constraint Programming (CP'01), Springer, Lecture Notes in Computer Science, vol. 2239, pp 716–729

Voudouris C, Owusu G, Dorne R, Mccormick A (2006) FOS: An Advanced Planning and Scheduling Suite for Service Operations. In: IEEE International Conference on Services Systems and Services Management, IEEE/SSSM06

W3C (2001) Web Service Description Language. http://www.w3.org/ TR/wsdl

W3C (2006a) Extensible Markup Language (XML) 1.0 (Fourth Edition) http://www.w3.org/TR/REC-xml/

W3C (2006b) OWL-S: Semantic Markup for Web Services. http://www.w3.org/

W3C (2007) SOAP Version 1.2 Part 1: Messaging Framework (Second Edition) http://www.w3.org/TR/2007/REC-soap12-part1–20070427/

Walsh W, Wellman M (1999) Modelling Supply Chains Formation in Multiagent Systems. In: Proceedings of the IJCAI-99 Workshop on Agent-Mediated Electronic Commerce, Stockholm, Sweden

Wang Y, Thompson R, Bishop I (1999) A GIS-based Information Integration Framework for Dynamic Vehicle Routing and Scheduling. In: Proceedings of the IEEE International Vehicle Electronics Conference (IVEC'99), Changchun, China, pp 474–479

Weatherford L (1994) Optimization of Perishable-Asset Revenue Management Problems that Allow Prices as Decision Variables. Working paper, University of Wyoming, Laramie, WY

Weatherford L, Bodily S (1992) A Taxonomy and Research Overview of Perishable-Asset Revenue Management: Yield Management, Overbooking, and Pricing. Operations Research 40(5):831–844

Wedel M, Kamahura W (2000) Market Segmentation: Conceptual and Methodological Foundations, 2nd edn., Kluwer

Weerawarana S, Curbera F, Leymann F, Storey T, Ferguson D (2005) Web Services Platform Architecture: SOAP, WSDL, WS-Policy, WS-Addressing, WS-BPEL, WS-Reliable Messaging, and More. Prentice Hall

Weil G, Heus K, Francois P, Poujade M (1995) Constraint Programming for Nurse Scheduling. IEEE Engineering in Medicine and Biology 14(4):417–422

Winters P (1960) Forecasting Sales by Exponentially Weighted Moving Averages. Management Science 6(3):324–342

Wittgreffe J, Dames M, Clark J, McDonald J (2006) End-to-end service level agreements for complex ICT solutions. BT Technology Journal 24(4):31–46

Wölfl A (2005) The Service Economy in OECD Countries. STI Working paper 2005/3, OECD

Wooldbridge M (2002) An Introduction to MultiAgent Systems. John Wiley & Sons

Woods J (2005) RFID Enables Sensory Network Strategies to Transform Industries. Tech rep, Gartner

Wren A, Wren D (1995) A Genetic Algorithm for Public Transport Driver Scheduling. Computers and Operations Research 22(1):101–110

Wu T (1992) Fiber Network Service Survivability. Artech House

Wu X, Schulzrinne H (2002) Programmable End System Services Using SIP. In: 2nd New York Metro Area Networking Workshop, New York, NY

Wu Z, Boulos P, Orr C, Ro J (2001) Rehabilitation of Water Distribution Systems Using Genetic Algorithms. Journal of American Water Works Association

Wurman P, Wellman M, Walsh M (1998) The Michigan Internet Auctionbot: A Configurable Auction Server for Human and Software Agents. In: Sycara KP, Wooldridge M (eds) Proceedings of the 2nd International Conference on Autonomous Agents (Agents'98), ACM Press, Minneapolis/St. Paul MN, pp 301–308

Yano C, Gilbert S (2004) Coordinated Pricing and Production/Procurement Decisions: A Review. In: Chakravarty A, Eliashberg J (eds) Managing Business Interfaces: Marketing, Engineering and Manufacturing Perspectives. Kluwer

Yau O (2002) An Empirical Investigation of the Impact of Business-to-Business Electronic Commerce Adoption on the Business Operations of Hong Kong Manufactures. First Monday 7(9), http://www.firstmonday.org/issues/issue7_9/yau/

Yeoman I, McMahon-Beattie U (2004) Revenue Management and Pricing: Case Studies and Applications. Thomson Business Press

Zave P (2003) An Experiment in Feature Engineering. In: McIver A, Morgan C (eds) Programming Methodology, Springer-Verlag, pp 353–377

Zave P, Goguen H, Smith TM (2004) Component Coordination: a Telecommunication Case Study. Computer Networks 45(5):645–664

Zeithaml V, Bitner M (2003) Services Marketing: Integrating Customer Focus Across the Firm, 3rd edn., McGraw-Hill

Zeng D (2001) Managing Flexibility for Inter-Organisational Electronic Commerce. Electronic Commerce Research 1(1–2):33–51

Zhang G, Patuwo B, Hu M (1998) Forecasting with Artificial Neural Networks: The State of the Art. International Journal of Forecasting 14(1):35–62

Index